THEATRE LIGHTING DESIGN
CONVERSATIONS ON THE ART
AND LIFE

THEATRE LIGHTING DESIGN: CONVERSATIONS ON THE ART, CRAFT AND LIFE

Emma Chapman and Rob Halliday

methuen | drama

LONDON • NEW YORK • OXFORD • NEW DELHI • SYDNEY

METHUEN DRAMA
Bloomsbury Publishing Plc
50 Bedford Square, London, WC1B 3DP, UK
1385 Broadway, New York, NY 10018, USA
29 Earlsfort Terrace, Dublin 2, Ireland

BLOOMSBURY, METHUEN DRAMA and the Methuen Drama logo are trademarks
of Bloomsbury Publishing Plc

First published in Great Britain 2024

Copyright © Emma Chapman and Rob Halliday, 2024

Emma Chapman and Rob Halliday have asserted their right under the Copyright, Designs and
Patents Act, 1988, to be identified as authors of this work.

For legal purposes the Acknowledgements on p. 227 constitute an extension of this copyright page.

Cover Photograph: *Lighting a Show – Les Misérables – The Staged Concert at the Sondheim Theatre, London.*
Directed by James Powell and Jean-Pierre Van Der Spuy, scenic design by Matt Kinley, costume design by Andreane Neofitou and Christine Rowland, lighting by Paule Constable and Warren Letton, sound by Mick Potter. Photographer: Johan Persson

All rights reserved. No part of this publication may be reproduced or transmitted in any form or by any means, electronic or mechanical, including photocopying, recording, or any information storage or retrieval system, without prior permission in writing from the publishers.

Bloomsbury Publishing Plc does not have any control over, or responsibility for, any third-party websites referred to or in this book. All internet addresses given in this book were correct at the time of going to press. The author and publisher regret any inconvenience caused if addresses have changed or sites have ceased to exist, but can accept no responsibility for any such changes.

A catalogue record for this book is available from the British Library.

ISBN: HB: 978-1-3502-9593-3
PB: 978-1-3502-9592-6
ePDF: 978-1-3502-9595-7
eBook: 978-1-3502-9594-0

Typeset by RefineCatch Limited, Bungay, Suffolk
Printed and bound in India

To find out more about our authors and books visit www.bloomsbury.com
and sign up for our newsletters.

From Emma:

For Dom and Imogen, who wants to be an author when she grows up...

From Rob:

For my gang: Mary, Emily, Ben and Leo. For when they need something to help explain what I spend all my time doing!

CONTENTS

List of Images		viii
Introduction		**1**
Conversations		**3**
1	Neil Austin	5
2	Natasha Chivers	19
3	Jon Clark	31
4	Paule Constable	45
5	Rick Fisher	59
6	Richard Howell	73
7	Howard Hudson	85
8	Jessica Hung Han Yun	99
9	Mark Jonathan	111
10	Amy Mae	127
11	Ben Ormerod	141
12	Bruno Poet	157
13	Jackie Shemesh	173
14	Johanna Town	187
15	Team Conversation: *Billy Elliot*	201
Glossary		217
Acknowledgements		227
About the Authors		229
Index		231

IMAGES

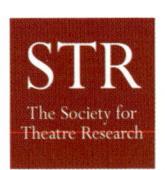

Pictures supported by a research grant from The Society for Theatre Research.

Front Cover: *Les Misérables: The Staged Concert* in production at the Gielgud Theatre. Photographer: Johan Persson, © Cameron Macintosh (Overseas) Ltd..

Back Cover: Jon Clark lighting *The Lehman Trilogy* at the Ahmanson Theatre, Los Angeles. Photographer: Rich Booth.

Introduction: *Crazy For You* at the Gillian Lynne Theatre. Photographer: Rob Halliday.	1

1:

Neil Austin. Photographer: Johan Persson.	5
Company at the Gielgud Theatre. Photographer: Geraint Lewis / ArenaPAL.	9
Harry Potter and the Cursed Child at the Palace Theatre. Photographer: Manuel Harlan, courtesy of Sonia Friedman Productions.	11

2:

Natasha Chivers	19
Message In A Bottle at Sadler's Wells. Photographer: Helen Maybanks / ArenaPAL.	22
Macbeth at the Tramway, Glasgow. Photographer: Manuel Harlan / ArenaPAL.	28

3:

Jon Clark	31
The Inheritance. Photographer: Marc Brenner.	34
The Jungle at the Young Vic. Photographer: Leon Puplett.	40

4:

Paule Constable	45
The Ocean at the End of the Lane at the National Theatre. Photographer: Manuel Harlan / ArenaPAL.	50
Follies at the National Theatre. Photographer: Johan Persson / ArenaPAL.	55

5:

Rick Fisher	59
Swan Lake. Photographer: Mike Rothwell.	63
An Inspector Calls at the National Theatre. Photographer: Ivan Kyncl / ArenaPAL.	68

6:

Richard Howell	73
Guards at the Taj at the Bush Theatre. Photographer: Marc Brenner.	79
Jekyll & Hyde at the Old Vic. Photographer: Manuel Harlan / ArenaPAL.	82

IMAGES

7:
Howard Hudson	85
& Juliet at the Shaftesbury Theatre. Photographer: Johan Persson / ArenaPAL.	87
Romeo and Juliet at the Garrick Theatre. Photographer: Johan Persson / ArenaPAL.	96

8:
Jessica Hung Han Yun. Photographer: Morgan Eglin.	99
Equus at the Theatre Royal Stratford East. Photographer: The Other Richard / ArenaPAL.	105
Seven Methods of Killing Kylie Jenner at the Royal Court. Photographer: Helen Murray / ArenaPAL.	109

9:
Mark Jonathan. Photographer: Matthew Ferguson.	111
Aladdin – from the front, and from behind the scenes. Photos courtesy of Mark Jonathan.	118–19
Sleeping Beauty – Royal Opera House. Photographer: Johan Persson / ArenaPAL.	123

10:
Amy Mae	127
Sweeney Todd at Harringtons Pie Shop. Photographer: Bronwen Sharp.	130
Sweeney Todd at Harringtons Pie Shop. Photographer: Bronwen Sharp.	133

11:
Ben Ormerod	141
Der Ring Des Nibelungen at Longborough Festival Opera. Photographer: Ben Ormerod.	144
Zorro: The Musical at the Garrick Theatre. Photographer: Elliott Franks / ArenaPAL.	146

12:
Bruno Poet	157
Tina: The Tina Turner Musical at the Aldwych Theatre. Photographer: Manuel Harlan.	162
Frankenstein at the National Theatre. Photographer: Catherine Ashmore.	169

13:
Jackie Shemesh. Photographer: Chisato Shemesh	173
Misty at the Bush Theatre. Photographer: Tristram Kenton.	177
The Seagull at the Harold Pinter Theatre. Photographer: Jackie Shemesh.	179

14:
Johanna Town. Photographer: Colin Grenfell.	187
Orfeo ed Euridice at The Grange Festival. Photographer: Craig Fuller.	190
Frankenstein at the Royal Exchange Theatre Manchester. Photographer: Johan Persson / ArenaPAL.	198

15:
Billy Elliot at the Victoria Palace Theatre, London. Photographer: Rob Halliday.	201
'Grandma's Song', from *Billy Elliot*. Photographer: Rob Halliday.	210
'Angry Dance', from *Billy Elliot*. Photographer: Rob Halliday.	211
'Once We Were Kings', from *Billy Elliot*. Photographer: Rob Halliday.	216

INTRODUCTION

Crazy For You at the Gillian Lynne Theatre, London. Directed and choreographed by Susan Stroman, scenic designer Beowulf Boritt, costume designer William Ivey Long, lighting by Ken Billington, sound by Kai Harada. *Photographer: Rob Halliday*.

Sometimes, on a journey, you find yourself on a different route from the one you expected. Sometimes, at the end of a journey, you find yourself somewhere entirely different from where you expected. Sometimes both make a result better than you expected. That's very much how we feel about the journey of this book.

The journey plan originally proposed was a book about 'advanced theatre lighting design'. That felt like a big topic, and a hard one to pin down. We knew it couldn't just be our opinions. Fortunately, one of the joys of theatre lighting has always been the enormous generosity and kindness of its community, its willingness to share experience and insights. So we called some designers to see if they'd help us by sharing their experiences in work and in life as professional lighting designers – which they did, in a series of fascinating conversations.

A moment of enlightenment along the way came with a realization that perhaps part of the very definition of 'advanced lighting', or more particularly of being an 'advanced lighting designer', is that you'd no longer want to read about it. When you're starting out you need the basic, practical information about how to do things. With a bit more practice and a bit more experience you crave a bit more advice, a bit more inspiration, sometimes just something to shamelessly copy: how do other designers do things? Which kind of lights do they use? Where do they rig them? Which colours do they use? We've all peeked at lighting plans in textbooks and magazines, lifting things from them to try.

Then at some point, perhaps without even realizing it, you stop peeking. You have things you know work. You have other ideas you want to try. You know how to enjoy them if they work as expected, you know what to do if they don't. You have your own opinion, and you trust it over and above the opinions of others. That, surely, is being an advanced lighting designer – when you know your mind and trust your judgement. That, actually, is surely being an advanced anything, particularly any craft or any art or anything that is the perfect intersection of the two. Stage lighting is certainly that.

So, no need then for a book prescribing how to do it. Down pen and move on. And yet, those conversations were fascinating. Each fascinating on its own. More fascinating still read together, for the things the lighting designers agreed on – but more so for the things they approached differently or even disagreed about completely. These were lighting designers spanning a range of ages, experiences, shows, work and life. Even to us, both working lighting designers, listening to their answers was fascinating. And reassuring. Not the 'use this colour, it will work' reassurance we craved when we were starting out. A whole other level of reassurance, that our choices – whatever they are – can be the right choices, that lighting is hard, that sometimes there are bad days, but sometimes there are good days, that the show you loved working on most might not be your biggest hit. Plus the occasional 'oh, I'd never thought of that' moment...

So maybe something for advanced lighting designers after all – but actually for lighting designers of any level. A chance to dive into how designers approach their work, where their ideas come from, how they collaborate with their creative and technical teams. But also how they live their lives in lighting, balancing the demands of technical rehearsals with those of family and life. The balance of what can be both a lonely profession, but also one that relies on collaboration and teamwork. Interesting for those who work in this field, but just maybe also of interest to others merely interested in light – performers who spend their lives immersed in it, other creative professionals who see their work brought to life by it. Maybe even audience members who just experience it, perhaps without even thinking about it at all.

Which is how we ended up here, at our unexpected destination. Fifteen conversations. Fourteen of them wonderful chats with fourteen wonderful lighting designers. And then since all of them talked about their reliance on their teams, one group chat where the key people involved with *Billy Elliot* over the last twenty years talk about the show, its lighting, and just what made it the hit it became.

We thank them all for their time. We loved hearing their responses. We hope you do too.

Emma & Rob.

With thanks also to Joshua Carr, who was there at the beginning of the journey and was a fantastic supporter all the way through.

CONVERSATIONS

NEIL AUSTIN

Photographer: Johan Persson

Neil graduated from Guildhall knowing he wanted to be a lighting designer, but fell into doing every job in theatre – flyman, carpenter, sound op as well as lighting work, as an electrician, as assistant to, in particular, Mark Henderson, and on the team of design firm Imagination for some of the zones at the Millennium Dome – to earn a living, squeezing in his own designs around the edges.

After some years of that, during a lunch with friends around Christmas 2001 he announced that he was going to concentrate on what he really wanted to do, being a lighting designer purely for theatre, by saying no to everything else.

During the next fifteen years, he carefully sought out new directors and designers, working around the country but forging a particularly strong relationship with director Michael Grandage and designer Christopher Oram during their time at the Donmar Warehouse. He won his first Tony Award for their production of the play *Red* in New York, subsequently winning two more Tonys alongside two Oliviers. He lived the theatre lighting designer's life of having to light a lot of shows in a lot of places just to earn a reasonable living until there finally came that rare but perfect intersection of talent, experience, luck and timing that brought him to *Harry Potter and the Cursed Child*.

www.neilaustin.com

Emma What are the pros and cons of being a lighting designer? What would you have liked to have known twenty years ago?

Neil That you will have no life for a long, long time. That you will work from 9am to 10pm, or in America 8am to midnight, six days a week. A lighting designer only really earns money in tech, because most of the detailed process is in tech, and so you go from show to show, tech to tech as fast as possible. A director might do two or three shows a year, so maybe six to eight weeks a year where they are doing those sorts of hours, but as a lighting designer or sound designer or video designer, all of which are pretty much comparable and have similar work practices, you will do a tech every fortnight. At its worst, I did twenty-four shows in one year in order to earn a living – that was too many. I had a student ask to come and see us on *Company*; we worked from 9am through to 10pm, and I said, you are welcome to come to as much or as little as you'd like. They turned up at 2.30pm and disappeared at 5pm. Right there, you could say this probably isn't the right job for you...

On the flip side, I was very happy doing the crazy hours in my early career, because I was taking every opportunity that was thrown at me, not knowing where anything would lead. There are an awful lot of seemingly blind alleys, which are individually rewarding in themselves but don't seem to lead anywhere – then years later they will suddenly be the thing that blossoms into something. That director who I worked for at the Battersea Arts Centre in 1995 and didn't hear from for years suddenly took me to the National Theatre. Who would have known that was the one?

Emma Our tools have also changed over twenty years. What are the benefits and challenges LED has brought?

Neil I think the challenges early on were the standard of the technology, the quality of the technology. In the fifteen years or so we've been using LEDs, quality is what's changed. We've gone from brightness being the only metric, 'mine's brighter than yours', to manufacturers understanding that now the final gain to be made is 'mine is higher quality than yours'. We've got to that quality stage where the dimming is really very good, and the quality of light sources is pretty much indiscernible from tungsten and way better than the arc sources that we had before. So the tech has become a great tool for the craft, and better in terms of energy consumption too.

Emma In terms of colour, how has it changed your process? Presumably it no longer starts with choosing gels in a swatch book...

Neil Gels were hard. If you went to someone now and said, 'I've got this great light, it's absolutely brilliant, it's this colour at full... but 99 gently different colours as it dims', that would be the craziest thing in the world – but that's the colour change that happens as tungsten dims. In a musical, you'd choose that lovely, crisp, really clear pink that pierces through. Then you'd dim it and it would go a warm, muddy orange – how annoying because it turns out I didn't want to use it at full, I wanted to use it at 27 per cent. So I actually really love the fact that LED doesn't colour shift, which I didn't think I was going to. But I really appreciate that you pick your colour, put it on stage and that's the colour no matter the level.

Emma So when you start programming for a show, do you put set colours in?

Neil It's interesting. Certainly, there's been a nice crossover period where there has been a mixture of LED and tungsten, so you put your scroller colours in and just mix those. I think the great innovation for theatre has been the ETC Lustr being colour matched into the ETC console colour libraries. On the show where I used the Lustr 2 for the very first time, I needed some colours to go in traditional Source Fours to make fireworks. I'd forgotten my swatch books, but we could bring up all of the different colours – colours I'd never heard of – in the Lustrs, then order those gels. Someone had bothered to get that information into the consoles, and it wasn't Rosco, Lee or Gam. I wonder whether they will end up entirely defunct because they haven't made themselves into the Pantone – the reference for colour – for theatre.

With entirely LED rigs, any colour is possible, but how do you describe colours that don't exist in gel swatch books? I want that particular shade of pink that's in my head. Trying to describe that is frustrating. So just let me have the encoders, because they're in the hands of the wrong person: why do I have to talk to that person and say 'a little bit more blue, a little bit less red', try to find language to describe something when it would be much easier just to do it myself. But the next problem is, what do you call these colours? Pink 1, pink 2, pink 3, slightly less pink, slightly more pink? It's problematic.

Emma Has all this changed your relationship with a director? Do you find a director or designer gets more involved because you have all these colour options, or do you still have the control that you would have had when you picked a gel?

Neil You still have ultimate control, but it's always been a collaboration. I remember doing a show at the Sheffield Crucible with the designer Christopher Oram and he came up to me and talked about the colour of a scene. It was the first time he'd ever talked about the colour, and he was like, you know the protagonist's purple suit, and I was like, yeah, it's lovely, and he responded, yeah, it's not purple. Well, that was an aberration of this particular gel and tungsten and having such a red section of the spectrum; this blue I was using still had a massive amount of red in order to let the heat out along with the light without burning out. Sure enough that actually was a blue suit, but it had gone purple under that colour, Rosco 78, which is like Lee 200 but with a lot more red in it. So, I went whoops, OK, let's go to Lee 200 and try that, urgh, the face looks green but the suit looks blue… the costume designer's happy, the director's not.

In general, I think colour is still in your control, but isn't it great that people can say, I see that scene as red when you've decided to light it in green. It's so easy to change colour now, rather than ordering different gel, waiting for it to arrive, waiting for a work call to change every light to that gel – that process used to take a couple of days, now it's instant. So, it's much better for everyone and yes, you make colour decisions later.

Here's the interesting thing about what you are saying: it used to be that you, the LD, chose colour long before showing it to anyone else in the theatre. If you were lucky, you'd made the right decisions; if you were unlucky, you'd made the wrong ones. If the team were unhappy about it you had to find ways around it because it was difficult to change.

I've just done an interview with the V&A Archive and I said it's great the set designer can make a white card model and show it and everyone comments and they go away and refine it until it's right, then they make a colour model and get that to where they want it before anything's signed off, before it's in rehearsal. The costume designer draws for ages and eventually shows the director the drawings and they have a conversation – this isn't quite what I was thinking but how about this? They get this very prolonged process. The sound designer, the same thing: that period during rehearsals that you can play sounds to the director and discuss them before everyone goes into the theatre. The actors and director have had five weeks to try out different ideas and try out every permutation in a relaxed, nurturing environment with really no one else watching – the rehearsal room is often closed, to allow the actors to create without pressure.

But the lighting designer works under exceptional pressure, in front of everyone else, live. The producer will be behind you saying time is money, there is no audience in this theatre, this is really expensive for us. The actors are getting bored standing on stage waiting for you. Everyone is waiting for you, and everyone has an opinion about what you're doing – not like that, like this. Bang goes all sense of that nurturing, protected environment. It's incredibly pressured.

Emma How do you convey your ideas to a director or a designer? How does that collaboration work prior to going into the theatre?

Neil You try and talk about it, you try to describe the indescribable – light is invisible until it hits something and is exceptionally hard to describe even to people in the industry.

An interesting case in point is *Company*: there was a big discussion about the expense of having some black masking fly in just behind the main set. It would have splits in it so actors could appear and disappear quickly, but what would that really look like as performers came through a bit of serge? It would be pretty ugly, and the lighting would catch it. I said cut the black masking, you don't need it because I'll have some haze in the air and I'll provide a backlight shaft through the haze – it's a terrible word but it helps everyone understand the sort of intensity of the beam of light. Adolphe Appia and Edward Gordon Craig wrote about it, Svoboda actually managed to achieve it, David Hersey refined it, and now the manufacturer GLP have refined it even more for all of us with their X-Bars. You can create a curtain of light which comes all the way down from the unit to the deck, and people will suddenly appear as they walk forwards through it – just like with the black masking, but way more elegant. The team agreed to try it, in order to save the cost of the masking, but one bar was left free in the rig and a section of the budget remained ring-fenced because no one quite believed what I had described until they saw it. So, I think it's often impossible to describe lighting in advance.

Emma How do you form collaborations, and how do collaborations change?

Neil It's interesting. In old, trusted collaborations there is remarkably little conversation about lighting in advance – 'we're doing this show next!' You read the script. You look at

Company at the Gielgud Theatre, London. Directed by Marianne Elliott, choreographed by Liam Steel, designed by Bunny Christie, lighting by Neil Austin, sound by Ian Dickinson. Photographer: Geraint Lewis / ArenaPAL.

the set. You turn up to rehearsals. You draw the plan. You arrive at the theatre. You light the show. You're there because they know what you are going to deliver. That's trust, isn't it?

I worked with Lyndsey Turner on a show, *The Treatment*, at the Almeida. I'd never collaborated with her before but quickly realized she's really wonderful. She completely challenges everything and questions every minute decision. We ended up going with hugely deep saturated colours on the show. There were entire scenes in deep, deep green, purple, orange, blue or yellow – it was an amazingly freeing process where we kept trying different and unusual looks and colours. It was a piece which could take that treatment, a Martin Crimp, therefore absolutely non-naturalistic. It allowed a level of abstraction in the lighting design. You do a show like that and it throws you in completely new directions, which is exciting.

On the few occasions where you are absolutely the wrong fit for the team, or you haven't predicted in advance what the rest of the team were thinking, it's horrible because there is no time to change it.

Emma And then, of course, there is your collaboration with your team – the electricians, the programmer. How do you work with them?

Neil They're your closest friends and collaborators in the room. They are utterly essential to the process, and the people who can really help save you in tough situations. I think individual LDs collaborate with them differently, though.

I was reading an article about what programmers do, obviously written by someone in the concert industry. It made it very clear that in that industry there is a huge onus on the programmer to actually come up with a lot more of the visual look than we would ever expect or allow as a lighting designer in theatre. The programmer Dan Haggerty ended up doing a gig with a big-name rock-and-roll lighting designer and got an email saying, in advance of the job next week can you break the numbers down. What does that mean? So, he called Andy Voller, a programmer who's worked a lot in that field, who said that means they want you to timecode the number and put in all the cue points where things will be happening, in advance. But isn't that the designer's job? There is a difference in expectation between their part of the industry and ours.

Whereas I remember at the National Theatre saying, there are bombs going off far away, but the only thing which is going to flicker here is the light bulb as the electricity responds. This one single light bulb needs to flicker; I just need you to create that. I need you to do twelve different versions of this flickering light bulb, slightly different lengths, and we'll pick for the different scenes. Or sometimes, you have to be very prescriptive. It depends on the programmer.

I got asked by the programmers at Rose Bruford College – what skills do you want in a programmer? Slightly flippantly, I replied, 'type fast and shut up. . .' It's rude but there's a truth in there. There are times when I really appreciate your thought and your input, and there are times where I really need you to just leave my headspace clear and just type as fast as you can.

Emma In terms of developing equipment with the manufacturer, how does that process work?

Neil I think there is less money in theatre than in other lighting disciplines – we buy many fewer units than the concert industry. But what is interesting is there is a thriving rental market that manufacturers can sell to, and as they've moved from brighter, brighter, brighter to more quality, more quality, more quality, they've been listening to theatre more because I think we are the fussiest out there. And we are the fussiest because we have to deal with human skin and with storytelling live, so we are not so interested in movements and sweeps and flashes and quick colour changes – except for certain points in certain shows, of course – but what we are really interested in is that beautiful smooth two-minute-long fade, good colour changing, really slow movement through the gobos.

In terms of new equipment, *Harry Potter* was great because it was a brand that was so powerful the manufacturers understood the possibility that it would be worth working with us. Mark Ravenhill of GLP has always been very open to theatre. I approached him because they'd just released the X4 Bar. I thought it was wonderful but needed more work to make it theatre-ready. Because the show was *Potter*, he recognized that it might have legs, that there might be a few productions of it, so it was probably worthwhile

Harry Potter and the Cursed Child at the Palace Theatre, London. Directed by John Tiffany, movement director Steven Hoggett, set design by Christine Jones, costume design by Katrina Lindsay, lighting by Neil Austin, video by Finn Ross & Ash J Woodward, sound by Gareth Fry. Photographer: Manuel Harlan, courtesy of Sonia Friedman Productions.

them getting involved – there would be enough demand that it would make some money back. The problem quite often is that we demand quality, but we only buy five. If you demand quality and are going to buy four hundred, potentially more than that, then the maths on the spreadsheet works. *Potter* currently has seven productions worldwide, so GLP's investment in development paid back for them.

Emma How did you work with them?

Neil I thought the X4 Bar was probably the right unit for *Harry Potter* but wanted to test it against my favourite unit at the time, the DHA Digital Light Curtain. I had some of those on the play *Photograph 51* at the Noël Coward Theatre in the West End with Nicole Kidman. I took that theatre for two days, taking an X4 Bar as it existed at the time, putting it up at exactly the same height as the Light Curtains, doing the same shaft in the same theatre and tested everything about it. I'd been complaining about haze on that show because it seemed to only be high up, but what you saw with the X4 Bars was that the haze did come all the way down. Having a more parallel beam with less divergence revealed that. That was interesting. It was the right unit. But it had some issues.

The X4 Bar was as bright as the DLCs in Lee 201. But as soon as you got to L202 and lighter, warmer colours, the Light Curtain's warm tungsten source was winning out.

I went back to Mark with my findings. I thought the source was wrong, the dimming was too steppy, the movement was jerky, and the beam had bad chromatic aberration. He replied, 'so you like the unit, but you hate everything about it!' We spent the next six months working together to finesse all those elements, so that I could specify it on the show.

The X4 Bar was using an RGB-Cold White chip. I found out that Osram also made a warm white version of that chip – but unfortunately not an RGB-warm white. We tried to get a meeting with Osram to see if they could make an RGB-warm version. It was a disaster – too many barriers 'we have no time to make what you want', 'you'll have to pay for a prototype to be made', and that would take two and a half months. There was no space in our schedule for that. So we went with the original chip on the London production, but GLP developed the RGBY chip version for the next iterations of *Harry Potter*.

The other example of our collaboration is with the beamlight followspots. In the London production we'd been using the Superbeam 1.2k 80 volt beamlights as followspots, with a 15" scroller which made them heavy and large and less than ideal for the operators. By the time it came to specifying the rig for the Broadway transfer, Superbeam had gone bust. We went to Reiche & Vogel, who made an older beamlight, and got this heart-breaking email back saying, 'I'm sorry, we stopped the company a number of years ago, we just did not get enough orders so we had to close down'. That's when having a relationship with a manufacturer is great: I called Mark Ravenhill and went, here's the problem, can you help?

I went to Germany, taking a traditional beamlight with me, and we looked at it and all the options, with Osram's new RGBY chip in GLP's existing X4-XL fixture. We couldn't get the beam narrow enough without a bigger lens, at which point it became too dim, so I decided I would have to deal with a 6-degree beam rather than the beamlight's 4-degree beam. We added handles, faders, buttons. You press a button that releases the motors so you can move it, the moment you let go the motors engage and hold it where you left it. We mixed the colours next to the original beamlight, and it's pretty much indiscernible from the R&Vs – people standing in the room couldn't tell who was standing in the tungsten one and who was in the LED one.

Emma And how about new tools that aren't new lights?

Neil Lightstrike would be an example of that, which, again, *Harry Potter* let us develop. I wanted to be able to take the positional data from the automation system and convert that to moving light positions, so lights could track the movement of a revolve or a flying piece. I approached a very clever friend of mine, Dan Murfin, who was then head of programming at the National Theatre; he was intrigued, but sceptical. A few days later, he called saying, 'I haven't slept for days now, but I think I've got a way of doing it!' So we commissioned him to develop the software, which is now available for anyone to use. It has so many uses; it's an extraordinary tool, and it only exists because that show gave us the means to create it.

Or Vor, another piece of software which has totally changed the way I work. It imprints cue data from lighting, video, sound, automation or timecode onto a video you make of the show, with an audio track of the PSM or DSM cueing the show alongside the show audio if you like. It was developed by Jess Creager and Scott Tusing, my US associate and programmer on *Potter*. They showed me an early prototype and I pushed them to develop it into a product everyone could use. It completely changes your workflow for the better when doing notes during previews – you can discern immediately why something wasn't working. I find directors, choreographers and producers crowd around my desk to watch it, like an action replay from a sports event.

Emma Going to more of the role of the lighting designer: lighting design as a storytelling element. Could you talk a little bit more about how lighting design can help tell a story?

Neil It doesn't matter what your role is, whether you are an actor or a director or a musical director or orchestrator or set designer, costume designer, crew. You are all doing the same thing: helping to tell a story convincingly for an audience. We sometimes get a little bit too involved in our own department to remember that what we are doing is a collaboration, together.

At its most basic, you start with the script. Take a naturalistic piece: there, you have to tell the time of day, location. It's the things that Richard Pilbrow talked about all those years ago, which he was very right about: location, time, mood and atmosphere. You need to give an indication of where you are, sometimes when you are, and that's something lighting can massively help with on a piece which changes time, changes century, changes past, present and future. Acting, costume design, scenic design can also do this – if there's enough money, you can do some kind of physical change, but the quickest, easiest way of saying now I'm no longer in that reality, I'm in another reality is lighting. Now I am the narrator talking to you directly as the audience versus having a dialogue a moment ago. Lighting is very quick at doing that – there is nothing quicker at changing a location than a snap lighting cue; there will never be a set which changes that quickly. Video is a component of light, so I sort of count that as part of us as it can do the same, though that is certainly something that needs a collaboration where you are at least equals and talking – a nice collaborative conversation between the two designers helps there.

Emma In terms of being able to get the lighting positions you need, that negotiation with the designer and other departments – when they want a ceiling...?

Neil Christopher Oram has said from the very first moment I met him, from the very first show, I've always cut holes in his sets – for twenty years! So, when I go and see his models now, he hands me the scalpel and says, 'get on with it!'

It is a negotiation because that's why you are employed, I suppose. That person, the scenic designer, can't necessarily and shouldn't necessarily understand everything about what we might be needing lighting-wise; that's why you are there. You don't want to completely ruin the design and go, absolutely not, take the ceiling off – but you want to find ways of finding a compromise which could serve the piece and allow you to serve the director for the vision of what they want it to look like, and also serve what the scenic designer wants it to look like. But the scenic designer is slightly focused on that physical form at the moment, whereas you are having to think ahead to what happens when the person stands here and you say to me, I don't want to see their shadow on the back wall. It's a collaboration, the whole thing; that's the fun, isn't it?

That starts when you are brought on board. Sometimes you are brought on board super-early, and you are involved in a lot of those conversations. Sometimes it's crazily late, and then it's very hard to make those changes, but it's still worth trying if you can, or you have to come up with another route, or you pre-warn everyone. There, a conversation about lighting is possible – where you can warn someone that, just so you know, there are going to be shadows on the back wall if someone goes and stands too close to it, but here's where I can manage not to do that, or this would be a method of coming through the doorway with a big shaft of light.

As an example, *Company* is small boxes, scenic nine-foot squares and not very tall at all. One of the big negotiations was having a small slot downstage and a small slot upstage of the boxes, so the downstage was used a little bit by me and a lot by sound to have foldback speakers, because obviously it was a musical and they were needing to hear the band in there. The backlight bar was just enough to get some GLP X4 Bars in, and in single-pixel mode you can widen them and get them to flood the whole box or go to a single spotty special, which we used at times. There are moments when they were invaluable, but by making those apertures you haven't, hopefully, ruined the intent of the set – that's where you need to be careful.

Emma In terms of cue structure, do you work that out in the rehearsal room, before you get into the theatre, and load something into the desk?

Neil Rehearsal rooms are really useful on the first day of rehearsals if you've got enough time to sit and hear it, but mostly reading it is enough. The next two to three weeks of rehearsal, I always think, are pretty useless for us as that's about text, meanings and motivation, which is wonderful for the cast and director but not so much for the lighting designer. When they start to put a couple of scenes together and run them with a moment in between, and they begin to think about that moment, that's when it's really useful being there. It's from that moment you start to get your cue structure.

By the final run-through, I've produced a script with all the cues I can imagine in it, numbered and labelled, which I hand to the DSM to transfer into their script. Then I'll type that into the lighting desk: I love labelling my own cues! The label column is for me. I don't want fourteen parts that are unlabelled so that when I come back to that section of the show two days later or two months later or years later when you are transferring something, you don't know why that part was there. I've just had a show transfer twelve years after we last did it – the labels were a huge help.

Emma What do you think the skills of a lighting designer are?

Neil You have to be a good communicator. Apart from that, no idea! It's a horrid process. It's a very, very, very stressful period in tech. It's the most stressful for the lighting designer: you are the one under super-intense pressure at that moment, and that takes a certain personality. People react differently to that. There were people in the past who were known for being shouty, screamy. You are trying to remain as calm as you possibly can. Whether anyone ever achieves that is entirely another matter. Inside you are screaming, aren't you?

Emma Do you think it's an art, a science. . . ?

Neil I don't think it matters – that's for someone else to judge. It's semantics. It's a collaborative form. I'm very careful not to say a collaborative art form. It's a job like any other; if it's art or not is for someone else to judge. I think it's certainly a craft; I would agree with the idea that there is no difference between an artist and a craftsperson, they are one and the same.

I do firmly believe in the idea of practicality. I do find it helpful that I started rigging lights for other people, and actually, early on in my career, was doing everything trying to earn some money: I was a flyman in the West End in the evenings while building sets during the day. I went on tour with the English Shakespeare Company as a sound operator in the era of reel-to-reel tape – that was probably the scariest moment in my life! Being a production electrician. All of that is helpful; if nothing else, it ought to give you an empathy towards the other people you are working with and an understanding of what they are doing and how what you're doing can help or hinder that. Even now, lighting designers are sometimes the one person on cans in the auditorium during tech, so being able to talk to everybody else and at least relay information back to the director and designer is helpful. I might be the person who can help say, well actually, what they wanted to happen was this. If you know a little bit about what's going on, it's helpful. I'm in no way trying to big up what the lighting designer does, it's just there is sometimes that moment where you become a conduit about other stuff because you happen to be on headset.

Emma You are working with everyone in the team, aren't you?

Neil Exactly. Sometimes you've heard stuff the DSM hasn't or the flyman hasn't, or there is that thing where you are able to ask either through the stage manager or if they are busy, you can often ask directly, 'could that go any faster. . . ' Live events are very fragile; quite a lot of the time you are relying on individuals who are all invested in the process to do it rather brilliantly every night. It's kind of wonderful when it works out.

Emma Taking a show abroad. . . If you were to tell someone who had never taken a show from the UK to the States, for example, what would be your key advice to them?

Neil Yeah, the States is interesting. Taking a show abroad full stop has become easier. Taking a show abroad to anywhere which wasn't 240 volts or 220 volts was a really interesting prospect in the era of tungsten. I learnt that lesson really hard the first time: I was re-lighting someone else's show, touring it all the way around the world just using house par cans, 1k Fresnels, 2k Fresnels and profile spots, essentially lighting the whole show to a pretty standard rig. Then we did it in America and the director turned to me and said, why is that blackout taking so long? And I said, I don't know – it does seem to be taking a long time, it's no longer a snap, why is that? Oh, well it's because I'm using a bundle of 2k Fresnels at 120 volts which is roughly the equivalent of a 5k at 240 volts; it's a very large filament and it's taking ages to decay. That was a big lesson, so I used to say if you used a par can in the UK use a Source Four Par 575W in the US because you will get something close to your snaps.

That's all become easier now, with the LED fixtures which are multivoltage, so you get the same units here you get there. That makes transfers easier. But LED also makes it harder if you have to use a different LED product: how do you make the same colours you had before, if you have no reference and no old unit to compare it to? Again, someone needs to create Pantone for theatre lighting.

Emma And in terms of the working process in America?

Neil Yes, the systems of working are different – not off-Broadway, which works remarkably like the UK, a non-unionized bunch of enthusiasts doing it for not very much money and a lot of love and dedication, just like here. The difference when you get to Broadway is that the unionization means that the jobs are more delineated, so you cannot cross over and do anything belonging to somebody else's job, which is a very good way of making sure that the management does not conflate roles.

From a lighting designer's point of view, that means you are slightly more removed from the process, especially because they put associates in there as well. So, the associate goes off and talks to the electrician, does the focus, comes back to you and says, is that good? You say could you bring that shutter in a bit more, and off they go and bring that shutter in. It's fine. It works well. They get paid very well, and it's really nice to know that you can go somewhere in the world where in any role in the theatre, as a member of the crew, as a followspotter, as an electrician, you can afford to buy a house, have a family, put your children through college and retire. There are lots of things which aren't great about the system, but the thing to admire about it is that it is an industry where people are respected. In London, when you say you work in theatre, people look at you in a slightly pitying way. In America, especially in New York, if you say you work in theatre, it's like, oh, wow, you are one of the essential industries that makes our city what it is.

Emma Preview periods: how do you use a preview period, how do you respond to what an audience is seeing in terms of the work you are doing?

Neil Preview periods are a time to finesse and refine and hone and add the grace notes, whether that be in plotting, in the picture, or in a musical with cues that literally go with the grace notes. It's your time to do the detailed sketching that the scenic designer did when they were putting their paint finishes on their model or the costume designer did when they were looking at fabrics. It's that process, for us. Everyone else is finessing as well but I think there is probably a much greater difference between first preview and last preview for us than there is for a scenic or costume designer. My goodness, we'd all love to get to first preview and go right, that's perfect, I'm off now, but that never happens. It's your chance to check every level of the theatre, every extreme sightline, to check that all the audience are getting the best possible show no matter where they're sitting.

If the preview period is long enough, a night off in previews is really useful just to go away and become a normal person again. You come in the next day with a much clearer head. Also, having friends come and watch during previews: having someone else beside you who is making you watch the piece through their eyes, I think, is illuminating because it makes you step outside of your own view. Otherwise, I often find that press night is the first time I've relaxed properly and really watched the piece – if you see something wrong then, there is nothing you can do about it!

Emma What and who influences your work? Where do you find inspiration from?

Neil Anywhere. The natural world is a great place for inspiration because some of the stuff you see in the sky they would never believe if you managed to put it on stage. Sometimes you're out on a walk and you are up on the side of a mountain and this sunset is wow, how is that range of colours possible? Everything. Photography. Art. I tell students who come to me it's really important to go into the art world because that becomes common ground – we talked about how you talk about lighting, and because you can't talk about it, what you end up doing is having to rely on shared experiences. I always slightly hate it when directors say, you know, that thing that person did on that show. That's not a great shorthand. But this piece of art, that piece of art – that's a great shorthand.

I worked with Kenneth Branagh, and he would say, I don't know anything about lighting. But I would get texts from him every now and then saying National Gallery, Room this, that painting. That would be how he would talk to you.

Film references are often a way of talking to each other. All of those things are an inspiration. Your imagination as well, because you need to take all of those inspirations and then take the next leap. Imagination is probably fuelled by all of those things, subconsciously.

Emma How do work with a budget?

Neil That can be annoying! On *Company*, they didn't tell me the budget before I'd designed the rig and sent it to the rental company, and it had come back at a reasonable price for a musical, except they didn't have a musical's budget, they had half a musical's budget. So, then you hone and hone. It's hard to work with a budget because if you pick the right kit, which the rental company has in stock, which nobody else wants, you sometimes get a lot for your money. If you want the latest whiz-bang-flash, you inevitably don't get so much for your money. It really depends on the maths they are doing – do they think your show is going to run? There are times that I have said yes to shows, and I've been working on them and thinking, yes this is great, this could run, then you get a price back from the rental company and go, oh, they don't think so . . . they often have a very good inkling.

They are, in effect, investing in shows. *Harry Potter*, both in London and New York, is way cheaper per week than the rig should be because both rental companies have taken a very long-term view on it. In order to get the job, they wanted to be involved with it, which is lovely, but in order to do that, there is going to be a lot of competition, so they are not doing their usual, which is, will it pay back within a year?

There are other times where you get nothing of what you want, and you have to make massive compromises. You eventually cut it down to the money, and you have a little plead about whether there is any more money.

Emma What's been the most exciting show or most satisfying show you've done?

Neil It's weird, isn't it – you are never completely satisfied with anything. I went back two nights ago to watch *Harry Potter* in London for the first time in a long time and remember thinking, oh, that could be better. I wish I'd solved that. The frustration is that you hadn't quite managed to solve all those issues. There are moments where you go, I should have done something different there, or I know that's not quite right, but I don't know what the alternative is.

The shows that I did for director Howard Davies were amazing and rewarding. It was a weird relationship as it was absolutely professional – never a dinner or a drink, just in the theatre. I'd worked with him as a board op for Mark Henderson, then as a re-lighter. But beginning to work with Howard myself at the National, on *Philistines*, *The White Guard* and *Children of the Sun* in the Lyttelton and *The Cherry Orchard* in the Olivier, all with Bunny Christie and Howard, then another with Vicki Mortimer and Howard, *The Silver Tassie*. He would never want to stop in tech – he'd go, what are we waiting for and you'd reply that you just needed a moment… But it was a really rewarding collaboration, though not a word was really spoken about light.

Emma Thank you, Neil. This has been a fascinating conversation.

Neil Thank you.

NATASHA CHIVERS

Lighting takes skill, talent, tact, diplomacy, sensitivity, calm and a good eye. But it also takes getting on with people, forming relationships, maybe even becoming friends. Sometimes the friendship comes first: you find people and realize you want to make shows with them. Natasha has lit shows regularly for director John Tiffany and movement director Steven Hoggett and the company he formed, Frantic Assembly. But she'll confess that she's known Hoggett since their teens, and that her first non-theatre job was waitressing in a restaurant in Huddersfield – with John Tiffany.

She trained in stage management and technical theatre at LAMDA. After college she became part of a group called Arts Threshold, who set up a theatre in a basement in Paddington. Colleagues there? Composer Max Richter, designer Katrina Lindsay and director Rufus Norris. She continues to make new colleagues and friends on shows of all kinds now, directors Robert Icke and Kate Prince amongst her many regular collaborators across a career recognized by an Olivier Award (for *Sunday In The Park With George*), a UK Theatre Award (for *Happy Days*), a Theatre Critics of Wales Award (for *Praxis Makes Perfect*), a Drama Desk award (for *Prima Facie* on Broadway) and a Tony Award nomination (also for *Prima Facie* on Broadway).

www.natashachivers.co.uk

Emma What is your starting point for researching the world of the piece?

Natasha I work enormously on instinct so I'm always aware there are all sorts of things going on inside before I've even realized what's happening. I guess I'm always interested in what's discarded. I often ask the set designer what the ideas were before they got to this version because I find it useful to dig into why they ended up where they did. I always ask a set designer for their reference material and if there is anything in particular I should look at that they've followed. I have an archive of books on photography and art, and sometimes I go into those to dig ideas and images out to show to directors, to see if anything resonates.

Emma If there is a script, how would you approach it?

Natasha I read it once for enjoyment and don't make any notes and just try to let it wash over me. Then I would make notes of just practical things before meeting the director and set designer. I make most of my detailed notes at the read through. It's just about using your time better. I used to wait until later before I started the cue sheet. Now I realize I can just start an outline, a summary document that then turns into a cue sheet.

Emma Do you put your cues into the desk before tech?

Natasha No, but I always go in with a cue sheet, pretty much always a detailed cue sheet. That's become more refined over the years in terms of how I'll put blocking cues in one colour, times of days, changes of mood cues in another colour. I will always go in with a document. I will always give the DSM that document as well. I want to get the information over to them, then just speak to them about things that have changed rather than starting from scratch during tech week – I find it too much to be making the state and telling someone where it goes at the same time. And the DSM feels more relaxed and happier because they have something in the book. Then it's just a dialogue about let's just move that a little bit earlier, or we don't need it.

Emma So do you go through it with the DSM beforehand?

Natasha No. I email it to them as early as I can. Obviously, if I'm caught out by directors not sharing the work until the last minute sometimes it might be like the Sunday night that the DSM gets it. What I've learnt is the sooner I get it to them, the sooner they can go through it. I always say come back to me with any questions and if there is anything you don't understand or doesn't make any sense.

The other thing I do with anything that is particularly complicated is have a video, and I make sure the DSM has the same video, so I can put a cue on 3 minutes 43 seconds when she raises her arm or on that beat of the music or exactly at this point so that they are up and running on their own. It's slightly so you can go, I did say it was there. I guess it's also about getting older and expecting people to do their job to a high standard. I'm never not kind, but at the same time I've had some DSMs who've tried to make the process just about them when it isn't about them, when it has to be about lots of elements coming together, but of course they have a job to do. I used to be a DSM, and I know it's not always easy, but you do expect them to step up. To be fair, most of them do, and most are really good.

Emma Do you like to have a lighting session before tech?

Natasha I always keep it in there because schedules get knocked on, and it ends up being the final bit of the focus or moving light focus. There might be one or two things that I want to see or to try. I'm not so bothered about it as I used to be. I think quite a lot of the more complicated jobs you find that nothing's set up properly until you start the tech. So, you can demand a plotting session with people to fly and walk in, but most of the time you don't get it anyway and no one takes it seriously until the tech starts.

Emma When you start creating a state, where do you start?

Natasha I tend to start with backlight and sidelight and form and then fill in faces, but I've become much more into face lighting as I've got older. I think that's because I've got better at learning how to make things look good but also access people's faces at the same time. It seems to have taken me quite a long time to do that. I guess my route is quite architectural; I think I'm interested in the big stage picture. The director Vicky Featherstone and I have had a frank discussion where she's said to me, you know you fill the faces in last, and that's fine when we've got time, but sometimes we are racing to fill them in. It was great she said that to me because you don't really know what the other person sees. I appreciated her saying it because I know her well enough, and she knows me well enough to say that. It taught me something about myself and about something I needed to be careful of, because obviously you want to work and you want people to feel happy with what you are doing.

Emma How do you find the lighting language for a project?

Natasha Instinct. It's so funny that's the answer to so many of these questions on lighting, it really is just instinct. Once you start to see the model, you go by that, but even then, what you are putting in it might be quite different from what the model dictates – you might be going against it. So, it's all just a feeling and an instinct.

Emma If you have a model which you look at and struggle to see how you would get any light in to, how do you approach that situation?

Natasha Well, I guess experience is really great, and collaboration. If I think it's not going to be good because you can't get light in, I call it out these days. I let the director and designer know what they potentially will get with that set and ask them if that's what they want, if it's enough for the production. It's a shared responsibility. I think when I was younger, I used to freak out and go I'm not going to be able to do this, that and the other, but now I go, OK so you want a false ceiling. What that means is there won't be any backlight: are you good with that? Or, do you want to light the back wall so you can get some sense of shape and sculpting there? When I was younger, I was quite anxious, and I used to take a lot on as my responsibility, but now I'm happy to bounce it back a bit. That's what I did on the last show I did at the Royal Court. The set designer was great and said I've done this before and we put some LED tape on the

Theatre Lighting Design: Conversations on the Art, Craft and Life

Message In A Bottle at Sadler's Wells, London. Directed and choreographed by a regular collaborator of Natasha's, Kate Prince. Set design by Ben Stones, costume design by Anna Fleischle, lighting by Natasha Chivers, video by Andrzej Goulding, sound by David McEwan. Photographer: Helen Maybanks / ArenaPAL.

floor. So, we tried that and it looked great, and I put some other lights in and it worked really well. So, I think keeping your cool.

I think the problem with the early process is when you get a white card model, what you actually need is the plans. You're asking very specific things about positions and angles and what's possible and what's not possible. To work those out, what you actually need is to be able to draw the beams of light, whether it's on a computer or on a bit of paper, in order to answer the question. You need to work out what the shots are. But no one gives you that at that stage. That's a problem. Even if it was just a scruffy drawing and they'd pencilled on the shape of the set, you could ask them more clearly. That is something which I think needs to be addressed as you need to be able to give concrete answers to some things.

I do think everything begins and ends with stressing less. When you are stressed, you are not seeing clearly, and you are not communicating clearly, and you are not collaborating clearly.

Emma It's all about collaborating isn't it, because you can only get light in if it's physically possible to.

Natasha Exactly! I think physics becomes your friend, actually, as you get older. When you are younger and a bit insecure you think someone else could do something better – but if you are drawing a beam of light, it either will go from point A to point B through a particular aperture or it won't. You learn that no one else can do physics better than you can!

There is a limited number of ways you can suggest to solve a problem, and once you've offered them all up, if there is still a problem and no one wants to help you solve it, then it's worth calling that out again and saying I'm a bit stuck because you don't want this, but you do want this and I'm not quite sure you are going to get what you want. It's not taking it all on yourself. It's being as smart as you can and offering as much as you can – I can't do this, but I can do this.

Emma What other experiences influence how you light a show?

Natasha I'm hugely influenced by music and sound these days. Music I've always been influenced by, but sound much more now. I work with Tom Gibbons a lot and it's kind of changed my practice totally in a way that I could never have predicted, because of what he brings and the conversations we have early on about what we are doing. We generally feed off each other now; he inspires me and that's been really joyful. I never really noticed sound before I started working with him. Now I know when the sound could be more and I miss it. I miss working with him. That's been a huge inspiration.

I think gigs influence me a huge amount these days, more than anything else. I put my festival tickets through on tax because I tend to learn more from gigs than probably going to see theatre pieces. I tend to be influenced more by the way people light music.

Emma Is that because there is a freedom?

Natasha There is a freedom, but I think also because they tend to be a bit ahead of us in terms of what's possible. Maybe because they have a bit more money, they get the toys first, so I'm often seeing things being used at gigs that I've not seen in the theatre. When music is lit well, that engages me and excites me. I just find it exciting. I try and bring that excitement into theatre and dance.

Emma How do you talk about light?

Natasha I find quite a lot of directors don't want to talk about light. Some of the more experienced ones do. It's a miracle when someone really knows about light. They either know a lot or they know nothing about light, you don't find a lot in between. Some of them are quite happy to admit they don't know a lot, and some feel a bit embarrassed.

I think if you get a sense that they have a sophisticated understanding of light then you can use terms like sculptural and architectural and talk in terms of colour or things being full or stylized. If they don't know anything and they are a bit overwhelmed, then I tend to show images. I've just done some dance in Sweden, and I was struggling to get into the head of one of the choreographers who I'd not worked with before. The piece he was making was not like anything I'd ever lit before. He wanted it to be quite odd and quite alienated and unusual colours. I struggled with finding a way in until we started to look at some of the specific images of Gregory Crewdson. That was a much easier dialogue to start because he could understand what I was talking about, whereas before I don't think he would have done.

Emma When you read a script do you create an emotional journey? Do you look at it as an emotional journey and then try and run that as an arc?

Natasha Yes, I think there is nothing more exciting than getting a play, a great play, something like *Who's Afraid of Virginia Woolf*, and knowing you are starting somewhere and ending somewhere else and how are you going to do that. How are you going to mirror that with light, what is your journey? The start of the evening full of potential. A full warm appealing room that tells the audience they are about to see something and by the end you know everything has gone to pot – and you are allowed the freedom to take the light on that journey.

I do get quite a lot of complex, multi-location, moving set-type pieces. When I get a play in a room where I can throw all the gear at that one room in different ways and colours and take it from cue 1 to cue 64 at the end, you realize you've nudged it along. You realize that cue 1 and cue 64 are so radically different, but hopefully nobody's really noticed that happen. It is intensely satisfying to be able to work in that kind of detail and mirror the emotion of a piece.

Emma When you watch previews, what do you gain from watching it with an audience?

Natasha I've realized more recently that until I've taken the cans off, I don't really watch it properly. I don't think there is any way to shortcut that journey because I think you have to get to a certain place with cans on. When you've got the cues in the right place and you've got to a certain point, you are a bit out of touch with the detail of the emotion of the piece. You kind of go back to the final rehearsal room run-through on first preview. That's the beginning of the next part of the journey.

Emma So the previews are a honing of the work?

Natasha Yes, definitely, and also occasionally, things that you've got slightly wrong or misunderstood from that final rehearsal room run-through, or maybe the actor's performance has developed or the director's gone in a slightly different direction. But I've realized getting the cans off is a good thing, even if what's exposed to you is that you are still a bit of a way away. It's a step which needs to happen.

Emma How do you progress your ideas from the script onto a lighting plan?

Natasha I can't do anything until I've done one draft, and what tends to happen is that I do a first draft which is about seventy per cent, and then I change it, which I think is for the best as the first draft is about getting something out and then the second draft is about me finessing it and being a bit bolder. Sometimes practical things lead: what your positions are, what you can afford.

It's interesting when we do the Michael Northen bursary judging for the ALPD: what you realize is the submissions seem to split normally into two groups. The top submissions are the type of lighting plan where someone has gone for it entirely and they have designed something that if it doesn't work then they would be a bit stuck because they might not have lots of moving lights, but what they've gone for is something so bold and so clear that if it works it's going to be great. The other is the one where someone has come up with really good results through designing a rig which makes sense, so it could be that they've got lots of movers and they've put those up with a bit of other cleverly designed stuff, and they've proved they know how to light things because they've come up with images that are appropriate whether it's a musical and it's sculptural or has really strong looks or a play where they've used that rig well. I guess what you want to be doing is going somewhere in between. I think a smart lighting designer is a lighting designer that covers themselves if they don't know the director, in case they don't like what they're doing. I think I've always aimed to be bold, but occasionally that's not the right response to a job.

Emma How do you work with a budget?

Natasha I normally speak to the hire companies myself rather than giving a list to a production manager or head electrician. I like to be involved in that process and explore what the options are and what's in stock. I guess otherwise it's like being a chef and not going to the market. It feels a bit odd not checking whether things are available and how many you could get, and if you had this, how many of these and how many of those. Lighting designer Paul Anderson, who also runs Sparks, a lighting rental company, once said we were quite similar in that we were able to work with different kinds of lights. That we were quite versatile designers, and while occasionally there was something we knew we had to have for a specific job, we would make it work.

I think coming up through the fringe is incredibly powerful because if you've got six Patt 743s and some par cans you move them round until you come up with something that works. If you have to get some sun floods in, you can be really creative with that. I think it's a great grounding.

Emma How do you keep pace with the technology coming in? Do you make time to go and look at new products?

Natasha No; I go and see shows or gigs. If there's something I like at that gig, I will find out what it is, or I will just store it up in my head and wait until I need that particular thing. Sometimes I wish I was going to demos of new lights; I think it is quite sensible to do it, I just never seem to make or have the time.

I do find you are introduced to a lot of things because venues buy them. It's not long before someone's got one, and you are lighting with it, and you're testing it, and you think, did I really need to go to that demo, giving up an afternoon?

Emma How do you work with a programmer and how do you see that relationship?

Natasha Well, it's everything isn't it, it's just essential. I find it difficult not to work with people I like. That sounds really obvious, but it's quite a personal relationship, but at the same time I do like to try and give younger people a chance. It's about picking the right job for the right person at the right time.

Emma Has your visual language changed through your career?

Natasha Yeah, I think it's become slightly more sophisticated. I've always loved colour, I'm unapologetic about that. I know that there was a fashion for just using colour correction, and there felt like a slight sort of snobbery associated with that, which I found quite irritating. I will say I think that I have moved in that direction, although I've never been afraid to use colour. I'm still not afraid to use strong colour, I absolutely love it, though I would say I probably have moved away from it. I think my lighting's become slightly more elegant.

Emma LED means you are now able to have any colour. How has that affected how you draw a lighting plan and how your relationship with a director works when there are so many options?

Natasha I know my traditional gel colours well, and I've found it fascinating to call up a colour and work out if it is really that colour. It's an ongoing process. When I did *Sunset at the Villa Thalia* at the National I thought that because it was a show that took place on a Greek Island and started in the morning and went through sunset, Lustrs would be my friends in terms of doing a kind of directional sun from two sides. But actually, I found that Lustr front light was unsatisfactory. It seemed like a great solution because I could change colour temperature constantly throughout the show, but I didn't enjoy having LED front light. So that was a big lesson.

I don't feel overwhelmed by LEDs as an option. I think I would have really considered my scroll colours before, and I think now I probably only use the Lustr colours that would have been in the scroll. I go in knowing what the colours are and maybe a director goes, could it be a little bit warmer and I might notch it up to a colour that I might not have put in the scroll. It feels exciting to have any colour available – but I think I'm glad that I'm far enough into my career not to feel overwhelmed.

Emma How does colour affect an audience's perception of space and atmosphere?

Natasha It's funny because I run workshops on this. I think what you realize is everyone is an expert, they just don't know they are. I think everyone's an expert because we all encounter colour. What I find fascinating about the workshops is that when you talk to people about colour is when they realize they know a lot about it. I think it's one of your three big tools. I would put what type of light, where the light goes and colour as your three big choices. So, I think it is a third of the power of a lighting design.

Emma It's a massive element. Are there particular colours that you like to have in the rig?

Natasha Yes, I think so, not every rig, but these days I'd always want a full set of colour correction, I'd always want Lee 711 cold blue, those are my colour staples. Some rigs I like a nice L709 lavender.

Emma How do you work with colour in sets and costume?

Natasha When I first started, people used to ask me about paint finishes and things, and I had literally no idea. They'd show me a sample of something splattered this way and splattered that way, and I just made it up. Now I do have a sense of how light will react to a certain colour or a certain texture or a certain finish, and I'm able to offer something more intelligent about what needs to happen to a surface and if we'll be able to access texture and things. I think the reason I don't worry so much about costume is I pretty much always have a rig which is able to change colour on the people so that allows me not to worry so much. Whereas the backlight, until fairly recently, was part of a wash where I had to choose the scroll colours, so I'd have to pay a lot more attention because I wouldn't have limitless opportunities. Normally, I'd make sure that on the people I could change colour a little bit. I guess it's less likely to be as saturated as well – and if you get it wrong, the chances are you can get at the lights to change it, which you can't for the overhead lights.

Emma And the importance of the real source – tungsten, fluorescent – if you have a show where you want to use those sources, do you feel the actual sources are the best ways of achieving that?

Natasha I think pretty important, though bizarrely it's probably one of the last things I came to. For a lot of people it's the first thing, but it took me a long time to get my head around it. I got my head around other things quicker, like positions and colour. I knew what fluorescents were, but it took me a long time to talk about the quality of light and understand the quality of light. I think other lighting designers got to it much more quickly. In the last ten years, I've really got it.

Emma How can lighting add to a story? And what can lighting add to an audiences' understanding?

Natasha I think you can put characters in an environment which supports them or doesn't support them. It's the classic manipulate the audience into feeling particular things. I'm thinking about the show I did last week at the Royal Court, it's another sort of *Virginia Woolf* answer. . . It starts off with the daughter returning back to see her parents, and it's not a naturalistic set so you kind of know something might happen. The lighting is quite even then, but by the end of the show it's almost exclusively lit by footlights, and it's like a footlight Punch and Judy. You are presenting them in a way which shows that everything is quite warped, and they are quite warped, so you are influencing the audience in that way.

I did a one-man *Macbeth* set in a Victorian hospital. The idea was this guy was locked into a secure hospital, and he had sort of psychotic personality disorder, which meant he had to play out, he'd done something and he didn't know what he'd done, so he had to act

Theatre Lighting Design: Conversations on the Art, Craft and Life

out the whole affair and play all the characters as part of his psychosis. In situations like that you can support that narrative by putting that performer into lots of different worlds, to show that he's conjuring up these different worlds in order to now be Lady Macbeth. So it can sort of support the ideas and the emotions in that way by taking the audience up certain roads and sometimes bringing them back.

Emma What is the biggest thing you've learnt from someone else which has unlocked something for you as a lighting designer?

Natasha My friend Steven Hoggett, I've worked with him for years, the thing he taught me is: never be the smartest person in the room, which I think is really good. What he means is, keep working with very smart people so you grow. He's been a great influence. The other person whose been a big influence is Vicky Featherstone. She's fascinating not just as a director but as a producer, she is just so creative. What Vicky has taught me is always to really listen and to ask the question 'well we can't do that but what can we do?' Always be creative within the limits of what you've got.

Emma In terms of collaborations, has your process changed?

Natasha I think I've become easier to work with because I think I've honed my communication skills, and because I get less stressed and anxious. I think sometimes I came across as a bit grumpy or defensive because I was anxious and working so hard to

Macbeth, with Alan Cumming, performed at the Glasgow Tramway and then in New York. Directed by John Tiffany and Andrew Goldberg, designed by Merle Hensel, lighting by Natasha Chivers, video by Ian William Galloway, sound by Fergus O'Hare. *Photographer: Manuel Harlan / ArenaPAL.*

process everything and work at great speed. Now, I'm comfortable disagreeing with people, and I don't have a problem with that as I did when I was younger. I think my collaborations are more detailed... actually that's probably not true as in some ways the more lighting you do, the less you talk about lighting, but I think you tend to be able to go more quickly to the things that need to be discussed, to have that understanding of the key things. I think people would say I'm a better collaborator.

Emma What would you tell your younger self?

Natasha I would tell my younger self to worry less, to do some training on myself and stress management, and spend some time on how to worry less and to have less imposter syndrome and have a little more faith. I feel I've lost a lot of time worrying, and it's a shame. It's just such a waste of energy, and I know everyone needs to grow and there is always going to be a process, but I do think the industry is desperately in need of training on stress management and mindfulness. I think as freelancers you are a little bit out on a limb, and there is a lot of stuff that you have to find your own way through. I wish I'd found it a bit earlier.

Emma The imposter syndrome is hard, isn't it?

Natasha Yeah, I even still get it now sometimes, not often, but now I'm able to see it and go look at this, isn't it amazing you are doing this, who would have thought, and smile a bit more. But sometimes it might be two or three days from having that feeling before I notice it and go, get a grip.

Emma Thank you, Natasha. That's an important lesson for us all. It has been great talking to you.

JON CLARK

Many of the designers featured here just launched into lighting with no specific training. Some trained in theatre production, some lighting design. Jon studied more broadly, taking the theatre design course at Bretton Hall. Perhaps this helps understand his constant striving to define, shape and control space, almost architecturally, rather than just lighting each scene, his style perfectly suiting plays staged in more abstract settings and the worlds of opera and dance. He seems to thrive in particular when presented with spaces some might consider unlightable, such as the low-ceilinged rooms of *The Jungle* or the rotating glass box of *The Lehman Trilogy*, which won him a Tony Award. He has become the go-to lighting designer for directors such as Stephen Daldry, Jamie Lloyd, Sam Mendes and Katie Mitchell.

Away from theatres, Jon lives outside the hustle and bustle of London: like many lighting designers he has escaped to the sea, a neighbour of Paule Constable's in Brighton, the train journey in and out of the capital the perfect time to get ahead on reading a script or preparing a cue list so a little more time is left free for family life.

www.jon-clark.com

Emma When you read a script for the first time, what is your process from reading the script to drawing a lighting plan?

Jon I don't think lighting can emerge from the cold reading of a script alone. For me, lighting design is about defining and re-defining space over time. The narrative drives that, of course, but for me, it's mostly driven by what I see and feel in the rehearsal room. I'll read the script, of course, but I find it very hard to respond to a script in isolation.

With *The Inheritance*, though, I was absolutely sucked into it, as with an extraordinary novel. I read it straight through, two four-hour plays as it was then. So compelling and brilliantly structured as a piece of work. It was like reading a novel; your mind makes your own pictures for it.

But then, of course, you start to wonder what on earth the set designer will come up with! It was a play that moved from location to location to location, and I thought, I hope this isn't going to be a million things just flying in and out. A designer might present just a sign or a light bulb for a scene, but nothing else will have physically changed in the space. There's nothing to suggest any kind of ceiling or compression. It's just a piece of furniture on an open stage. How on earth will I constrain this scene dramatically?

Alongside that, there are always the mechanics of being a lighting designer. I've read a play, I've seen a set design, but the theatre needs to know what the lighting rig is, what they need to hire, a specification. I sometimes struggle, shy away from that because I don't know yet what sticks the two things together; I haven't yet got a connection to the people and the space. It's more about architecture than script, I suppose, as I don't know what choices the director is making.

So I sit in the rehearsal room and I scribble and scribble ideas, and then suddenly it is something. I'm responding to seeing humans in space, to hearing it, and suddenly it gets the juices flowing. I can get excited about it and start to see how I'm going to define it. I see what I need to do.

Emma How do you then translate that?

Jon It becomes which single direction of light best forms the relationship between these two people and the space they inhabit. That's the fundamental question through the rehearsal process; it releases everything, really. Making an instinctive choice about the direction of light for a scene is liberating, because it's one decision made – a structural choice from which you can hang later decisions. How do the choices for this moment or scene then relate to the scene before or the scene after? How can they all exist in one coherent world?

Emma Taking the ideas from your time in rehearsals and drawing them on a plan – how do you do that? Do you have systems you like to use?

Jon I get wedded to directional systems of light that describe the space. Using multiple sources from one direction makes the idea scalable without compromising the honesty of the direction. I don't like calling them systems as in that classic lighting terminology; that suggests to me a saturated rig of tried and tested ideas repeated irrespective of the particular show, which is the antithesis of what I'm trying to do.

Breaking that direction down into elements lets the idea be scalable and selective. I love clusters of lights, par cans specifically. It's such an honest source of light, and has such a range within it: very intense light at full or a thick, warm blanket of light burning away gently at twenty or thirty per cent. I use them time and time again. The design for *The Jungle* followed this pattern, but with 500W tungsten sun floods instead of pars. Three floods on a low ceiling at one hundred per cent are harsh and hard to look at directly, but at twenty or thirty per cent there is a love and warmth and honesty and humanity to the light. With these clusters, I can describe the stage, open and close the space over time in a repeatable way. It's about exploring space and exploring time and connecting people or fracturing space or separating people. That's what I like to do.

Combining that with crosslighting means I can make choices about how faces are informed without making any unintentional statement across the rest of the space. I can then choose the light that informs how they connect to the surface and the world they're in. I can make a choice about the perceived ceiling or volume of the space – whether that's something coming in low or whether it's above, or far away, or close. The balance of these things and shifting that balance throughout the piece is the structure that I find gives me freedom to craft the narrative. It's about where the light comes from, is the space open or closed, and then how it keeps shifting between those two places through the piece. Temperature of light is the next thing, I guess, and then when, if anywhere, is there any need to be bold with colour.

Emma How or where do you find your inspiration for how you define that space?

Jon It is mainly just a response to what you see in front of you. Nine times out of ten, you will have a response to what's going on, to the choices that have been made. In a way, it's just instinctive – about where the light should be coming from, about what you need to do to balance the boldness of a picture. It may not be democratic, so it may not give everyone an even quality of light, but it should be directionally or dramatically the right thing to do in terms of who is seen or isn't seen or is close to the heat of the light.

I do think if you give anyone a room for a month with some objects and five or ten or a hundred lights, people will make aesthetically pleasing choices with the lights – it's not so hard to do that. But the other part of what we do is that it's harder to deliver strong, clear images one after another quickly, under pressure. That's definitely a muscle you have to exercise, a skill, something you get very much better at delivering. I don't think I'm brilliant at making beautiful pictures, actually, but then I don't think that's what really interests me. I don't think a good lighting design is a series of beautiful pictures in isolation from each other. This is all generalizations, of course; there are so many variables. But for me, a very clear, readable design has an arc – how space moves in time, how it opens and contracts, how that supports the production dramaturgically. Someone watching the show may not be aware of it, but subconsciously they understand how it all fits together.

The closest I've got to this ideal, so far, has perhaps been for *The Inheritance*. Rather than all those flying pieces I'd feared, Bob Crowley created a simple grey rectangular platform in a black box. Stephen Daldry, the director, said two key things to me during the rehearsal process. That he thought of it as being like a contemporary dance – I thought, great! That's brilliant! That's instinctively how I had been approaching the design, so we are thinking the same thing here. So much information and reassurance came from that single comment.

The other was, don't feel you need to light it locationally, just light it emotionally. That was really empowering too. It would be stupid to try and make rooms out of light for six and a half hours, but that's what it could have become. Instead, each scene became an exploration or a response to one or more actors in a space; the volume of the space is re-defined to make sense of this emotively and dramatically. The first half is almost entirely monochromatic, colour-corrected light from above. Light expands and contracts the space; the text and the staging tell you everything about the direction you're heading, the choices you're making. It's also about trusting when not to make a change, understanding the broader language of the production so that not every change of blocking or facial expressions is underlined by a shift of lighting.

The Inheritance at the Noël Coward Theatre, London. Directed by Stephen Daldry, designed by Bob Crowley, lighting by Jon Clark, sound by Paul Arditti and Christopher Reid. *Photographer: Marc Brenner.*

Of course, these rules of engagement are different every time…

In opera, there's also then the music, which contains so much information – it is the dynamic journey which defines the whole piece. For the most part, it will be instructive in the choices you make, though occasionally there might be good reason to push back against it. There is a global decision you make about when you heighten moments and when you don't, and that means you've already got some rules, some kind of structure and intention before you start. You discuss that with the director and everyone early on. Then you can be proactive about other suggestions. It's lovely to have those conversations where the set designer lets you into their process, and you collaborate and bounce off each other. It also means you've opened that relationship for when you're further along, in the theatre.

Emma And having worked out the direction and how to define the space, how do you define the colour palette?

Jon I'm not terribly reliant on colour. I like to use it sparingly and for effect – like putting a cold slice of pineapple into a dry mouth; there's an overwhelming rush of the senses, a zinginess, a fruitiness to it. That's how I like colour to work. Conversely, if you ate the whole pineapple, that initial impact would fade.

So, I think about the temperature of light first. Beyond that, I don't want to make colour choices by theory or science but rather to find a human response to the world of each production.

Emma What for you is the practical process of transferring your ideas from the rehearsal room to the stage?

Jon I aim to be in the rehearsal room as much as I can. In the last week there I would hope to see the piece several times before it gets on stage, even if that's staggered run-throughs before a full run. I video the last couple of runs as it's vital to have that information to return to on a busy production. Structurally I'll get all the cue points into the script, but those won't be prescriptive choices about the contents of the lighting so much as identifying dramatic intentions and events – an instinct that something needs to happen. I feel very confident in my ability to do that wherever I feel an emotive response to what's going on on-stage rather than necessarily when something has to happen lighting-wise. I have no interest in following one person from a chair to a table, and I resist the urge to make a tightly framed picture each time an actor moves.

I use Sam Smallman's Stamp software, which lets you add notes or cue numbers to the video you're recording and ties those to the exact point on the video. In tech or during previews, it links directly to the lighting console and automatically adds the cue information to the video. Later on, you can go back and see exactly where cue 100 ran in the preview the previous night. I don't do my lighting notes in response to the video but in response to what I saw in the rehearsal room or on the stage, but Stamp makes it faster and more accurate to analyse events and cue timing. I'm better informed to respond to a note rather than trying to decipher what I've scribbled in a rehearsal room or in the dark during a preview. It's a tool – the simplest idea, but it has changed my life.

After the last rehearsal room run, I will sit down with the DSM and talk through the cues with them; doing this in person means you also learn so much from them – why something has happened, how that's happened because of this. You can gain so much more information about the production and the relationships of people in the production from the time you spend with the DSM.

I'll then go through the script and put each one of those cues into the console showfile. I'll label every cue and give each a time – I don't beat myself up about it, just a rough guess that feels about right. Sometimes I'll do that on the train coming in and out of London, sometimes I'll do it in tech trying to keep ahead of myself. But it will always be there before we tech those scenes. Having a cue structure in place gives me the freedom to concentrate more on the stage during tech rehearsals.

Emma Do you pre-visualize shows?

Jon Only really at the Royal Opera House; it's not bullet-proof, but it's very useful for building presets and checking angles, especially in that environment where it's like an opera factory! It's interesting talking to students about that: it's very hard to impress on them the kind of skill set you have to develop once you've graduated in order to be able to do the job at any level. To rock up at the Royal Opera House and light an opera there takes a broad range of skills and experience. I've walked away sometimes during stage rehearsals with my head in my hands, saying, well, it is lit to a standard, but it's certainly not a work of brilliance!

Emma What do you think those skills are?

Jon I think you have to have stamina. It's repeatability, to make all those choices as quickly and accurately as you can – follow your instincts and deliver something on stage pretty quickly as you get very little time. International opera houses vary hugely in how they approach putting on a production. At the Royal Opera, there is one day, a 'technical Sunday', when the set is put on stage for the first time in the morning, followed by focusing for a couple of hours in the afternoon, followed by plotting cues in the evening. A director who's never worked there before may have wildly different expectations about what's achievable over the course of the day. They may intend to work methodically through the whole thing. Sometimes they are completely disinterested, or something comes up technically that they are so worried about that you just do that all day. At 7am the next day, you do what more you can in an hour and a half, then the cast are on and you do a stage and piano where you literally whip through the whole show, and you just keep lighting.

If you've been in those kinds of sessions before, then you have the experience; you can manage the expectations. It's about having the confidence to adapt your process and make use of the limited time effectively. I use these rehearsals to explore the space. If I sit back then we are going to run out of time, so I hack around and hack around until things begin to stick. I need to know what my intention is. I'm prepared for things not to work, but, crucially, it gives me a chance to understand the space so I can move forwards.

I don't work from a paper plan in tech now. I work with magic sheets on the console, because it allows me to organize the lights in a visual form which works for my brain. It's like a low-res snapshot of each cue, which is great to scan through to get a shape of the directions and choices I've made for each cue. It's also brilliantly selective in a rep environment where there's a house rig, large chunks of which aren't relevant to this production. I don't need to see things that have no purpose in this show. So I'll have a large touchscreen flat on the table in front of me for the magic sheets – bang, glance down quickly and see which lights are doing that. It's about having quick access to the information you need at that precise moment to help you make quick decisions.

Emma How do you work collaboratively with a director and a designer?

Jon I am more empowered by when we start making the work in the theatre than the time before that. I want to be invested in all the conversations before that, but often you can only offer words and references, so I always feel like you can't quite demonstrate the potency of your ideas. It can feel as though you have nothing solid to offer until the point you can share the actual light.

Those first days of tech are then really interesting – responding to what you are seeing, going, OK, what is it that isn't working? Managing the expectations of directors and designers and their understanding of what they're seeing on stage – 'what is Jon thinking?!' – especially if they're new relationships. At the same time, I'm trying to make sense of the space for the first time, the reality of what the real light is doing in the real volume of space on the real surfaces, human and scenic. It's a process that can only occur at this point in time; you have to recognize that, which becomes easier with experience. What I've learnt is to be more confident, to say this isn't working as it's meant to and, crucially, to be able to identify why. But I see tech as the real start of a process which doesn't end until the very end of the preview period.

An experienced director will often appreciate all this, especially at the start of tech. They might say two or three pertinent things, or they might say nothing at all, but you will often know full well they don't think it's right either. Crucially, that then gives me the space to find out what it is for myself. That's the best gift – to get pertinent directorial notes. Ah, we are on the same page, or, I see it that way, or it could be one comment as they pass in the corridor. I thrive on being given the space to find something out; I think the process is impossible without that.

That's different from not working collaboratively. But if you lose ownership of what you're trying to do because someone says do this or it should be that, then at some point I won't own those choices. All the choices I make should belong to one central design for that piece. I essentially need notes to be dramaturgical or practical. It's OK to have some notes which are prescriptive, but you must interpret those notes yourself. If they say, it needs to be brighter over there, the tendency can be to just react and throw up something terrible to achieve that. They say, great, we can see them now, you move on. But those lights shouldn't be on in my world, so now I have to go back and manage and edit, stay on top of and continually re-evaluate the choices I'm making.

Emma Can we talk about all of those things in context, with *The Jungle* – a play about the residents of Europe's largest refugee camp, presented in a closed-room environment designed very much to feel like that camp, and lit almost entirely with practicals. Can you talk about the show a little for those who weren't lucky enough to see it?

Jon When you go in, the room is under-exposed. It invites you to look around, to make sense of the space you're in. There is singing, and you're welcomed into a friendly atmosphere by the performers. Then suddenly, the room is smacked into very bright light, and noise. You have no idea what's coming next. The first ten minutes are a bombardment, almost incomprehensible. You experience a huge tension, people running around shouting. You're at the end of the story. You are desperately trying to piece together who's who. Then there's an invasion by the police and it stops dead. You can take a breath and say, now I can begin to make sense of this. It's an interesting device; you experience first-hand what the characters experienced.

I never thought of *The Jungle*'s lights as 'practicals'. I never thought of it as lighting with practicals, though I suppose it is in the sense that they are not conventional theatre lights. They were just the right lights to light that show with.

The first conversations were along the lines that there shouldn't really be any lights in the space at all! Joe and Joe, who wrote the play and spent a long time in the camp in Calais that it takes place in, and Miriam Buether, the set designer, had a massive file of reference photos. We all worked from those, trying to obey the rules visually and aesthetically. There is practically no compromise scenically – the ceiling is a little bit higher than it would have been, and the space is a little bit bigger, but the aesthetic is accurately re-created, so the lighting fixtures needed to obey the same conventions. I love rules like that, restrictions. The challenge is to find the range with whatever lights you can have to explore the space. It's cheating to say maybe we could put these tiny Fresnels in here or maybe we could just do it with birdies.

I wanted to be clear from the outset with Justin and Stephen, the directors, and with Miriam that this was great, and if these are the rules, then this is what we'll do. No conventional theatre lights. We did briefly discuss other ideas – could we justify using old theatre lights with a narrative in our heads that they'd been donated to the camp by a theatre company? But there were no visual references to support this, and it felt like a compromise.

At the first model showing, there was a very accurate model of the whole room in which the entire play would take place. It was entirely covered by a fabric ceiling. Everyone was peering in through the windows; I mindfully put the anglepoise above the ceiling and it gave this brilliant quality of diffused light to the room below. It immediately felt like daylight; I remember thinking, oh wow, that's a gift, we've got to be able to do that.

I was straight over to Paul Arditti, the sound designer, and Anthony Newton, the production manager, to talk about minimizing the amount of equipment above the ceiling. That worried me – shadows of rigging or speakers would give the game away, but we managed to find a way and then improved it each time we moved the show.

On the original version at the Young Vic, we had a very tight budget, but since it was a National Theatre co-production we were begging, borrowing and stealing everything we could from the National, then adding what we could afford to hire, which wasn't very much at all. There we top-lit the ceiling with HMI Fresnels. We didn't have very much throw between the ceiling and the grid, and there were all kinds of unavoidable bridles and bits of zig-zag rigging. In the West End, the rigging was cleaner; we used Martin Encores because fan noise was an issue. In New York, the throw was even more limited, so we took a different approach and used ColorForce LED battens with their very wide lens option – 36 battens spaced above the whole ceiling. It worked brilliantly; even where there were obstructions the beams overlapped and fuzzed out the shadows.

Then I went back to the reference pictures, and what I saw time and time again were pictures of the real Jungle in Calais: these make-shift structures at dusk, with the grey-blueness of daylight then a tungsten light or a fluorescent CFL twirly-whirly bulb hanging inside one of these structures and that was it really. The cold, depressing light of day or the never-ending landscape of hopelessness outside with this warmer kind of love coming from inside, and people who were trying to make something of the moment – eating, drinking, worshipping. There were little shops, cans of coke, crisps, a shop with a little sun flood with a bit of twin-and-earth wire to a small generator outside.

It was prevalent across the camp, and it became the central structural idea: diffused light for outside, essentially daylight or darkness. It could be on or off, and you could change the temperature of it. It made you aware of the outside world and that scale of life outside. Against that, light from inside, which would be sun floods or fluorescent lights. Sun floods mounted to the underside of the ceiling could be harsh and brutal at high intensity or, at a lower level, would give a warmer light and a sense of humanity inside.

I looked at the reference pictures again – they'd clearly used whichever lights they could get from the local DIY places. That led me to the 500W sun flood. I have always loved what you can get out of these £10 lights. You get a lot of love out of that burning tungsten wire!

So: I drew a plan where I tried to use as few units as possible but tried to have a key direction into each area, uniform up to a point, across the space. I had to make a best guess; I knew the light was going to go everywhere, I did some beam angle calculations to make sure the coverage between each unit would work, but I didn't really have any sense of where the heat would be. Surprisingly, there is a tiny bit of heat in the middle of the beam at close proximity. I allowed myself the scope and theatrical licence to channel the floods individually, to give us a degree of selectivity – as selective, at least, as a little floodlight could be.

The Jungle at the Young Vic, London. Directed by Stephen Daldry & Justin Martin, set design by Miriam Buether, costume design by Catherine Kodicek, lighting by Jon Clark, video by Tristan Shepherd, sound by Paul Arditti. *Photographer: Leon Puplett.*

We got it all up and focused really quickly – it was all a bit of a rush – and that was it. The light went everywhere! I'd spent a lot of time in rehearsals as they'd devised it, so I knew the piece very well and knew the choices they'd made and how things had evolved over three or four weeks. When we got to tech I thought I had a pretty good idea about the choices I'd made about light inside and outside the room. And there were the torches, an idea Stephen had brought. We did a lot of R&D in the rehearsal room – torches of different sizes, other portable light sources. The torches I chose could be focused really tightly, so they could essentially function as makeshift followspots with the cast lighting each other, or they could be pushed soft and wide for close-up torchwork.

Emma When the floods were on, you were aware of the body of people, and the audience were the other people within the camp, whereas when it went to torches it was that isolation and loneliness and it being at night so the storytelling suddenly took on a whole other level.

Jon It works brilliantly because with the torches you instantly forget about the walls and ceiling; it redefines the space you are in. So you believe you are outside: your relationship with the space changes. The torch beams travel horizontally rather than light being pushed down vertically from the ceiling floodlights. There is an air and space to the light outside the tent, but then a deliberately oppressive visceral feel to the floodlights that are in your eyes giving you a headache, which I kind of love as well.

So, we started the tech and we started with these sun floods. I hadn't worked with Stephen before. We got to the first tea break, and he came up to me and said, it doesn't really work, does it?

At the end of day one, we talked about swapping the floods for theatrical lights. By this stage, we had done two sessions of tech and I was beginning to get the feel of how the floods were working: it was a very democratic light coming out of them, but there was no selectivity, one flood lit up a third of the room. So, we started the process of putting Blacktak foil masks on them; you could put a strip right across the front, just narrowing it a little bit, not focusing it just on to the deck but controlling it to a degree. It was definitely improving it, and to my eye, that was really starting to work.

Stephen came in the next day and noticed we hadn't added any theatrical lights, hadn't changed anything. I explained we'd done a few things and added a few more floodlights. We got through that day, and I began to see something coming together. We got to a point before the dress rehearsal where it was still just bubbling along, and I asked Stephen what he thought I might have done. He said, 'I thought you might put one big light there and one big light there'. Ah, OK – his expectation was that it might be lit like a studio theatre show, like the Royal Court Upstairs, a light in each corner. The problem with that was the ceiling was so low one performer would instantly block all the light for the others behind them. I explained that, and he immediately understood it.

But, there was still a lack of confidence around the floods. Although the cast were very well lit and they looked good, there was little in the way of selectivity. The show in the Young Vic's studio theatre had just finished its run, so we took half a dozen of the 650 W Fresnels from there and, in a tea break, screwed them to the ceiling next to the sun floods. It ruined the aesthetic we'd been striving for. I hated them. But I left them there for a day and a half, and we turned them on every couple of scenes. It just didn't work. Practically, they weren't wide enough. And they looked utterly ridiculous and out of place. It was a brilliant provocation. Without saying a word, we all totally knew they didn't belong there.

Then we did a dress rehearsal. All of the Young Vic's FOH staff were invited to sit in as audience members to see how it was going to work with people in, primarily for the cast. But it had the brilliant effect of focusing all of the action for the viewer, so it was no longer a vast open space but was suddenly full of bodies and clothing. It gave the cast a focus that the lights alone couldn't quite achieve. Suddenly the intention of the lights being selective for different areas, opening and contracting the space was heightened massively by the fact that there was now definition, positive and negative space rather than a big void. It defined itself, then everything the lighting was already doing came in to focus.

The director came straight up to me at the end and said he now totally got it, that it worked really well. It was one of the best moments of the year – it's very good when directors are able to tell you the good things as well! The principle worked and I could carry on, and I knew that my hunch was right and holding your nerve is important. You have to believe in the rules you have used to define the piece, and knowing that it has come from the right place because you've put the time in, in rehearsals, so you know what you're trying to achieve and not to throw your instincts out before you've had time for them to be proven. Then if it still isn't working, you need to do something else; it's a totally valid part of the process to throw something out and try something new. But only then.

Emma And the fluorescent fixtures?

Jon That was because the play needs to move between brutally different locations. It's about the shift of focus and the shifting of temperature. The reference pictures showed the odd fluorescent tube, so they were valid. I wanted to go somewhere which was clinical and oppressive for the French detention centre, to contrast with the real environment of the room on the camp. The fluorescents let us do that.

Emma It also emphasized the architecture of the space in terms of the set and the lights, the delineation.

Jon That was exactly the idea, kind of an aesthetic relationship as well. They were used in the women and children's centre as well and combined with the diffused light from outside the space gives you a different impression, less oppressive. The light is diffused and indiscriminate in both cases but different to the visceral feel of the floodlights. It gives you a sense of relief and release; you feel like you are in a safe space. It was a valid source of light in this environment, and by going from one to another, it had the effect of instilling that. They were sketch ideas I had, instinctive ideas about what is valid and what the rules were for the design.

Emma How do you work out the rules?

Jon You can tell the story with anything. You can open and close the space with whatever you put up, so you don't need a rig full of moving lights to give great variation. In fact, all those moving lights can quickly become a nightmare as you can do anything if you don't have any rules of what you can and can't do. That's not to say moving lights aren't useful, but you must define your rules in a very clear way.

I always try to have rules of engagement of what I can and can't do, derived from the rehearsal process and understanding of the space and architecture the show is in. Without that, you don't know why you are making any of the decisions you are making, I think you get yourself into a right old mess...

Emma You can! And we should all try to avoid that. Last thing: is there any piece of information or advice you've been given that you now think was a turning point? Something you really hold on to?

Jon Katie Mitchell would often use the phrase 'hold your nerve'. That often comes into my head when making new work. When she said it to me, I'd always assume I was displaying weakness, but the more I think about it now, the more I'm aware that that's not what she meant at all. It is, don't capitulate on what you're doing, stick to your instinct because your instinct is good. There is clarity in the idea. Keep going. Interrogate what you're doing, don't just throw it away. Follow your instinct. Beauty can be in one person lit by one light, which may look kind of brutal – but often, the honesty of that brutality is the right thing for that moment.

I also go back to the work of Josef Svoboda: space and time. There's a good quote of his, about how every time he sits in an empty house and looks at an empty stage, he is gripped by a fear that this time he won't know how to penetrate it, and about how it's ultimately that fear which is the secret to creativity. Someone of that stature, with that body of work over the years, is admitting that each and every time there is a fear, that it is never easy – that I find reassuring. If it's easy, you are not invested enough.

Emma Thank you, Jon, for sharing your amazing insights.

PAULE CONSTABLE

If you need a lighting designer to put on the radio or television as part of a campaign, Paule is the likely choice because the public recognize and connect with some of her biggest hits, particularly *War Horse*. Fortunately, she is also happy to be a campaigner, an early voice arguing theatre had to improve its sustainability, part of the campaign to protect tungsten light sources from legislation, and more recently, helping establish the Freelancers Make Theatre Work organization during the pandemic.

She began as a rock-and-roll lampie while a student before starting to design her own shows, an early success being *Street of Crocodiles* for Theatre de Complicité. She spent a lot of time lighting shows across the opera houses of Europe, her personal highlights including *Satyagraha* for ENO and *Billy Budd* at Glyndebourne, before a run of huge successes at the National began with *His Dark Materials*, she formed a long collaboration with Matthew Bourne, and found commercial successes such as the re-invention of *Les Misérables*. She has won many, many awards for her work and is also a Royal Designer for Industry. Beyond theatre, she'll be found at home with her family, or out in nature in the oceans or hills.

www.pauleconstable.com

Emma What drew you to lighting design?

Paule Lighting design discovered me. I didn't know it was a thing. My first relationship with lighting was purely accidental. It was about being introduced to the backstage world. It was technical, it was physical, it was mercurial. But I didn't really understand what it was. It was finding a tribe of people and a kind of world that I found compelling and interesting, and that seemed to wake things up in me. But I didn't even know there was such a thing as a lighting designer in those days. I started lighting doing gig lighting. You just did lighting – you put lights up, you pointed them around, you turned them on and off.

I am scared of the dark. I'm very claustrophobic, and I think that darkness is quite claustrophobic. When I was little and people would burrow to the ends of their beds and sit there with torches, I couldn't imagine anything worse. And my claustrophobia's got worse with age, as most phobias do, so I'm frightened of the dark. I love being in the open air, because I love being in the sky. So having a relationship with the sky and a horizon, I realize now, is incredibly important to my mental health, but it also sort of feeds me, and that's always been true. So yeah, they are the two things that made me realize lighting was the perfect thing for me: controlling a lack of light so I never went into an abyss, or living a life where I sort of walk along the edge of something that I find really frightening. And also playing with an element that, naturally, I find I'm very drawn to and find exhilarating.

Emma How old were you when you thought, this is what I want to do, or began to dabble and realized this was interesting?

Paule I was at university in London, so I was probably about 21 when I first started helping out in a theatre, learning a bit about lighting and going, oh, this is fun. The idea of having a career in lighting design, I didn't really start to think about that even as a thing until I was in my late 20s.

Emma What were you reading at university?

Paule I read English at Goldsmiths. I'm drawn to English for many reasons, but one was that part of me thought I might end up an academic and part of me thought I might end up working in TV or something. I was quite interested in lots of things. Eventually, I changed to English and Drama because I realized all the kind of people I found interesting and who had a sort of more physical relationship with text were Combined Honours students, doing English and Drama. So towards the end of my first year, I applied to change. The lighting bit came afterwards – but what was great is that we only did one practical module each year in the drama department because we were a very academic course, but in my second and third year I was able to do lighting as my practical module.

Emma Did you meet people you then collaborated with at university?

Paule Not really, no. Ian, my partner, was working for People Show and the world of fringe theatre. So I was meeting lots of his cohorts, at People Show, Lumiere and Son, companies like that in London. But at that stage I was working in music. Trussing, climbing around and stuff. So as that sort of technology started to be used more and more in theatre, particularly experimental theatre and fringe, which is where he was working, suddenly the line between personal and professional was getting blurred and I could go help him out or work for companies who he knew, as part of that pool, that creative backstage workforce who would move around gigs in London.

At some point I met, through Ian, a lighting designer called Stevie Whitson, who was a New Yorker who used to light lots of shows for DV8, for People Show. He was utterly brilliant and insane. I met him as a technician and loved doing shows with him. We worked for Station House Opera and we did festivals on the South Bank and things. And it was him who told me to go and be a lighting designer. I'd said to him, why didn't you ask me to do this European tour at Station House Opera? And he just said, just fuck off and do your own work girlfriend. And I was so mortified – but actually it was a gift. He made me realize that I needed to be creative.

Emma And so what was your first theatre show?

Paule I suppose the first proper show where I was employed to be the lighting designer – where it wasn't just a question of load the van then turn lights on and off and all the rest of it – would have been *The Resistible Rise of Arturo Ui* at 7:84 in Scotland. Ben Ormerod had been doing lots of shows up there. And I'd been doing a lot of assisting for Ben, and touring his shows; he couldn't do the show and he said, ask Paule. And so I got on the train with my bag and my stencils, and off I went to Glasgow.

Roanna Benn directed it; she went on to be very senior at Channel Four television. It was designed by Rae Smith – it was when Rae and I met. I had no idea what a designer was or how they worked or what they were, really. And suddenly, here I was with this woman, and all these thoughts I was having, this way of conceiving things, thinking about things – Rae encouraged me to think like a designer.

The show had a company of six or seven in the cast because they played all the roles between them. And that six or seven included Ashley Jensen and David Tennant, who were both doing their first jobs out of the Royal Scottish Academy as it was then. So yeah, it was hilarious, absolutely hilarious – and a bit of a baptism by fire! I got paid. I stayed in digs in Glasgow. And I felt like, wow, I'm really doing it; there's a label on the door, and it says – Lighting Designer.

Emma Looking back on that, if you had to give a piece of advice to somebody starting out in the industry now, what would you say?

Paule I think that's really hard, because I think the whole idea of a career… you know, I didn't have to pay to go to university. There was a welfare state that would hold me up in-between times. It was a very, very different environment. I think the huge advantage it gave me was I was able to follow my heart and I wasn't doing it because I wanted to be anybody else – I was doing it because I was sort of just really drawn to it. I didn't think, when I grow up, I want to be David Hersey. I didn't look to the National Theatre and think that was where I wanted to be. I just wanted to make work and meet really interesting people. And it was an adventure, but I had the luxury of being able to be open to that sort of adventure. I'm not sure that's so easy anymore.

But I do think there are so many roles in the lighting department, indeed so many roles in making theatre. Some are very, very different to how we perceive them when we are young. I think we are compartmentalized too quickly. So, I'd say, don't be in too much of a hurry to decide what you are. I quite like the language a lot of young theatre practitioners use in describing themselves as makers; when I worked with Complicité that was very much the kind of vein that we worked in. I was the production manager, I was the ASM, and I was the lighting designer – I just kind of contributed what skills I had to that room.

Emma Were your parents in the arts?

Paule No, not at all. My father was a fighter pilot, so I travelled a lot as a kid, went to boarding school, was used to being with lots of groups of new people, often abroad. So yeah, no understanding of the arts at all.

I think I was drawn to Goldsmiths as a way to reject that kind of very conventional middle-class background I'd been brought up with. I think for quite a long time my parents were looking forward to the day when I might get a proper job. Now I think they kind of love it, love what it is, enjoy it. And they've come to see much more of it, and it's become more accessible to them.

Actually, if I think about it, my dad took me to see the new Lloyd Webber's, took me to see *Cats* and *Starlight Express* when I was a kid because he loved that kind of thing. But I never related that kind of spectacle to what I was doing in fringe theatre in London. It was never, I'm doing this because I want to be lighting *Cats*. It was like *Cats* was riding a bicycle and I was knitting a jumper – just a completely different thing.

Emma In terms of who and what influences you, you've talked about the natural world. What other things do you draw inspiration from?

Paule I suppose from people and other work, so people like Jennifer Tipton and Jean Kalman and Wolfgang Göbbel and other lighting designers who are doing work that makes you kind of go, wow – work that feels different, that kind of makes your senses very alive. I was very drawn to that. I did Art History at A-Level, so I suppose I'm quite visually literate, but I think a lot of what you're doing working in lighting, particularly working in articulating ideas in lighting, is that you're learning to look. That's sort of the job of being a lighting designer – a kind of heightened awareness, a lifetime of learning to look.

Emma When you start on a new show, where do you begin?

Paule The idea of a new show – that conversation starts way before you even start to think about lighting. I start with a conversation with myself around what I think I need to help me do my best work. Or be the best colleague, the best collaborator I can be. So, I measure every project in terms of really simple criteria. Do I have the time to do it? When someone asks you to do something, you need to assess what the level of input from you is going to be. There are shows that are going to be very light touch, like the *St John's Passion* broadcast I've just done, where they just needed me to be there to show the space for them. But then there's doing something like *Ocean At The End Of The Lane*, putting a Neil Gaiman fantasy on stage: you know that's going to take a lot of time and a lot of front foot. So, time is a big factor to me.

Then, voice. Thinking if it's something I want to be part of telling – is there something in me that feels like I might be an appropriate person to do that work. I can't engage with something that I don't like or don't have a way into. There's got to be a reason for me to do it, for interest to spark.

Then who's doing it. You know, I tend to only work with about ten different people. I'm very conservative. And that's not only fear about trust.

Then where – it's really hard trying to achieve good things in Austrian opera houses where the system is very loaded against you, for example, so where is a big part. Then my kids growing up – was it a time when I was happy to absent myself or not? And then money: that comes down to thinking about what's been asked of you. I think you can decide to do something for free – I think that's fine. But I think you need to decide what you think is your value in that room. I say all those things because I think you need to make sure you're taking on the right things before you start even thinking about lighting them. And why are you taking them on, because if you don't ask yourself that, then when it's really hard later on it's going to be really tough to remember, or you're going to unravel. That's happened to me before.

Beyond that, I tend to start, I suppose, in simplistic terms. I think what often happens is that a director will engage a designer, and the director and designer will create a sense of how they want to do this. Is it a big open space? Is it a composite space? Is it a room? Is it a row of deck chairs? Is it an abstract? And I think as soon as they have that sense of how, that's when I get involved.

I was talking to John Mcfarlane a few years ago, who's a painter and a set and costume designer, and he was talking about being asked to do a ballet that he'd already done once before, a *Swan Lake* or something, and he said, I've done my *Swan Lake*. That's not the same for a lighting designer, because every *Swan Lake*, every *Cosi Fan Tutti* will be different because it will be interpreted by another – the director and designer will decide how they're going to do it. I then react to that. I bring that to life. I look for the suitable lighting response to what they are proposing. And I might unpick it a bit and I might help push it to become more extreme or slightly different by asking questions. But you know it's funny when people say, is there anything you'd really like to do? I think it's quite difficult to see anything as an entity in its own self with lighting, because I'm such a collaborative, reactive part of the creative process. More craft than art, I would claim.

Emma And how do you communicate your ideas with the director and the set designer?

Paule I tend to communicate more with a designer than a director, I would say, partly because I think that with a designer you can be talking about the nitty-gritty of the section and what you can fit where, but at the same time you can be talking about textural

The Ocean at the End of the Lane at the National Theatre – Dorfman, London. Directed by Katy Rudd, movement director Steven Hoggett, puppetry director Finn Caldwell, set designer Fly Davis, costume and puppet designer Samuel Wyer, lighting by Paule Constable, sound by Ian Dickinson. *Photographer: Manuel Harlan / ArenaPAL.*

qualities and bouncing ideas and visual references, you can explore. So, with a designer you can have that kind of brilliant, multi-layered conversation where it's about quality and problem-solving simultaneously. I love that.

Whereas with the director, it tends to be more about the kind of delivery of the beats, delivery of kind of the corners of the show, the broad-brush strokes of the structure and what those elements have to carry and communicate to an audience in terms of story. For that, I don't often use visual references. I use them for myself, more often than not, to articulate things like a palette or a particular sense of quality. And if a designer has done storyboards or moodboards or has other visual references, I'll use those. And it might be that I pick up on one or two of those and offer them to a director and say, do you mean like this, or use that to explore. But more, I tend to communicate those ideas just by being there and talking and unpicking and imagining, and I don't find it's a formalized presentation because I tend to sort of work more underneath something than on the outside, if that makes sense.

Emma And do you spend a lot of time in rehearsal?

Paule In an ideal world, yeah. It's my happy place. I love watching rehearsals, because there's a three-dimensional, living, breathing thing in front of you. And, you know, because there's that thing with lighting that we don't get process, we don't get an opportunity – you can workshop odd ideas and you can try bits and pieces, but ultimately you are on your own. So, I think it's really nice to kind of just be around. If the show becomes familiar enough to you, it almost lights itself. You have that stage of the model and developing ideas and working out why light is there and what it's going to do and how you're going to achieve that. Then once you start in rehearsals, you're mentally testing that, but also mentally imagining it as a kind of moving thing.

I go through this stage where I scribble in the script as things are happening, or just absorb, and then I'll articulate that into spreadsheets of cues and timings and things. And it just ends up being a series of instructions, like instruction one – houselights fade to black, instruction two, this appears in the downstage-left corner and it's gentle and it's soft. And I'll write myself the story of the show. And it can change, of course, when I'm in the theatre. But it just gives me a structure to hang everything on to start with. So yeah, rehearsals are really important.

Emma And when you then start to light onstage, where do you start? Do you start with your keylight? Do you start somewhere else?

Paule You have to start with the idea. You have to identify however you've broken a piece down, even if it's a four-act structure, you'll know the character and the quality and the function and the sort of shape and the idea of the light for each one of those four acts, or each one of your scenes, or whatever it is. You have to strip that back to its most pure form. That's what I do. And I put that on stage, and then I put twenty dummy cues in or whatever it is, and then I put a block in. Then I go for my next big idea because I think with lighting, it's really easy to just end up creating a mess, so I think it's really good to have a sorbet, to have a palette cleanser, to strip something back. It's only in stripping it back that you can really see what else you need.

Emma So do you put those big ideas in before you start with the cast on stage, and then your dummy cues you are filling as you go?

Paule Yeah. It might be that you've got ten minutes before a tech session starts and I'll come in and go, OK, cue 1, just put this light at this level, bang, OK, cue 20, which is the next change, this light this level, bang, cue 30, this light this level, bang. So, you never go into an empty cupboard. It means you can keep working. The DSM has got all these cues in the book. Everything can change, but they're not going, what page do you want that cue on? You are just going, where I gave you LX cue 10 can you take it three bars earlier, or can you put an extra cue in. I do all of this because what you want to be doing in tech is looking, you don't want to be scrabbling around to find pages in the script or lights or going what happens next. You just want to clear all that away, so in the end, you are free to look.

Emma And your relationship with your programmer and your chief electrician, how has that evolved as things have changed and boards have become more technical?

Paule Your programmer is like your right hand. It's great when you get to the point where your programmer is riffing with you, where they're kind of guessing what you're doing. I like working collaboratively with creative teams. I like working collaboratively with colleagues. I like problem-solving. And, you know, some of my best friends are programmers, they really are. I think if you were to identify the role that enables me to do my work in the most exciting way, it is the programmer. For the production electrician there's the building up, they're spinning off and doing all these things, and it's amazing. But the kind of alchemy of making the show, you really feel your programmer is in the bubbling bit of that, whereas your production electrician is monitoring all the instruments.

Emma In terms of LED and moving light technology and how it has changed the way you light, could you talk a bit about that? Because it feels to me that I've been so lucky to grow up with tungsten and to have learnt to look at colour in that way through gel books, but that there's a new generation to whom those gel books are becoming obsolete. That there's so much choice now that actually, in some ways it's overwhelming, but then in the other there are infinite possibilities. . .

Paule Yes, I was talking to Lee Filters the other day about what the function of a swatch book will be in the future, is it that it's a means of communication to get you close to something? I agree. I feel really lucky to have grown up with tungsten, but then who's to say what the generation who don't have that as a benchmark will do imaginatively. It may also be a millstone around our necks. I think being in a generation who have a foot in both camps is. . . sometimes we're trying to harken back to something that might not actually be as valuable as we believe it is. Is that really the benchmark? I do like light to be painterly, and I like it to be gentle and dark and coercive and complex, and that was the frustration with LED technology to start with, but now it's meeting our sense of what we want to do with it much better. But we're still on the edge of what it can do. It's interesting that often I think we take a technology into theatre, and we sort of put it to a very extreme place to get it to bend to our will. I think that's the nature of our processes. I think things like moving light technology and LED technology, they've allowed us many interesting things, but I don't think they necessarily make things better. But they are all just tools we use to make beautiful images, beautiful, appropriate moments in the theatre.

Emma Do you think LED technology or moving light technology makes you make decisions later, in terms of what you're going to do?

Paule It can be a curse, and it can be brilliant, can't it? I mean, I think the idea of focusing a rig of generics, committing to a large show that was all generics, would now be absolutely terrifying. And yet, of course, that's what we used to do all the time! Now that just feels like, how would you know what to allocate to do that job, to do this job? The moving light is there as a unit that I know can do all those jobs – but the idea of making them all individual lights? That would be really scary. It's funny imagining that now, isn't it! Yet I definitely grew up in a world where moving lights were unusual.

Emma Have your rigs got smaller, based on the fact that each unit can do more?

Paule Certainly with things like *Romeo and Juliet* that I did for Matthew Bourne, that needed to be quite a small, contained rig because the show was moving very quickly. Having a rig that could do a lot with a small number of units was hugely useful. *Curious Incident* – it's a really small rig, but everything that's up there does a lot of work. It's also that thing where you're sort of dictating the character of the lighting by the kind of equation of time and delivery. It certainly helps that I don't really get on with the whole Eurovision, *Hamilton*, that kind of flashy sort of whoop-de-do, complex moving light stuff. Is that something going through its test cycle, or is that actually lighting design?

It's so weird for me because there is a whole other school of lighting design, which is about lighting stuff rather than the stuff of light, you know, the kind of thickness, the quality. And that's about casting. I wrote to Howell Binkley after I went to see *Hamilton*; I said, I don't know how you do that. And I would never want to do that. But you're very good at it. It's like it's a different job. So, when people ask me what I would like to light, I can't really answer that question. But I can say that I don't know that I've got a jukebox musical in me. I've got no idea what I would do!

Emma Well, you are such a storyteller. That's why your lighting is so beautiful. I remember following you on *The House of Bernarda Alba* at the National, goodness knows how many years ago now, and I just remember the beauty of it, the absolute beauty of it. And the respect you had from the team, and therefore how much goodwill there was in the space was something I will never forget.

Paule That's lovely to hear. It is stories that interest me – telling stories. That's why I love it. And I think, it can be beautiful. It can be brutal. It can be extreme. It can be so many things. But it's carrying the story, which is the interesting thing, I think. And also, that's what's so magical about it, isn't it? Telling stories, but also creating the space where we can sort of press the space and press the space between the audience and the performers, and the whole idea of us looking at ourselves, us thinking about ourselves relative to what we're experiencing, and hearing, feeling that that's important. Because it is. It is why we do it.

Emma In terms of colour, do you have colours that you go back to? I remember at one point you said to me, I have set colours, then I add one on every show to push myself out of that comfort zone...

Paule I really try to. I mean, most production electricians who have ever worked with me would say, if you give me a Paule plan, I could probably colour it up for you. You slightly grade how cold the crosslight is – is it Lee 202, or is it 203? That makes a big difference to me. I don't particularly like saturated colour unless it's really thick and there for a very clear reason, to communicate a strong idea. I spend most of my time in 202, 203, 205 territory. Even 201 feels too much to me quite often. I like sodium colours, 650 and things like that. I like colours that are sort of industrial, that have a quality of something you are trying to grapple with, like big sodium or streetlights or sunlight or interior fluorescents. I love fluorescence. I love that kind of flat quality. I love that kind of greyness. So yeah, I don't often go into the pink world...

Emma Why not?

Paule I just find it terrifying. I kind of don't know what it's meant to be. So I go, well, I'll leave that for people who live that, I'll just live at this corner of sludge!

Emma If you had to not pick one, but pick a few shows where you would go, that was really special – can you describe why? What the alchemy is?

Paule I think *Ear for Eye*, which was at the Royal Court, was really special. It was really special because it was a really fucking good play, and because working with debbie tucker green as both playwright and director was really amazing, and it's one of those things where it felt entirely elusive. So, trying to articulate what the response was from us as a creative team was a question of taking steps of trust. I love that process, and what we ended up with was so abstract and yet informed – so you're twenty-five foot over the edge of the cliff, but you feel safe, you know you're out at sea, but you are together in it. That felt really good, and I think we made something that you couldn't have anticipated what it was going to be until we made it. But the steps were the right steps to get us where we got to, and it landed something that felt like it articulated the piece. That was great.

The other extreme would be something like *Follies* at the National, where again, everything about the process was right and in terms of the whole thing, of what I think storytelling can do, and also being somebody who is the age of the older disillusioned characters in that piece. That it sort of celebrates theatre and dramaturgy and loss and pain and dereliction, so the idea of beauty meeting brutality and different periods bumping into each other, the nightmare of trying to navigate a route through there, that made sense to me. And also, that it celebrated, for me, my relationship with Vic [the designer Vicki Mortimer]. There were so many things that were special to me. So, between those shows, both of them are absolutely pure theatre, both celebrate the extremes of how far you can take an idea, one pushing you to an unknown territory, the other pushing you totally to craft.

So, yeah, those are two I'd hold onto on my Desert Island Discs!

Emma And in terms of spaces, which inspire you?

Paule I have a very complicated relationship with the Olivier at the National Theatre, but I made *Follies* in the Olivier, I made *Saint Joan* in the Olivier, I made *War Horse* in the Olivier, there's clearly something in that space. I made *Beyond The Beautiful Forevers* in that space. It's really hard. It's really, really, really, really, really hard. You can't ever be back foot in there, you can't ever be passive, and I love that about it. So really, it's a pig. Nothing is easy in there. And that's quite exciting, because it puts you on your mettle. So, the Olivier. I love the Young Vic because I grew up in there, and I think it's a perfect scale of space, and you can do so much in there. So, they're probably the two.

Emma In terms of how you approach a play to an opera to a musical – are they different things to you?

Follies at the National Theatre – Olivier, London. Directed by Dominic Cooke, choreographed by Bill Deamer, designed by Vicki Mortimer, lighting by Paule Constable, sound by Paul Groothuis. *Photographer: Johan Persson / ArenaPAL.*

Paule I don't think they are. I think doing opera taught me a lot about planning and being prepared because you have so little time. But now I take that process and apply it to everything I do. So, there's been different learning, but I think what you're concentrating on is the story you're trying to tell, the kind of space you're trying to put the audience in to hold that moment, hold that production, hold those words. I think that's true. I worked with Complicité a lot when I was younger, so I did a lot of devised theatre – I approach almost everything as if it's devised. It's trying to find the clues that let you into a way of making decisions that lead an audience through something that's whatever it is. That's all you're doing.

Emma And your best collaborations? You talk about Vic? What makes them so special?

Paule Well, in terms of designers, I think about Vic, and I think about Rae, and I think about Bunny [Christie]. And it's interesting, we're all women of a certain age, aren't we? So clearly, there is something in who we are that I think is a shared thing; we work with other people, but I certainly think there is a sense of understanding. There are so many things you don't need to say because the shared experience is stronger, greater, even though we're all very different as people. There's trust. And I think with directors I've worked with often, it's so much easier. You can take more risks if you feel less like you're being judged for every step you make. And then humour. That's true of the gorgeous programmers I was talking about earlier, and so many people I love working with. People who are really good at what they do, and are really silly!

Emma Absolutely!

Paule Such a stupidly stressful job, isn't it?

Emma It is, because as you said earlier, you're the one who hasn't had a process, and suddenly you've got goodness knows how many people sat looking at their watches...

Paule Judging your work. It's so stressful.

Emma And time is money. You must have felt that so much, particularly when you did the work with Cameron Mackintosh, that every second is money down the drain in his book.

Paule Actually he's really good because he will also spend money if he needs to. You know, he would never watch a clock. He would rather get it done – actually, it's the opposite, it's trying to stop that is quite hard! And I think part of his success is that he'll allow things – I mean, he's impatient, but he's impatient because he's excited. The problem with lighting is it's the thing you can change – make it blue, make it pink, make it yellow – stop! The speed is about excitement as opposed to you've got to stop in a minute. Opera's the place where, once you've got an orchestra involved, you can't fuck around.

Emma And being a woman in this industry, you are a pioneer. When you started, how did you find that – and how do you think that's evolved?

Paule I think that there were other women around. It's such a massive conversation, isn't it. There you are, being a mum through this. I think that's a whole other book. I think what's interesting is, I do think our work is different.

Emma In what way?

Paule I remember a long time ago going to a Georgia O'Keeffe exhibition and walking away at the end of it and going, what she is articulating is a gaze that relates to her lived experience of living as a woman. You know, I was quite a tomboy when I was a kid, I loved climbing trees and all sorts of things, but my lived experience comes from how I've been treated by my fellow human beings, and that's complicated and difficult at times, and at other times not, but it is different to the men in the room. Actually, we're all just trying to find a way to do it, aren't we? I don't know whether that's true of all women who are lighting designers, that their work is different. But actually, every lighting designer's work is different, isn't it? And I think one of the things that's really interesting about it as a medium is, none of us really know what it is.

Emma Can you talk a little bit about darkness and light?

Paule I have a lovely artist friend. She lives down in Penwith in Cornwall. I went to see her and there was an artist, film-maker by her studio and when he asked me what I do, he said, oh, what's your hierarchy? And I said, darkness, you know, that's what controls everything I do. I definitely carve images out of darkness. It's more interesting what you leave out than what you put in, isn't it?

Emma What has been your biggest learning curve, and why?

Paule Are you talking about life or lighting?

Emma Well, I guess slightly both, because I think the two are so interconnected. This job is a passion – it's all encompassing.

Paule Yeah, it really is. So, my glib answer is, if in doubt, go to black and start again. And also, not to be frightened. You have to be your own harshest critic. So, if you think how many notes you get after a preview, how many notes you get given versus how many you write down, I think is a really interesting one. Of course, you've really got one area of concern most of the time, but you need to keep asking yourself the questions.

I always believe that you can solve every problem with better lighting – whatever the problem in the show, I always think it's my fault and I can make it better. But it means that if I make bad decisions about the work that I do, then the moments at which I make those decisions are lacking in integrity and lacking in rigour. That makes me incredibly unhappy, and I find it really difficult. I don't mind if something's wrong or it's rubbish as long as it's got there in the right way. And you can stand by the decisions that you made. If you can't, it's incredibly painful. To the point where it's nearly broken me several times. I go back to earlier in our conversation, about making good decisions and knowing why you were there. If you know why you're there, you will engage in the right way. If you engage in a way that's right for you, you will make it better. So, the importance of that, I think, is probably the biggest, hardest learn for me.

Emma How do you work within a budget?

Paule We are doing a new Matthew Bourne show, and we know that, kind of back of fag packet, that it's going to be two-thirds of what *Romeo and Juliet* was, and *Romeo and Juliet* was pretty small. So, it's going to be smaller than that. But beyond that, I kind of go, OK, I can imagine something that is going to kind of sit in this space. It's trying not to let your creative response be restricted by the budget, but also trying to allow your create response to be framed by it. It's trying to see that as a space to be in rather than something to stifle your imagination, which can be hard. The reality of it is it's going to be much harder as we get back to work post-pandemic. It does worry me that we're going to be pushing to get more for less money; that means necessarily that the pressure gets put on the people.

Emma So in some ways, the budget is a parameter, in the same way as the space gives you parameters that you work within. So, there are benefits to it as well as challenges?

Paule You don't want a blank sheet of paper, do you?

Emma Thank you, Paule. This has been such a joy.

RICK FISHER

Rick is perhaps the beating heart of the UK lighting profession, and arguably a key reason it continues to be such an open profession, happy to share information and encourage and support new designers. That was the driving goal behind his eleven-year tenure as chair of the Association of Lighting Designers, of which he is now vice president, and as a co-founder of the lighting industry support charity Light Relief, which subsequently expanded into the backstage charity Backup Tech.

Alongside all that, he's lit an enormous quantity and range of shows since moving to the UK from his native US in the 1970s. The best known are perhaps the trio of Matthew Bourne's *Swan Lake*, the National Theatre's *An Inspector Calls*, and the hit musical *Billy Elliot*, the last two with his long-time collaborators, director Stephen Daldry and designer Ian MacNeil. Those shows, and others, have earned him two Olivier Awards, two Tony Awards and many more, and been seen worldwide. But ask him, and he'll still name *Room*, a tiny show he lit at London's Oval House, as one of his key works – still relishing the joy smaller shows bring of just being able to reach up and move the rig around until finding the perfect solution.

Emma What drew you to lighting design?

Rick It was really accidental. I became interested in the theatre. I didn't see a future in performing, but I found that I liked working with the people backstage, making a show. The camaraderie, the sense of single shared purpose was all very attractive to me and gave me a new sense of family, which I was looking for at that time. I gravitated to being the stage manager because they very much had a finger in every pie. I moved to Britain temporarily – forty years ago! – and started working at fringe theatres where in those days the stage manager did everything, including the sound, the lighting, the scenery, collecting the props, tearing the tickets, fixing the building. But I slowly found I had a bit of an aptitude for lighting.

I was resident stage manager at a place called Oval House, where a lot of performance art groups came. They would describe to me their lighting needs because that was something they couldn't provide for themselves. They were developing non-script-oriented work. So, they told me what stories they were trying to tell. The images they were trying to create were often very visual, and I was using a couple of handfuls of lights and a little manual desk to rig, focus and plot. Fast forward again to doing slightly larger scale work with the Bush Theatre as a more traditional stage manager and finding that actually I enjoyed the lighting more than anything else.

I went freelance as a general technician/stage manager, particularly doing a lot of lighting calls and working on certain shows as a lighting designer. When it came to billing myself in the programme there were the writers, the directors, the designers, the performers, and there was me doing everything else. The best credit I could get for myself was for lighting. So, I billed myself as lighting designer and that's how I became one. I called myself one and people started thinking that I was one.

Emma What do you think was the draw to lighting over stage management?

Rick Even moving up from the Oval House to The Bush, I found stage managing was actually not as creatively involved as I was hoping it would be. You were more task oriented, note-taking and facilitating, than actually being involved. And because of the way that I had been a little bit more creatively involved in some of the fringy performance art shows, I found going back into a bit more technical work less exciting. So, that first experience maybe ruined me for traditional stage management. I was a stage manager who never called the show because I would have been talking to myself. I never said go with fly cue 7 as I was literally pulling little bits of nylon line, because that's how small scale we were. It was a great way of learning: rigging, focusing and plotting lights teaches you what the lights should be doing, teaches you the power of them without having to draw a plan. Because it was just me putting them up without having to explain any concept to an electrician. When it's you running up and down the ladder, you make better decisions.

Emma Who and what were your biggest influences as your career progressed?

Rick I think I'm a magpie. I like looking at everybody's work; I get excited when I see good work. Very early at the Oval House there was a crazy British-based American lighting designer called Stevie Whitson, who sadly died young. He was this outrageous figure, who I was warned about when I took the job: don't let him touch anything because he just blows everything up! What I quickly learnt to admire from Stevie was that he was passionate about working on shows, and what he provided was a lighting designer who also was a genuine collaborator. He made lighting look like fun. He made it look like you didn't have to be just a technician because he was reasonably technically inadept as well. But he was creative. And that was a big inspiration to me.

Another influence was Chahine Yavroyan, another lighting designer and collaborator. He was cool, inscrutably cool at times. And, you know, when you're 22 and you're thinking about a career, seeing someone who's kind of cool makes you think, oh, maybe this is OK.

Emma What other mediums affect how you light?

Rick I think everything impacts. I enjoy going to art exhibitions, seeing films, looking at photography. I would say steep yourself in as much as possible. I have noticed at any given moment there are half a dozen references in the zeitgeist of your directors and designers that people constantly come back to because they don't know how to talk about lighting. The great light artist, James Turrell. Hugely influential, hugely inspirational, not really theatrical, but there's something about what he does that I sometimes try and bring into my work. The photographer Gregory Crewdson: I didn't know who he was when he was first mentioned to me, but once somebody alerted me, I started seeing some images of his work and finding that my directors, my designers were all talking about him. Then Rembrandt, Caravaggio, Edward Hopper. I'm working on a production that's set in Norway, so you get Hammershoi, a Danish painter who painted very grey paintings. Candlelit films like Stanley Kubrick's *Barry Lyndon*. All those glamorous 1930s, 1940s silver screen, silver print film star photos beautifully lit. There are probably a dozen or so references that you're going to hear all the time that you probably want to have at least some feeling for. You don't have to know everything, and you are constantly learning by seeing what other people are inspired by.

Emma In terms of talking about lighting to a director or designer, how would you go about that?

Rick It's hard and I'm not very good at it. Sometimes I think lighting designers, myself included, cloak ourselves in technology and the practical conundrum of how to deliver light to the stage, to stop us talking to our collaborators. You have to forget all of that and try to discuss or demonstrate the quality of light we're looking for. Interestingly enough, as I've gotten further along in my career, I find that those conversations happen less, that people just trust you to do something and hopefully comment when they like it or give notes if they do not.

Emma When you receive a script how do you approach it?

Rick I read it. I try to not read the stage directions the first time around, then I'll go back and look at them. If there's anything that is written about light, I try and discount that pretty quickly and see whether or not the piece suggests those things to me on its own.

Similarly with the stage directions if it's a show that's been done before, as they often recall the original production. So, I just kind of feel it.

If I'm then presented with a set design, a lot of times I don't have a huge hand in what has evolved. The idea that you might all work and sit in a room together and come up with a way to stage these things does happen, but often I'm not there. I miss that old collaboration which we used to have in the fringe days, really coming up with these things together. But in reality, I often get presented with a first draft or a white card model and I kind of know that's probably what it's going to be. I can say, wouldn't it be useful if there was a way to deliver light this way or if that wall was a bit higher or the window was there, those kind of practical type conversations. Can I deliver light? Which way can I deliver light? And then, what sort of light do I want to deliver from each of those angles and/or positions?

Emma If you end up with a set which you feel you can't deliver the light that you think the script demands, how do you approach that?

Rick I write long memos, which I'm not sure anybody reads! It doesn't happen very often, but I try and say, look, if we're going to do this, this is the choice, these are the options, or these are the types of light I cannot deliver. And it's fine as long as we're all agreed. But if you say you want one big backlight to cover the whole stage, putting a ceiling there is going to make that impossible. If you want an even gobo coverage, but you put it in a box, again, that may not happen – but it doesn't mean we can't say we're outside in different ways. It's just so that other people realize what the ramifications are.

Emma Do you think that's a benefit of the amount of shows a lighting designer does in comparison to a set designer?

Rick Yes, often the case. And sometimes I'd like to hope that when people ask me to do shows, they are thinking, I want someone who's got 35 years of experience in this business. Sometimes I'm finding that people don't want that because they want to learn by making their mistakes together, which is also how I learned. That's also how you develop your language, and doing the wrong things might produce a much better solution.

Emma How has collaboration changed since you began?

Rick It's changed dramatically, a lot for the worse in my experience. In the old days we used to sit around and have endless cups of tea, go out to lunch, cook together, spend time together in the same room talking about what we were doing. Now, too often, and maybe it's because I'm further on in my career and some of my collaborators trust me by reputation or by previous experience, but we might have one conversation or watch a couple of rehearsals and then we turn up at the tech. I think that we have so many more means of sharing information, though actually what we're doing is sharing a lot less in person.

Emma And you retain so much more face to face.

Rick Even a telephone call. I mean, you understand when someone's getting bored with what you're saying, you can hear them drifting off. You can hear when they don't kind of get what you are talking about. Whereas in an email you don't always get that.

Emma So your advice to somebody coming into the industry is to try and orchestrate those meetings?

Rick I think so. Just being together. Even if it's not so useful, sit and watch rehearsals. Even the early days. Be a little fly on the wall and just see what the process is like. You'll learn something. I'm lucky I did that a lot when I was starting, I think it's helped me pick up a shorthand. Sometimes I do just see a run and then have to start a lighting session. That's regrettable. The years of experience make it a little bit easier, but when you're starting out, try and talk as much as you can.

Emma It's like when you pick up the dynamics of the room and how it works.

Rick Exactly, and who's doing what and what's not being thought about, what's being assumed, because we all make assumptions all the time.

Emma In terms of materials and finishes of things: how do you get involved in that?

Swan Lake, directed and choreographed by Matthew Bourne, designed by Lez Brotherston, lighting by Rick Fisher. *Photographer: Mike Rothwell*.

Rick I wish I got involved a bit more. One of my little pet hobby horses is the sad demise or imminent demise of scenic painting. The artists who work with paint in the theatre and just know how to paint a flat wall not flat, how to interpret inspiration from a picture grabbed off the Internet with too many pixels. The over-reliance on projected or digital imagery to set the scene is worrying and, I think, ultimately, anti-theatrical. It has great potential to take theatre into different places than it's ever been before, but using it to set location in a mundane way isn't very interesting. But getting the magic that paint can bring to even the most ordinary-looking set is, I think, really important. I would hate it if those skills go completely.

Emma How do you collaborate with a video designer?

Rick I used to try and stay out of the way with my light, but because I also think we all want to get the best out of what this technology can do, and we are working with someone who is doing that, I tend to be quite critical or have a critical opinion, positive and or negative, about what the imagery might be – though I try not to be too negative at the outset. I withdrew from *Sunday In The Park With George* at the Châtelet; it was going to be heavily projected, and when I saw the design concept I realized how limited the role of light was potentially going to be. I just said, I don't think this is for me. You need someone who is really with it – and maybe I'm not the right person for this project. I want to be an open collaborator, and I think on that one, I would have been a closed collaborator.

Emma That's a brave thing to do. An honest thing to do.

Rick I hope it was perceived as that. What you want for collaboration is the best ideas should win. We should all push each other to have even better ideas and have that freedom, which means the freedom to sometimes have bad ideas. And express them. I try to tell students when I talk to them, don't be afraid to say this is a really good idea or a really bad idea. You learn more about what the project should be from people's reactions. Or it may be the one thing that comes out of the blue solves a big problem, or even if that idea never lands on stage, it unlocks a conversation that leads to a different solution.

I've often said to directors, I think it should be like this. And they tell me, absolutely not. And then three days later, they've owned that idea and turned it into their own, and now it's part of the whole as opposed to just something that the lighting designer suggested. We want to get the best out of each other. So much as it's painful to have your ideas laughed at sometimes, it's better if you can then move on to get a better idea. That's a really useful thing.

Emma What do you think has been your biggest learning curve? What would you tell your younger self?

Rick Get used to the fact that you panic because it's never going to change. I still panic with a blank piece of paper. I still panic: do I know what I'm doing? I still think I don't have an idea in my head about anything. And maybe that just isn't going to change, and that's just the level of adrenaline I need to get the work done. I wish I could relax about that more. I wish I had better technical skills. I wish I had better art and collaborative skills and talking about what we might be trying to achieve.

I think also on larger scale shows, there's the challenge of managing the different people and departments you interact with, how you just keep everything moving forward in a positive way. That is still a challenge whether coming into a building like the National Theatre or into a big commercial theatre where the backup is different and you have to create an infrastructure to support you. That's been quite a big learning curve.

Emma Because you're so dependent on your team in creating the work?

Rick Yeah. And to be proactive and to make your crazy idea better and/or to give you a better idea than your crazy idea.

Emma With the advance of technology, how important do you think it is for a lighting designer to understand what new lights can do?

Rick It's impossible to understand what all the new lights can do. You have to try and keep an open mind, an inquiring mind to what's going on. But you basically want to develop a very good address book of people to ask, watch other shows, ask what did that, ask the hire companies what you might be able to afford to use instead of dreaming about specifying the latest you've just seen at a trade show, because if the hire companies haven't bought it or if they've just bought it and it has to go out at list hire price, chances are I can't afford to hire it. I might be able to hire what was hot three months ago or three years ago, depending on what my budget is. Very rarely in my 40-year career have I specified equipment that has been bought or hired-in specially. Even working at a Broadway or West End level, that often does not happen because the budgets are not big enough to make that financially viable for your suppliers. I like to temper the idea that there's all this stuff you have to be aware of by a little bit of a reality check of what you might actually get your hands on.

Emma In terms of a relationship with a programmer or a production electrician. Can they help with that?

Rick Absolutely. I also learned from a very early age, ask. The worst thing to come into any situation is to look like you know, and bullshit. If you walk into a theatre and say, can I put a light there or I'm trying to achieve a light that might do this, most people are really excited to tell you what they know, share their experience of what has worked or not worked before. Whereas some of my American colleagues, I think, have fixed ideas in their heads that they will put stuff down on a plan that just physically doesn't work and the electricians know it won't. They set up a combative process as opposed to, how are we going to make this work? Here's what we're trying to achieve. How can we do it? Let's do it the simple way and see if we can make it work before we make it difficult for ourselves.

Emma It's taking the team on a journey.

Rick That's right. I try and be collaborative like that. I probably don't always succeed, but that's what I hope to do. And getting the best out of your team of production people means they're more creatively engaged.

Emma With the evolution of LED and moving lights, the drawing of a lighting plan has changed. It's no longer you and your gel book. How do you go about defining a rig?

Rick When I was at the Oval House with my 30 lights and 12 dimmers, when I put up a light, it was an idea. I had an idea for each light, even if it was a non-idea, like this is part of the general cover.

Now, I rig opportunities. I know that's a good place to put a light. What sort of opportunities do I want to come from that light? And if it's able to be something more flexible, what are the qualities that light should have? Is it a spot or a wash? Is it just one colour, or do I need lots of colours? So, I now rig opportunities as opposed to ideas, and then I have to make sure that I'm managing where I put my resources as to where I need those opportunities the most.

Emma And do you find that it changes with the director because they know you have the ability to change things more quickly now?

Rick I think there's an expectation now that we can change anything at any time. When we were first doing *Billy Elliot*, Stephen Daldry, who I'd worked with a lot, asked if he could put someone there. And in my usual flippant way that I am with people I know very well, I said, you just direct them and I'll light them. He perceived it as, don't talk to me about lighting. What I meant, and later clarified with him, was: we have the resources that I can light them wherever you put them – because that's what I set out to design the rig to do, be a super-flexible tool so we can react to whatever happens as the show is made.

Emma When you went in to *Billy Elliot*, did you have an idea of how you were going to light every scene, or that came during tech?

Rick That came during tech, very much so.

Emma Is that more frightening?

Rick Completely terrifying. Also, the show itself kept on changing. I kind of had a sense of what it should look like. How we were going to achieve that, I didn't know, and we tried lots of different ways. *Billy* was a very long tech, and the benefit was the fact we teched the show three separate times for the three performers playing Billy. It meant that I had a lot of chances to experiment.

Emma How do you use a preview period as a lighting designer?

Rick Things keep changing and developing. Most of the time, some of your collaborators really won't even look at what you're doing until the previews. During the tech, they're too busy with their own departments, getting their own bit done. That can be quite disheartening if you've been working a lot on something, and then by the time the fourth preview comes around someone's telling you, I don't think this is very good. You think, well, you've been looking at it for the last two weeks, now you tell me! And that's because they really just haven't been looking at it for the last two weeks. So, shows change a lot in previews.

Emma How do you think the audience influence the evolution of a show from a lighting perspective?

Rick I think they influence how the show's developing. You just feel when the audience is with you or against you, whether they're responding in the way that you want them to. If it's a musical, are you getting them to clap when you want them to clap? Are you keeping the energy going in the right way? All those things, we just get a sense of. They can be influential. I think that affects every aspect of the show. Are they getting engaged or are they being bombarded? And you obviously want them engaged.

Emma How do you think light can help with storytelling?

Rick It is storytelling. In an ideal world, it should be completely directing the audience: where to look, what to look at, what not to look at. And it should be giving information about time of day, location, if that's important, or emotional involvement of the characters to the audience at any given moment. It can be giving naturalism; it can be giving expressionism. It can do all that. And sometimes it's doing all that together and in conflicting ways. Everybody always says the best lighting is not noticeable. My take on that is the lighting should look inevitable, like it just couldn't be any other way.

Emma How do you balance light and dark?

Rick As I've gotten older, I've become less tolerant of not seeing people well-lit on stage. Even if I feel it's supposed to be a dark world, I'd still want the lighting level on a performer to be good. I have spent a lot of time working on some of the things that I've learned from doing *Inspector Calls* at the National and so many times since. Lots of happy accidents have occurred at the National. Finding the kind of light that looks good on the performers in *Inspector Calls* was one of them: it is largely modified dance lighting or side lighting. So, the brightest thing that light hit was a performer, and the rest of the light went off into the wings.

What that taught me was that I could light people brightly sometimes but still make the world they were in look dark because we weren't hitting the scenery or the environment around the performer. And I could control the darkness by how we lit the backcloth or how we lit the floor or by colour on other occasions. Sometimes I think I even light people too brightly because I'm so excited that I can get light on them. And I think it doesn't matter, and often people will tell me it could be a little bit more atmospheric or a little bit darker, but I don't like seeing people in the gloom for very long.

Emma When you start with creating a state, do you start in a particular place?

An Inspector Calls at the National Theatre – Lyttelton, London. Directed by Stephen Daldry, designed by Ian MacNeil, lighting by Rick Fisher, sound by Paul Groothuis. Photographer: Ivan Kyncl / ArenaPAL.

Rick I start with trying to light the people. And sometimes, I almost stop the march when I feel like I've lit the people, and sometimes that's bad because I forget about some of the other things, like dressing the scenery in a nice way. My main obsession is about lighting performers to let them tell the story.

Emma Do you go into a show with the cue structure worked out?

Rick One of the processes that works for me is I sit and watch rehearsals as often as I can. Sometimes the first time I watch a run-through, if I have the luxury of seeing a few, I try and watch it without a notebook. A lot of times I realize that may be the only time I'm going to see it, so I note when I think something should happen whether that's activated by something really happening or the way I feel when I'm watching.

I will develop a cue list in my mind: their big speech – intensify, or they move over to the table, so we don't need the chair anymore. I just do a list of things that happen so the skeleton is there. When we start lighting sessions or tech, I have a list. I might make a cue, or I will leave a space in the cue stack for those moments and say, let's get a beginning and an end look, then once we get performers on stage, I'll just keep doing things. I know that maybe I'll fill that in later, maybe even in a dress rehearsal or preview.

Sometimes the director will come to you after the dress and say I think this number needs a lot more things going on. I am able to say these are all the things I think I want to happen – I just haven't had time to make them yet. They're on my list, don't worry, and that might calm them down. Sometimes they ask, can you do that on your own or do you need the performers to step through the piece with you? I sometimes say, let me try on my own, if it's not a priority for you to rehearse that number. Then there might be a moment when I say, now I need you to step through this number for lighting. I did that effectively with *Billy* because they rehearsed over and over again. So on some of the big numbers, I kept on working on my own, and then eventually I said, OK, now let's put it on the list. I just need to step through this, I need them to mark it through just so I can check positions. There are 40 cues during this number, and I need to make sure that each one of them is working. Hopefully by not wasting people's time, when you do ask for time, you get it.

Emma Sounds like a great technique.

Rick It's a good technique. There's nothing worse than being in a tech waiting for lighting. I'll say, don't worry, I'll take a note. Let's move on. Let's defuse the tension around this moment. Sometimes you need them to wait for lighting while you have an idea, while you discuss it with other people. But if you can just keep working in the background. I'd like to think that people enjoy working with you more because you're not so demanding of their time.

Emma If someone approached you and said, I'm taking a show from the UK to the States, what would your advice to them be?

Rick Well, first I would say get a really good assistant or associate, someone who knows how things work there. That's essential. The way you interact with the crew is very different. They're much more about the paperwork and documentation because there is the expectation that these people are physically going to supply, prep, rig, focus and maintain. We need everything completely written down and documented in a way that anybody could use it.

It is interesting: I've done shows at the National in the old days, in the Lyttelton, and there may be six areas that are broken down among six crew members. And maybe they would write it down on a scrap of paper that would go into a file in case they were sick when that show needed to come back. That used to work. I would see my less-good ideas and solutions lovingly recreated throughout an entire run of the show. I focused that light badly six months ago and here it is still focused badly. It was partly in their muscle memory, because they knew what it was doing, whereas if you did that in New York, you wouldn't expect that somebody would have that same feeling about what that light was doing. They would be able to say the lens was here, the shutter was there. They would get it all so it was picture perfect in terms of their paperwork, but they wouldn't necessarily look at what it's doing to say you know the hot spot is here as opposed to here. The light would look right as long as it looked right on the flat floor, but if someone stood in it, you can tell as a lighting person the heat's not in the right place, maybe it just needs a little lift up, and a change in the shutters, I'm obsessive about where my hot spot is. I always want it on people's faces.

But, particularly in New York: don't think you're going to go in and change the way things are done. You've got to go and work in the way that they work and get the best out of it. Help them see what the priorities are and what the priorities are not. There are people who have made a really good niche by understanding and helping to be the translator between the British and American way.

The system there can make you feel like you don't know what you're doing and you don't know how to present a lighting plan. Whereas we rely on somebody who works in a building like the National to rig a light the right way up if you draw it upside down, in New York they will rig it upside down. Somebody who can ask all those questions just so everything is clear for them, those people have been invaluable to me. Make sure it's somebody you want to spend a lot of time with – that's really important.

Emma How does it work in terms of time management, because you've got people who only do certain jobs in the States, whereas in the UK, whether I moved the chair on stage is immaterial.

Rick You just have to begin, and that's for your local people to advise you. It's never as dramatic as it sometimes sounds unless people start to think that you're trying to take the piss. Once you get to the point where you know everyone knows each other and it's like, oh, sorry, I just need to move this chair, is it OK for me to move that while we refocus? As opposed to, can someone call props, please? You wait five minutes for props to come and do that and move the chair six inches here. Technically, that's what should happen. A lot of that gets broken down and you realize that the props people are still there getting on with their own job. They're still being paid. You're not going to take their work away from them or have one less person on the crew, but a heavy-handed person will say, no you cannot touch that. But your local people will help you work your way through. Just advise you when to push something and when not to. Choose when to have your tantrum because you're probably only allowed one. And if you start to have three, you've lost it.

Emma In terms of taking a show to Europe, the thing I found really tricky at the Châtelet was the change of programmer. And the different skill sets.

Rick This happens a lot on the Continent. Particular people have a different work life structure. It happens in opera houses or state theatres all over Europe as they're on a shift system and they tend to work two of the three shifts a day, whereas we as lighting designers do the three shifts. You get someone who does morning and afternoon, you get someone who does afternoon and evening. You think, I'm here three sessions, why can't one person be here for three sessions for this week and then take next week off? But it just doesn't work that way.

Emma How do you work with rep rigs in theatres like the National?

Rick I love rep rigs because I hate drawing lighting plans. I know that when you come into the National, there's going to be a pretty good rig which is going to offer all the opportunities that I may want. That's liberating. I'll figure out what I don't have and ask for a few extras. I think that I like that challenge of how I can take a rep rig and make it look like it's my show at the end.

I work with rep rigs quite a lot in opera houses. At the Santa Fe Opera there's a rep rig that has been reasonably unchanged for 20 years. They refocus everything nightly between shows. They've added just a dozen moving lights. That's partly because the architecture of the building affects what a light can do, and to put an expensive moving light somewhere where it can only do one job or two jobs is not cost effective. I totally get that. And yes, we add lights all over the place, particularly booms and things like that, per show. But the real challenge is to pull apart the rep rig in a way that's useful to you but doesn't screw them up on their changeovers. That's part of the craft. I've seen people go into Santa Fe and try and fight the rep rig and make it do things it doesn't. If they just listened to the staff, they would tell them that kind of shot from that angle doesn't see through wood. And just get over it, have another idea.

Emma Do you have a show that you're most proud of, and why?

Rick Gosh, I mean, I'd like to think that I'm proud of them all. I'm still very proud of *An Inspector Calls*. I've learned a lot from that show through happy accidents that's given me a way of lighting people that I've found very useful, I think it has contributed to something a little bit distinctive that I may have brought to the world of lighting. I didn't invent it, but maybe it's distilled a little bit more on that show.

I'm very proud of *Billy Elliot* because it was a musical that didn't look like a musical, which was right for that show. There are certain shows that nobody's seen and I'm very proud of. I just lit a musical in Japan. It's a better night in the theatre than I thought this musical might have been, and I felt I was able to contribute to this by my involvement not only in the lighting but also in how we staged it, constantly asking questions of the designer or the director – asking, why are we making those choices? Sometimes the director would listen and agree with me, and many times she wouldn't. But again, by not agreeing with my suggestions she was defining better for me what it should be. Even if I didn't agree, I could appreciate that it was a considered decision and a choice. Working in Japan is also very different; it's much more hierarchical, and you have to really work hard to encourage the crew to use their initiative, despite the fact that they all have bundles of it and can create very good solutions to creative challenges.

Emma Why is that?

Rick They're just too hierarchical. Do as you're told, respect your elders, respect the boss, don't get out of line and do everything really fast and really efficiently but don't question. It's a lot less questioning culture. It's the only place in the world where you give a note and before the words are out of your mouth, you can see somebody running to get there. You know, when you're running through lighting cues, doing odd, random, sporadic lighting notes and your crew are listening to where you're going to and moving to the positions of where the performers are in that cue. The person on stage standing in the right place for you to light was the fourth electrician.

Emma How does a fourth electrician actually know that position?

Rick They're just watching and taking notes, paying attention. They're involved. They're not sitting in a crew room waiting to do something. They care.

Emma What an amazing system.

Rick It's pretty amazing. Learning to appreciate that, to harness that creativity and then a way to break down a little bit of the hierarchical structure, if it's useful to you, without losing your authority is part of what my game is there. I go in being silly and making laughter, making sure that we go out drinking and just start to talk, enjoy each other's company and enjoy working together. What we all try and do is to create a happy working environment because you are going to get better work out of everybody.

Emma Do they work three session days?

Rick They work! It's heart-breaking when you go home because, again, they don't work in the theatre, they are brought in as the crew for that particular show. They are completely your slaves.

Emma So they are all freelance? There's nobody in-house?

Rick There maybe one or two in-house people, but they're doing systems as opposed to show roles because the theatres I was working in were mostly theatres for hire. So that's a very different place to work.

It's worth saying if you are working in America, it's different when you work in a regional theatre or an off-Broadway theatre: the level of involvement is still a lot more than perhaps what we are used to here. American theatre is not just Broadway. But one of my main takes on the difference between the US and the UK theatre world is what people aspire to. The West End is a goal, but not necessarily the ultimate goal. There's as much esteem, recognition and pride at creating a great show at the National Theatre or the RSC or the Royal Court, the Almeida, Hampstead, the Donmar, Kiln, as there is in having a commercial show running in the West End – perhaps even more so. Whereas in America, the pinnacle of theatre is having a hit on Broadway. That's a very different, fundamentally different, world, and what it doesn't have are what those producing theatres do in fostering teams of people to support producing work rather than just installing shows. The result of that is the ability to make shows that jump over the parapet, like *War Horse* has, or like *Inspector Calls* did. Developing people who make theatre. Being able to work in those places, to me that's very special.

Emma Thank you so much, Rick. It has been fascinating to talk to you.

RICHARD HOWELL

Rich grew up wanting to pursue a career in radio, along the way being named 'TV Hits DJ of the Year' at the age of twelve, winning what he describes as a 'spectacularly awkward meal' with the European club DJ Sash. That may have prompted a change in direction…

Instead, he studied at the Guildhall School of Music and Drama, with *Anatol* at the Arcola in 2006 his first professional design. For the Donmar, he lit *Dance of Death* as part of their Trafalgar season of works by upcoming directors, and subsequently *Aristocrats* and *Privacy*. His career has spanned drama, dance, musicals and opera around the UK and further afield for the Gothenburg Opera, Danish National Opera and the Public Theater New York. In 2017, he lit *Guards at the Taj* at the Bush Theatre, for which he won a Knight of Illumination Award – the famous lighting sword.

Another designer to make his base outside London, Rich lives in Stroud with his partner Holly and their two children, Rowan and Anya.

www.richardhowell.co.uk

Emma What drew you to lighting design?

Rich I got into theatre at school. At that point, it was the sense of community that you get with theatre, with being together in a group, that I enjoyed. I was really shy and struggling to find a place to fit in, and that was where I found it. Then I went to Guildhall, where I met Paule Constable. I think that she crystallized what it was that really excited me about lighting, which is the ability to work with other people to create moments that are bigger than the sum of their parts.

Emma Did you go to the Guildhall thinking lighting was what you wanted to do?

Rich It certainly wasn't a done deal. As part of the course we did stage management and all the other stuff. Actually, some of the things I enjoyed most about Guildhall weren't lighting. We did a wardrobe allocation, which I never thought I'd enjoy, but I really did. Again, it was that kind of community aspect of theatre that had attracted me into it in the first place.

But there was definitely a moment quite early on when I saw that with lighting design there was an opportunity to have a career in something that I not only had an aptitude for, but that I could always get better at. I saw that long road as a real challenge, and that continues to be the case. There wasn't going to be a point where you were the best you could ever be; you could always keep getting better. I saw really early on that lighting combined everything that I was potentially good at, but also pushed me into areas I wasn't so good at. It really forced me to come out of my shell, to talk to people, to learn how to communicate – and that carries on. I think working in lighting makes me a better person.

Emma Do you draw inspiration from outside the theatre, and where does that come from?

Rich Yeah, I think we all do. I mean in terms of design work I think part of it is that you have to keep your eyes open. I now live on the side of a canal, which is a great inspiration. You look at natural light all the time, see what it's doing. Paule has that great phrase, learning to look, which is what it's about.

Emma So you met Paule – how did that come about, and what do you think the key things you took from your time with her were?

Rich I wrote to Paule, because we had to do a secondment in our final year, and I spent that with Paule and Hugh Vanstone one after the other in the Olivier at the National. At the time I still wasn't so sure about where I wanted to go or what I really wanted to do, and she put me on the right track.

And I learnt from her. I watched her ability to distil lighting ideas into really simple terms when she was talking about them. So, she made something that was quite complicated sound very simple. The key is the way she is able to articulate what she does. I watched her do that with directors and designers: she's able to just make it totally straightforward. That's a real skill.

Design-wise she keeps it really simple in big spaces. This idea of always stripping back, always focusing on the single source. She actually does the same thing design-wise that she does when she talks about it: keeps it really simple, clear and visually articulate on stage.

Emma Do you approach lighting from a particular view, and how does this influence your work?

Rich I don't come to it with a specific stamp that I want to put on it. I do think a lot about clarity. Certainly, my thing is trying to make the actors the most important thing on stage; that would be my starting point. I also tend to root my ideas in realism to start with. I find starting with more abstract concepts or spaces quite tricky. I always have to try and find a route back to something that's recognizable and real, even if it's just in my own mind. I think you have to find a common ground with an audience to start with, but then lighting can be really exciting because you can twist and push with it. You can start with light coming through a window, something we all understand, but then you can twist the colour or really push the intensity to hook up to an emotional story, too.

Emma What do you think the key skills to being a lighting designer are?

Rich I think communication across the board. You have to be able to communicate both through your work and with the team around you. It's about communicating your ideas, whether that's getting what's in your head onto the stage or talking to a director, designer or a choreographer about it. And communication means listening as well as talking.

Emma When you speak to a director about lighting, do you have a particular language or a way of explaining?

Rich I think it's all about trying to find common ground. That's all any kind of shared reference is aiming to do: find a way of talking about it so you're on the same page with an idea that is really hard to articulate. The more you can route it back to something that you both understand, the easier it gets.

Emma We've all had times when you're sat in a tech and maybe your vision and the director's vision have been different. Has there been a time when that's happened to you?

Rich Definitely, but as I've gone on, I've realized the skill is about always trying to stay open in those situations. Even now I sometimes struggle, but there are also moments that I can feel myself getting better at it. I did my first show at the RSC in the main space, which was quite a big deal for me at the time. I put my first offer onstage and the director said, 'oh, wow, that's not what I expected at all. I think that's probably wrong for this show'. I'm really proud because I didn't panic. We worked through it, and actually, although it wasn't completely right, it also wasn't completely wrong. So you just have to ride through those situations and listen and talk to each other.

Emma Have you found over the years you've become less precious about your original concept in order to have that creative process in the theatre?

Rich Yes, I suppose this is something that I've sometimes found hard in the past. I've actually been doing something in the last couple of years which has really helped me: I tell myself at the beginning of really tricky days, I may not be able to make this look brilliant today, but what I *can* do is really focus on communication and really focus on how I'm working as part of the team and being a positive presence in the room. Those are things that are in my control. There's such a pressure to go in on day one and make it look brilliant, but I've found that by removing that pressure for myself I'm able to focus on being a useful, open collaborator. Which does then let you go on to make it look brilliant.

Emma How much independent research work do you carry out on a production?

Rich I would like to have a more rigorous research process. I don't have a set way of approaching it. It's all about the people I'm working with. I might watch films or bring bits of research or images in order to communicate specific ideas. Anything that helps that conversation you're having. Often, it's thinking about a feeling or atmosphere you're trying to create rather than trying to find references that look exactly like what you want to create together.

Emma When you see a white card model – how do you approach it?

Rich I suppose the space dictates everything, so it's an exciting time. There's always questions about scenic finishes as well, all of that is so important. But I think most of the time when you initially see that model, it's clear what you need to do next, even if there are challenges. If there's a massive ceiling or you can't get light in, somehow that's almost as exciting as it being a completely empty space.

Emma Do you like to talk through what's possible with those things?

Rich The reality is that you have the conversation. I would tend to avoid asking to cut massive holes in bits of scenery. If there is a ceiling, it's normally there for a reason; you don't necessarily want to have a big gap in it to get lights in. I really do think the limitations imposed define what it's going to be. Often the hardest sets to light are the projects I'm ultimately most proud of because it pushes you in a direction where you can't do your normal thing.

I did a show really early on at the Gate called *Car Cemetery*, where the grid was sort of covered up, and the brief was no theatre lights visible at all. That turned out to be great. We lit the whole thing with desk lamps and angle poises. I was really proud of that show because at that point when I was just starting out, it pushed me completely out of my comfort zone.

That said, I think I would now make an effort to talk about things that are hard. I think when I started out, if there was a ceiling, I'd go home and worry about it. Now I would definitely talk to the designer about it because the set model exists to start those conversations. It's just having the confidence to really talk things through. I think sometimes you have to go out there and initiate those conversations yourself, which I wouldn't necessarily have done early on.

Emma How does your work and process change between genres and spaces?

Rich I guess I learned the basics of lighting design in small spaces. Now I've had a chance to work in bigger spaces, a lot of what I find is that I'm trying to hang on to those things I was able to do in smaller spaces, which is hard sometimes – clarity, single source, all those things. You can light a small space with a single light bulb, and I try to hang on to that purity in bigger spaces. I think the same across genres. Coming from theatre to opera it sometimes feels like it's a completely alien world, but it's all the same really. The same rules apply whether it's a studio theatre or a big space or dance or an opera. I think what you're trying to do with light remains the same, and I think the process is completely transferable.

Emma How does technology change the planning process, and what are the benefits and challenges of this change? Talking particularly about things like moving lights, where it can do all sorts of different things.

Rich There's a danger that having a rig of moving lights replaces the need to be specific about planning what your rig does, because you can put a moving light there and know you've got options later on down the line. But I think it only really delays the choices you have to make. You still have to make decisions about what you're doing. So you potentially encounter those choices later, when you're in tech – which is not the best time to be trying to tame a moving light rig. What is wonderful then is when the actor moves a little bit, and you can just tilt the light up back on to them.

Emma So when you draw a lighting plan, do you have a sense of where that light is going to focus?

Rich Yes, for a conventional. For a moving light I'll know roughly what its range of options are. For me, it is all about sculpting and angles. Where the light starts from, its journey to the stage, is really important – almost more important than where it ends up focusing in terms of how it is going to sculpt people.

I do definitely do my thinking about the design when I'm drawing it. I don't understand how people can get plans drawn for them. It actually did happen to me once when I did a show which went to America and they drew the plans for me. I did a sort of draft plan and they worked it up, they channel numbered it and did lots of stuff like that. I really struggled initially with that because I got into tech and didn't know the plan as well as I would normally do, because certainly channel numbers you'd normally do yourself. It felt like I'd missed a whole layer of the design process that normally comes with drawing the plan.

Though sometimes you're in a focus session, and something comes on pointing in the wrong direction, and it looked better than the light you'd intended to use over there. I think you have to stay open to those things as well, don't you?

Emma How do you work with a budget? How does that shape your design process?

Rich I find there's a process of putting an initial bid in, and then it's too expensive, and you have to cut it back, probably to a degree that is quite helpful.

On the fringe, part of my design process was, how many dimmers have I got? Then you'd have to do a big cut to the plan: all the essential ideas stayed and all the things you didn't really need went. When I started working in regional theatre, places with more dimmers, I didn't have to do that, so I stopped doing that. Now I try to do it even if I've got more than enough equipment: have a good sweep of that design and really strip it back out. I think constraints like that or like budget do shape things creatively. I try to see it as useful!

Emma How often do you go to rehearsal? How do you analyse the script? How do your ideas formulate?

Rich Obviously I start by reading the script or listening to the music, and have lots of conversations with the director, designer, choreographer and anyone else who is involved. I've never really done those shows where you're there right from the very beginning in the rehearsal room.

Of course, it is useful to be there to get to know everyone and to immerse myself in what's happening and how everything is developing, and also to work out my cue structure, which I'll tend to do directly into the Eos off-line software. I tend to be there as much as I can in the final couple of weeks. My ideas about the design form in a space somewhere between rehearsals and drawing the plan and those meetings with everyone.

Emma What makes a piece more than the sum of its parts?

Rich Well, I think that's entirely getting to the bottom of what we do. Collaboration, talking to each other. If you are all doing your job and listening to each other then things start to happen. You can really feel those moments where the motor kicks in and it sort of rises up, elevates above what you all do individually. But what exactly that is, I don't know. If you could churn it out reliably, it would be brilliant, wouldn't it?

I think you can know when you see work where the communication has been strong, and everyone's been pulling in the same direction. You can also pick up on it where there's a slight pull in different directions. You see it on stage. That's actually what really good directors do: get everyone pulling in the same direction at once, which is easier said than done.

Emma And you have to do the same with your team, your programmer, your electricians…

Rich Yeah, definitely. I think that's the phase beyond pub theatre: learning to be a team leader. You really have to communicate your ideas and your excitement about what you're trying to do. When you can motivate a team, it really works.

Emma The relationship between a designer and a programmer, how do you think that's changed?

Rich I really value that relationship with a brilliant programmer. Has it changed? I mean, it's changed more for me, I suppose, as in I've got the opportunity in the last few years to work with some really good freelance programmers. I think certainly when I first started working with freelance programmers, I was too all over them with specific syntaxes because I was used to working with programmers who weren't specialists. Now I've really learnt that a good programmer can just completely transform the process if you allow them the space to be creative and do their thing.

Emma How do you work with a show's stage management team?

Rich Good stage management makes all the difference, especially the DSM. In a live show that's changing all the time, it is so valuable to have someone who you know has an eye on it, and who is able to understand what you're trying to achieve.

Emma So you'd give the DSM your cues before going into tech?

Rich Yes, certainly the framework of it. There's so much to do in tech I try to set it up so I just have to do content creation rather than also having to explain cue points. So I'll try to have a conversation with the DSM, going through the cues rather than just emailing the list because I find that conversation often throws up things I didn't know were happening or things that were assumed from the rehearsal room. That's always a useful conversation to have.

Guards at the Taj at the Bush Theatre, London, for which Richard won his Knight of Illumination sword. Directed by Jamie Lloyd, designed by Soutra Gilmour, lighting by Richard Howell, sound and original music by George Dennis. *Photographer: Marc Brenner*.

Emma How can lighting enhance a story and add to an audience's understanding?

Rich I mean, in every way!

I'm most interested in the editorial aspect. Lighting can be like a film editor, picking the shots, controlling the pace of the story, how you're moving from one story beat to another, or one location to another. Often, I find one of the best ways to talk with everyone else about what I'm doing lighting-wise is in terms of camera sshots, whether you're zooming in or panning out at this moment. It doesn't have to be as literal as that. The zoom in is not a spotlight on someone on a dark stage, but you can zoom in on someone in different ways; even in a big open space, a single person can be made to feel isolated. That's the bit I enjoy. Everything you do in lighting is storytelling. It tells you where you are, what the emotional temperature of the scene is.

Emma How would you define the journey of a piece of work? Do you look at the whole arc of the piece, or do you look at component parts and link them?

Rich I think one thing the lighting can really do well is provide an arc. It can almost provide an arc when it's not there, for pieces that are quite disparate. I think you're always looking for ways to draw a piece together rather than split it apart. Quite often, the hard part of the job is when you're looking at something in isolation in a tech; you have to be very aware how you got there, what came before, what's coming afterwards. It's all about context. And I also try to self-impose a set of rules for each piece, particularly in terms of a limited palette of colours to hold everything in a coherent visual space to help draw everything together.

Emma When you begin to build a state on stage, where would you begin?

Rich Light the actors, which I know is maybe not what other people do.

Emma Do you prefer to light during tech rather than in a plotting session?

Rich Within reason. I think that does vary a bit between genres because obviously in opera you don't get the tech time in the same way, so you have to do a bit of pre-lighting, and the same sometimes with musicals because they can be so busy. I enjoy pre-lighting when it gives you the space to be able to play. And it's really useful for getting the basics – that allows you the freedom to be able to work quickly in tech, which I think is essential. But it's certainly only in the real tech that you get the chance to light instinctively, which is always when I feel I can do the best work.

Emma How do you balance the stage picture and allow an audience to focus?

Rich That is what we do isn't it? We're always balancing that picture. Again, this was something I learnt from Paule when I went to observe her lighting an opera really early on. She had hardly lit the people that were furthest downstage and had lit the people that were upstage, and I was like, why is that? And she said, if you block the stage picture too far downstage, if you make that too prominent, the eye will never see further upstage, so you have to kind of layer it back and draw the eye through. You're creating the picture in that way. I still often think about that.

Then there's a whole thing which I didn't even know existed, but which I was introduced to recently, where some people light from light, switching all the lights on and then sculpting away, whereas instinctively I do it the opposite way round, starting from darkness.

Emma So turn on all the fixtures and then?

Rich Not all of them, but you create a big bright look, and then you start turning lights off. It's a bit like a sculptor and you're creating a picture by chipping the light away. It gives you a safer way of approaching a tech, when you can't plunge people into darkness, or you worry straight away that it's underlit from the moment you start. Instead you can start to sculpt your picture out of that. I can't get my head around doing that, though. I need to start with darkness or a single source!

Emma How do you approach previews and how do you use them?

Rich I think the first dress rehearsal is a really vulnerable time, even more so than the start of tech. It's when you see it all the way through. It's your first time seeing it – and then you get a load of notes from everyone else as well. Staying calm then is a skill. The best situations are when the director recognizes that you're going in the right direction and just gives you the space to keep on crafting it and filling it out and providing what's needed. The opposite of that is the worst.

Beyond that – once you get over that initial fear of 'this is all wrong' in preview one, you can really use them. It's great to have an audience. I always try to go out and watch it in the audience, even in theatres that have a place set up where you can see a screen. I can't really take an iPad with me either – I prefer to get out from behind the desk and really see the show as part of the audience.

Emma Memory control desks. How have they benefited lighting as a craft?

Rich I can't remember a time before memory lighting desks! I imagine they let you be much more detailed. Obviously, it becomes a digital computerized process, which is arguably not as good as somebody operating it live, but I think part of our job is to blur those lines and make it feel as organic as we can. Once you can do that, of course, it lets you add the detail; you can really craft in a way that you couldn't if you were manually pushing up a selection of faders.

Emma What have you found are the benefits and challenges LEDs bring to the role of the lighting designer?

Rich Colour is the really interesting question. LED lighting gives you a huge colour palette, which is a great thing. The challenge I've really found with those sources is they can be overpowering in intensity. When I first encountered them, I definitely got caught out with that; the show becomes so bright that suddenly you're switching on a par can and it's not cutting it against them. You have to remember that brightness is relative. I wish I could go back in time and see the original *Phantom*, which I'm told was an incredibly dim show, but because it's all dim, it balances out fine.

I do think you need to be much more disciplined with colour, given all the options available. It's more important than ever to make sure all your colour choices speak to each other and live in a coherent place visually. But the colour LED offers is amazing. Certainly with Source Four Lustrs, which are a complete game changer in terms of what you can achieve.

Emma So are there now things that are almost part of your repertoire, that you couldn't have achieved before?

Rich Yeah, certainly in terms of live colour shifting, the way that stuff can move live from a single source – which is really about clarity again. Using fewer sources clarifies the whole image. Where you might have mixed two lights, it can now be a single source.

Emma Before you start in tech, do you put colour palettes into the desk? Do you know what colours you want to use in the way that you would have done in picking your gels and drawing a lighting plan?

Jekyll & Hyde at the Old Vic in London, directed and choreographed by Drew McOnie, designed by Soutra Gilmour, lighting by Richard Howell, sound by Sebastian Frost. *Photographer: Manuel Harlan / ArenaPAL.*

Rich If you think generationally, I'm probably one of the last to have grown up using gels. I do still certainly put the colour correction range, Lee 201, 202, 203, open white and into the warm colours, because it gives you a sort of benchmark. I don't know how that's going to work in the future because I think we will lose touch with that way of talking about colour. I'm really interested in how we communicate colour, because it's really hard. I love working with the subtleties of the colour correction range of gels, but with the Lustr you can be even more subtle – you can go between 202 and 203, pick your colour, then twist a bit of green into it. It's great.

You can also now be much braver with colour, because you don't have to commit to it in the same way that you would if you were cutting twenty bits of a weird green. You can just try it and ditch it, which I'm excited about because I think I am quite conservative with colour naturally. Though as I said, you have to be even more disciplined to make sure all your colour choices ultimately work together and fit into the set of decisions you've made for the particular production.

Emma Can you describe a project that you've been involved in which either stands out as rewarding, challenging or memorable? And what did you learn from it?

Rich *Jekyll & Hyde* at the Old Vic, which was a dance/theatre piece. It coincided with Rowan, my son, being born. He was born a week before we went into tech, which we always knew was a possibility. But luckily the timing all worked out, though I definitely did that show high on adrenaline and lack of sleep. We also had a short tech. I was proud of it because we did it really quickly, and it came off. It was a great set, designed by Soutra Gilmour. She really gets what lighting can do: it was just a big revolving skeletal scaffold structure, which gave lots of opportunity for lighting.

Emma If you could, what would you tell your younger self?

Rich I think just how long the journey is, so calm down and enjoy it – but then I also kind of enjoyed that period of being young, excited and slightly manic about it. I genuinely still love doing this job as much as I did, but I think getting a perspective on it is really useful.

Having found a community in theatre, I do now think there is a danger when that flips over into being your entire life. Certainly when you start linking your personal well-being, mental-health wise, to how your job is going, that's really dangerous. I've certainly found that having a family helps with that, but also, just having a life outside theatre is really valuable. It gives you that perspective.

Emma I couldn't agree more. Thank you for such an interesting conversation.

HOWARD HUDSON

If you kept an eye on London's fringe scene in the early 2000s, Howard's name was familiar for years before it burst across the bigger stages, lighting show after show and, in particular, musical after musical – a genre for which he seems to have a particular love. But some of those shows spectacularly outgrew the little theatres they began in – the Southwark Playhouse production of *Titanic*, in particular, expanding to big stages in Toronto and elsewhere. It speaks perhaps not just to the quality of the work but also to his fun personality that he still works today with many of the directors he worked with then – they still want him there as the shows become bigger. And designers he worked with on those shows recommended him to others, which ultimately led to his first West End show – *Romeo and Juliet* for Kenneth Branagh. His latest success is a new twist on the same story, *& Juliet*, now transferred to Broadway and netting him his first Tony Award nomination.

He began lighting at school and in amateur dramatics, but chose not to train as a lighting designer, instead taking a fine art degree at the Chelsea College of Arts – being there also gave him ready access to the London theatre scene. Now he works regularly there and around the world – letting him also fulfil his love of travel and exploring new places.

www.howardhudson.co.uk

Emma What drew you to lighting design?

Howard I did a lot at school, a lot of amateur dramatics in the early days, then started doing some fringe shows in London. I then went and did a fine art degree at Chelsea College of Arts, doing some painting and sculpture as a foundation and then a three-year degree. Throughout that, I was lighting my own stuff and doing some work with other people, finding my feet. Being in London, I had access to the whole of the theatre scene. I never wanted to become an artist, but I felt it was a better route into the world of theatre.

Emma Absolutely, and a fantastic route in terms of references.

Howard Of course, and most importantly, I think, was that we did these things called 'crits', I suppose like critiques, where you sit round and look at other people's work as a group of, say, fifteen people, and you talk for an hour about their work. That's a wonderful way of learning how to have that dialogue, how to be constructive without shooting ideas down, and I think all of that plays into how you collaborate as a team these days. Chelsea never taught me technique – we never had life drawing classes or were taught how to paint. It was more about discussion and analysis of an idea.

Emma How do you approach a new collaboration now?

Howard It's a weird thing because I never really know whether to reach out or whether I should wait for them to reach out to me. It varies hugely from team to team and person to person – sometimes a little like playing chicken with each other! If it's getting quite far down the line and I haven't heard anything, I will try to reach out and see if they want to talk about the show. It's also working out beforehand how that person works as much as you can. For some collaborators, lighting might be really high up their agenda, and they see it as integral to the piece. For others, they're happy for it to come along later in the process. Similarly, with some collaborators who I might have worked with for years, a lot of those broader conversations will already have happened, and so it's not as important to dig as deep with them as you might working with someone for the first time. Something I have learnt over the years is that first impressions can often be misleading, so I try to keep as open a mind as possible.

Emma And once you've made contact, how do you talk to a director about a show?

Howard It differs hugely from show to show: that's something which is brilliant about our business, all of the work we do is so different. Different pieces and people require different types of collaboration, so I think it's quite hard to talk too generally about these things. For example, I've lit quite a few of the classic American musicals now, things like *Kiss Me Kate* and *Guys and Dolls* and *On The Town*, where their structure is worked out to a tee. They've been tried and tested over years and years, so structurally, you know how the lighting will function – scene, song, transition, scene. So conversations with a director there might be more to do with how are we going to approach particular moments and what we might be planning for a specific number. What is our scene change language. What is the general look of the show. A new show, such as *& Juliet*, which we're about to take to Broadway, required a much bigger picture conversation as we had no idea what the show was or how the lighting was going to work through the whole thing. We knew it wasn't going to obey those existing conventions, so we had to really work hard to find that language.

I think broadly you could say I often sit down as early as possible and talk about the piece. That's my favourite thing, when you can talk very generally, and you're not talking about lighting as such, you are talking about the piece as a whole. I think that makes your work richer if you know what the bigger picture is and don't get bogged down too early in the specifics.

Emma When you get a script, what's your process from script to production?

Howard I've been doing a lot of work recently which has music, whether that's opera or musicals, so a lot of that, rather than reading the script, would be listening. I feel if you've got four or five shows on the go, the hardest thing is having to learn the music. You need to go into the theatre knowing it inside out, knowing the numbers, knowing the music, as that dictates what you do. With a script, I'd read it a couple of times, highlight things, circle very literal things and maybe that bigger picture stuff. Maybe sit down with the director and talk about what you took from that, if they are open to that. But a lot is ultimately led by the design, so the earlier I can get involved in that, the better.

& Juliet at the Shaftesbury Theatre, London. Directed by Luke Sheppard, choreographed by Jennifer Webber, set design by Soutra Gilmour, costume design by Paloma Young, lighting by Howard Hudson, video and projection by Andrzej Goulding, sound by Gareth Owen. *Photographer: Johan Persson / ArenaPAL.*

Emma In terms of putting together a cue structure, when do you do that?

Howard Some shows, I'll spend three weeks in the rehearsal room. Others I'll turn up at the end of the process to watch a final run. It really varies from show to show. I think for a new piece it is so important to learn the show as much as possible. I always think spending time in the room helps you see detail you'd just never see if you only watched once or twice – particularly with choreography. It helps me a lot to see the work being made, so you can learn the intention – what everyone's trying to achieve. And of course you can make suggestions, if you're allowed. It makes the piece better as a whole.

I mark up the score and script on my iPad; after the final run, I'll number the cues then send it through to the DSM. That's always the crunch point in the process as you're really up against the clock, but hopefully you've then got a framework.

Emma Do you put those cues into the desk before you start to plot?

Howard Yes, I would do the Eos offline and label the cues, maybe put the odd time on. I'd also sometimes make a very basic followspot crib sheet for the spot ops to follow in tech – just so we have something to start from.

Emma Do you like to pre-plot?

Howard More and more, yes. I went through a period of waiting until we do it in the tech, which for certain things is fine – it depends on how busy the piece is. I remember a show I lit in Sheffield where we basically pre-lit act one, which was only 180 cues or so but was a first, for me, in terms of getting so much in. Sometimes it's harder to unpick that, especially when you are using a big moving light rig – it's harder to then fix stuff, so it's easier to go with the flow in the tech. But I'm more and more of the mind that you should try to get as much in as possible if you have the time.

When you run out of cues in tech, it's like dropping off a cliff: you can see where you've lit up to, then it's nine-thirty and you don't finish until ten and you can see the end of the list. You have to work quickly then! The unwritten rule is that holding up tech is a bad thing, so I try to keep ahead and on top of it so as not to have people waiting for me. Though, it is hard sometimes.

Increasingly, pre-viz is becoming a useful option, particularly for busy sequences with lots of effects. For *& Juliet* we pre-lit most of the big numbers but just with the lights on or off and in open white – it was a bit like sketching, broad brush strokes, then we added colour and intensity in the tech when we had scenery and costumes. It's still pretty expensive and time-consuming to set up, but I think producers of musicals, in particular, are starting to understand that it will save time in the end.

Emma When you create a state, where do you start?

Howard I think a lot of the time I start with lighting the environment, so I light the scenery – create the background first, dress in what I need and then think about how the company might be lit. Define the space first. It depends on if there is something in the set that will dictate how it's lit or whether you are inventing that yourself. I'll think about how light enters the space if it's a more naturalistic set. Or I might be thinking about what colour the floor should be to make these costumes pop. I think of it a bit like background and foreground, effectively – so like in a painting, there is that undercoat of colour, that first layer, and then you add in the detail on top, which is the company. So I try to work more broadly initially, the bigger space, then I think of the company being the detail within that.

There is this phrase where people say someone paints with light. I've been thinking about that, and it's kind of a weird phrase for what we do, because it's thinking of our shows as being quite two-dimensional. I think what we do is paint but much more three-dimensionally – so our space is deeper than a single surface and has layers within it. It's more sculptural. And of course, our work exists over time and changes constantly, which is quite different from a painting.

Emma In terms of scenic finishes, with your background you obviously have an understanding of paints. How do you work with a designer in terms of getting the most out of the materials?

Howard It is so hard because even with a model, everyone is guessing until you see the thing on stage. But you can suggest things. I've done a couple of shows recently with really high gloss, shiny mirror floors, so you have to have the conversation early on that the followspots are going to bounce off the floor onto the back wall and any of the crosslight hitting the floor is going to skid off into the opposite side of the set. You just have to be able to explain that. They may say that's fine, in which case you run with it, or you may say, listen, if we just change that slightly to this...

I remember *9 to 5*, the Dolly Parton musical, at the Savoy. The set designer Tom Rogers and I discussed this a lot: initially the set design was a one colour grey portal-driven set, which is great as grey takes light very well and better to have that than a really saturated colour, which doesn't then take other colours very well. But I said, if we graduate that slightly going back so it gets a darker tint, it will just help me in terms of the foreground to the background, helping the upstage areas sit further away and not be so present in the picture, to allow us to pull things downstage. He was very happy to do that. You probably wouldn't even notice it, but it is very slightly darker towards the back. The good set designers are open to those changes – could you just darken this, help me lose this when you've got crosslight spilling onto opposite walls. It's brilliant when they are responding to what it is looking like, and you can explain there is nowhere else for this crosslight to spill off to, it has to hit something, I know that wall is looking very bright, so what can we do – help us!

Emma What do you take inspiration from?

Howard Art, I suppose. People talk about looking at paintings, at Turners and stuff. I don't really know; it's a lovely idea that you might look at a painting and be inspired. I suppose colour-wise that happens sometimes, but I think I'm more inspired by contemporary design of things and architecture. Instagram is brilliant for seeing stuff you'd never stumble across. Judd, Flavin, Twombly, Koons have been high up on the list. Those people. I don't look at their work and think, oh that's how I'm going to light a show, but I think they provoke ideas for how you can think about your work.

Photography is useful. It's contrast, it's not so much the pictorial or narrative, I don't often look at something and think I want to recreate that. It is what it suggests. The form of it, or the colour of something.

Some lighting people, and many directors, are obsessed with film. They could name you anything – and I think, oh I don't know that one, I should go and watch it! When I do, I often think it is so exquisitely beautifully lit – but there is no way we would ever be able to achieve that on stage; they can spend a week on one shot so they can refine it, and then they grade it afterwards to tweak all the colours and make it that beautiful. It's harder for us, having to do it live. But I think we can take away the essence of that.

Emma How do you balance light and dark?

Howard That's really hard. I often find that when you start a show – I think you see it in lots of people's work – the first ten or fifteen minutes of a show is often much brighter, much broader, and then you watch the rest of the show and you can see, ah, here they go, they are working out how it works, and they are taking more risks. It is something I really try to get on top of: don't over-light initially, in terms of contrast. But I also think that at the start of tech, everyone is finding their feet. No one really knows what the language of the piece is, and lighting is often quite high up on everyone's radar as we are one of the final elements to be added, so people are looking out for it. But as the tech goes on, the language of the piece might change completely, and it's important to try to get that continuity back into the start of the piece.

Emma When you draw a lighting plan, do you know what every unit on it does?

Howard I know what every unit could do, I suppose. We have to do our plans so early nowadays; you read books where people talk about, back in the day, drawing the plan after the final run-through, but with something like *& Juliet*, I drew it three months before they'd even started rehearsals. So, you draw a rig of moving lights in systems that you hope will give you what you need. There's a line of thought that you fill every position with everything so you have got every option, which we are being made to do more and more because you don't want to be in the tech without that available – but you haven't seen the show, you haven't seen rehearsals yet, and you are having to draw a big plan.

I think ultimately a lot of the early decisions are dictated by the set design. Something I think about is, where does the light come from – how will it look in the air, and how does it enter the space? What are the best angles I can achieve? The position of the units is so vital that it is worth fighting for that real estate from the other departments early in the process.

Emma What systems do you generally look to have?

Howard On a larger musical, generally I'll always want to have a toplight system, a high sidelight system, a low crosslight system from the sides onstage and from the front, then depending on the design (and where the loudspeakers are going!) whatever you can squeeze onto the proscenium. Backlight positions vary so much because you have to think whether you're working with a more single-source aesthetic or whether you're dealing with something more multi-source. If the show is going to be followspot-heavy, you might get away with fewer advance units. Then whatever systems of frontlight you can squeeze in or are required. I think the thing nowadays is just to make sure you have as much flexibility as you can in every position. People expect you to be able to adapt and produce new looks within seconds.

Emma And colour?

Howard That's definitely one of the things we can struggle with these days. With all the choice we have with LEDs and with the use of conventional lights and gel becoming rarer it's quite easy to become quite muddled, colour-wise. So what I try to do is have a system of sixteen or twenty colours for every show that I mix across every type of unit. So in the blue world, I might have what I call a grey-blue, a light blue, a medium blue, a dark blue and a saturated blue, then the same for the ambers, lavenders and pinks. I might make some specific colours that work for particular scenery or make certain costumes look great. Before the tech I'll go through all of these palettes and tweak them – so is this show a more greeny-blue show, or should the blues be more red? It takes time.

Working strictly in this framework means the show should have a continuity of palette. Though it does raise questions with how a show gets remounted or revived because we are not basing these colours on existing gel colours – so how do people know what they should look like in the future? Maybe there needs to be some system that lets us measure colour independently – a clever phone app. But I think basing our palettes on ancient gel numbers feels quite archaic now – I haven't got a swatch book out for ages.

Emma But if you do have any conventionals, do you have colours you'd always use in them?

Howard There are certain colours like Rosco 371, 372, 373 – if you want to light costumes very beautifully but in a very neutral white light, those are my go-to colours – and lots of other people's, too. They are slightly redder than Lee 201, 202, 203, so they are slightly better on skin, I think. The green-ness of the 201s is good at times, but the 371s are more like pastels. I very rarely use different front-of-house colours – maybe some lavender or pink tints sometimes. Oddly, I never really use any of the warmer gels at all. I think the taste nowadays is for crisper, whiter, cleaner-looking things. Open white is often the warmest I'll go.

Ultimately, colour is dictated by the piece, what the piece requires. And so much of what we are talking about ultimately is your taste, you have to have your own taste in colour. You think something might work for the piece, so you try it. If it doesn't, it's so easy to change now.

Emma The relationship with the programmer: how has that changed, and how do you see that collaboration?

Howard It works both ways, because you obviously want them to be engaged and involved with what you are doing, you don't want them just to sit there and type. Sometimes that can stray too much – you might have someone who can be too vocal, and actually, you just want them to be there for you and do a beautiful job programming the show. Then again, sometimes you do want them to be vocal, and you need them to chip in and help you if you run out of things to say. Help me out here, what can we do? It works both ways, and the good people are the ones who are sensitive to that and know when they can pipe up and when they do just have to sit back a little bit and let us work. If I'm having a conversation with the director, the programmer might be listening to that, and that would help them with where we might be going next with an idea.

Emma Describe a project which you've been involved in which stands out as rewarding, challenging or memorable?

Howard I did *Little Shop of Horrors* at the Regent's Park Open Air Theatre. Doing a show there is a very unique experience. You can talk for days about working there, and that was a special one, a fantastic show, really inventive by Tom Scutt, who designed it and Maria Aberg, who directed it. A drag artist as the plant, which had never really been seen before, and with the plant being in a show at the park – and being able to use a completely different palette of colours, into the green world that I've never really done before, proper green – we've all used tinty green stuff, but to go full-on green was really cool!

At the Park, they rehearse in a rehearsal room but then start tech on stage at one o'clock in the afternoon, so you are doing the opening of the show in daylight! So, I will then sit there under a little tent with the programmer, and we will just watch the rehearsal, and what we might do is just rough in some very initial moving light positions, literally flashing the light at full in open white and hoping that, if it's a dark enough day, we can vaguely see where it is.

I will already have a cue structure in the desk, which is absolutely vital if you are doing a show like that because if they are jumping around, you can see where you should be, you can see the structure, and you are not making cues up on the spot, then you might get to the evening session, and you are in scene 3, and you end up lighting – but of course what you are trying to do is light for when it will be in the show condition. So even though it might be very dark on stage when they are teching it, you know in reality it will actually be at 8pm and still very bright. The director might come up to you and say, oh Howard, I was thinking it should be a bit more like this, and I have to go, I completely understand, but I know it is going to be at 8pm so we won't be able to achieve that which is why I am throwing everything up at full to cut through the daylight. It is a huge guessing game – and weird that as the evening gets darker you have to turn the lights down, the opposite to what you'd think.

The first time you see it all properly in the evening is in a dress rehearsal later in the week; that's the first time you ever see it in real light, and it's genuinely absolutely terrifying to sit there – what is it going to look like! Of course, the followspots are in tech with you, so they are learning it during the day as you talk them through it. And the DSM is calling it during the day even though nothing seems to be happening with the lighting on stage, so you get all those little bits of the cogs working, then you just hope by the time you hit that dress rehearsal it looks OK.

The year before, for *On The Town*, we lost that dress rehearsal because of the weather, so the first time we saw it was in front of 1200 people! I was in a little tower by the followspots; I had my own lighting desk, so you are editing over previews along with the programmer. You just pray there aren't any holes. It's why the shows I've done there have been quite followspot-driven, because at least you know that people are going to be lit when they need to be lit, then you can creep that out or refine that over the preview period – but then of course they will come in during the afternoon and start re-teching and changing bits, so then you are having to do it on the fly without being able to see it again, going into a preview that night and hoping! It's a totally backwards but brilliant thing – it's really fun.

Emma Is there anything you've learnt doing a show at Regent's Park which has affected your process on other shows?

Howard I think that guessing thing – pre-visualizing in your mind what something will look like is really helpful when you draw your plans, when you know what a light will do from a position, setting the level – that guessing game.

Emma Changing direction slightly: what do you think the key ingredients of a great collaboration are?

Howard I think that the best collaborations are when you have a certain equality within the team, when everyone is allowed to chip in, within reason, to suggest things to other people. I think when you have those teams where there is a real hierarchy, where you have a big director, and you are all sort of working around that person, I think that's harder. I struggle with it if someone asks me to do something that I really strongly disagree with visually for the show and I'm not really in a position to say, or when you are sort of made to do it. I suppose ultimately, someone has to make that final decision, otherwise you would just be going round in circles. But it is lovely when you are working in a team where you are able to go to the pub afterwards and say, why was so and so saying that about that, and discuss decisions. I think the best collaborations are where you are able to say those things.

Emma Have you ever been in a position where you suddenly discover you and the director are on totally different pages, and how do you deal with that?

Howard Yes. It's really hard, and absolutely sick-making. It is one of the worst things, especially when you know you have another two weeks on a show. I don't think I've ever had it really bad, but there have been certain moments which have been stomach-churning. Or when they ask for a particular thing, and you know you do not have those lights in that position. All you have to be able to do is say, sorry, yes, we can spend lunch adding this and changing that colour. I don't know why we all get worried about it because ultimately, it's part of the process, it's part of working with other people, and that's the joy of why we do what we do – because we are collaborating with people.

That said, there is nothing wrong with being given a note. We all have to be given notes. The challenge is, we have a pride in what we do. If someone says, I wasn't sure about that, you go, oh no, I'm letting everyone down here. But really, it's a good thing – it's a collaboration. We have to get better as collaborators at taking on that information. I think probably you start to panic because it's so late in the process, and you feel there's not time to fix it – you start to panic that deep down there might be some misunderstanding of our shared vision for the piece – there's nothing worse. But ultimately, notes are good things, though it is something I battle with. It depends on how the note is given, especially if you disagree with it. I think we all have a deep-down desire to please, and when we feel we aren't achieving that, we kind of think we aren't doing our job properly and might get defensive. But I just try to remember our work takes time, and tech is where we're all learning about the show. Collaborators who allow you time and space to work things out are the best. Jumping on your back too early in the process can be unhelpful…

I sometimes think we're sort of the glue to the production, we come in so late, and there are all these disparate elements which people have been working away on, and then we have to unite all of that. Literally, it's filling in those gaps.

Emma How do you work with a budget?

Howard I've been in positions before where I don't know what the budget is, or haven't been told – which is kind of liberating, because if you know it, you have to work within it. If you don't know it, then ask for what you want and hope for the best. Then it's the production manager's problem – they then have to ring you up quite awkwardly and go, actually you've only got £x per week. So I sometimes try not to know!

Say it quietly, but I will always overdraw a plan if you're sending a kit list in. I will always add more, knowing that you are going to have to cut. Sometimes you get away with it and you don't have to cut anything, so you have a great rig. I suppose the good shows are budgeted properly, and the production manager and producer will sit down and go, we can see there's a lot of set electrics in this – if the set is a thousand lightbulbs, there needs to be money available. Sometimes you have people who don't understand that, and you then have to have those conversations. More recently, my agent will check all that beforehand; when she does the contract, she will ask what the weekly budget is and make sure that is confirmed. It becomes part of my decision-making about whether I do the show or not, so I can go, that is nowhere near enough money, there is no way I'm going to be able to achieve it on that sort of money. Then I don't think I can do the show, because you don't want to be in a position where you have no money, or don't have the correct resources.

Emma What would you tell your younger self?

Howard I think when you are starting out there is a desire to achieve a lot very quickly. It's very hard when you are in your early twenties to see contemporaries of yours doing very well. It's a very competitive world. I think now I've ticked a few of those boxes in my career, play in the West End, musical in the West End, international stuff, I can relax a little bit, so I wish I'd told myself you will get the chance to do those and actually not to panic.

I suppose when you are mid-20s, you don't know how your career is going to go, so it's very hard. Ultimately you have to say, I want to make good work, it doesn't matter where it is. That was my thing that gave me solace when I was doing lots and lots of fringe stuff and off-West End stuff for years. I was going, those shows artistically are as valid as something at the National Theatre, it just happens they are in a 90-seat theatre rather than in the Lyttelton. You are using the same lights, the same colours, the same desks to some extent. So artistically, they are complete equals – it doesn't matter where the work is.

Emma How did you make the leap between doing shows at the Finborough, for example, and doing a West End show?

Howard A big opportunity was through Christopher Oram, the set designer, who I had got to know a little bit through some of the designers who he had as assistants but who I'd worked with when they were doing their own work, and through Neil Austin. Neil was meant to be lighting Kenneth Branagh's *Romeo and Juliet*, but it ended up clashing with *Harry Potter*, and he had to pull out. So, then I snuck in, and Christopher got me seen for it, which was a massive leap because I'd done international and regional stuff but never a commercial thing like that. I went and met Ken and got it. It was the first proper big thing I did. It was absolutely terrifying! But it opened doors because in terms of box-ticking – which is a terrible thing – as a designer, when you've done that first West End show that opens doors, and it's sort of like people now trust you. It lets you exhale and go, phew. It took someone to take that chance on me and give me that break.

Also, producers and people you work with early on, they all rise up with you, and you hope someone takes you with them. It often doesn't happen because younger directors who do well early on get made to use more experienced people on their team, and often the lighting designer is an easier role to fill in that sense because we come along so late, whereas a set designer's involvement is seen as perhaps more senior, so they might have to fight to work with a lighting designer they've worked with before. But good directors who really fight to use their contemporaries, that's a great thing.

Emma In terms of the actual design work, how do you scale up? Are you using the same techniques that you learnt on the fringe?

Howard Mike Robertson gave me some of my earliest opportunities, doing some programming and assisting for him – I remember once teaching myself the Strand 520 console overnight before heading into tech the next day – but I mostly just churned out the shows for about four or five years, designing twenty-five or thirty shows a year after leaving college. All smaller stuff, the odd international thing, those are the shows where

Theatre Lighting Design: Conversations on the Art, Craft and Life

Romeo and Juliet at the Garrick Theatre, London as part of the Kenneth Branagh Theatre Company Plays at the Garrick season. Directed by Rob Ashford and Kenneth Branagh, designed by Christopher Oram, lighting by Howard Hudson, sound by Christopher Shutt. *Photographer: Johan Persson / ArenaPAL.*

you make your mistakes, and you learn about colour, about lights, you learn all that as you are going, but there you can really make mistakes, and few people see it. That was absolutely fundamental. You learn your craft and how to work with people on those smaller shows with no lights and no money, which is the hardest thing. It gets easier as the shows get bigger – the pressure is slightly higher, but it gets easier as you've got the kit. I did so many shows where a moving light would break, and I would literally be up a ladder trying to fix that moving light in the interval, knowing there was an audience waiting outside. I had years of that and cutting the colour and focusing the rig yourself. Also, it was such an important opportunity to meet people in those early days that I still work with today.

Emma When you take shows abroad – if you were going to talk to someone who had never taken a show abroad, what would you say to them? What would be your key points to them?

Howard You get paid a lot more! If you work anywhere outside this country you'll earn twice as much, easily, and that is an absolute fact, from my experience anyway.

I suppose you have to respect their way of working. You have to understand how they do things. It can be the most frustrating things, but ultimately you are not going to get anything done unless you respect that. I did a show in China last year. We took all the kit over because we'd heard horror stories of people going over, none of the kit being up to scratch. We were lucky that we took it all, but you have to be aware of what they've got in a general sense. Certain lights, like Robert Juliats, are much more popular in Europe, particularly in all the European opera houses; I see them much more than Source Fours there. But the biggest thing is having respect for their way of working. Recently on an opera in Bologna, the language barrier made things really hard, so it was adjusting to a slower speed and being respectful of their process and giving them the time.

I did a show some years ago in Toronto, and we were focusing some lights in a box. I was on stage and there were these two burly union guys up a ladder. I was saying – OK, sharp to shutter, bring this cut in, for a good five minutes, thinking to myself, how slow are these guys – before I realized nothing was happening. It turned out they'd gone on their union tea break without telling me, so I'd just kept talking to this box where no one was! Kind of embarrassing – but I learnt my lesson on how strict those union breaks are. That everything, absolutely everything, stops for lunch and dinner breaks. Those precious hours when over here our electricians would get tons of notes done – there the stage is left empty.

Ultimately, though, working abroad is a real privilege. You get put up in nice places. All your expenses are paid. You get nice meals in beautiful Italian squares. You are looked after. I'm all for working away, it's a big part of why I do what I do really. Any opportunity, I'll jump at to go to another country.

Emma Thank you, Howard, for sharing so much of your experience.

JESSICA HUNG HAN YUN

Photographer: Morgan Eglin

She'll smile and shake her head and dismiss it if you suggest that she's suddenly everywhere, but it does still feel like it's true, a meteoric rise from her beautiful, highly acclaimed and award-winning lighting for *Equus* at the Theatre Royal Stratford East and then in the West End. The director of that show brought her to the National Theatre for a complete change of style in their lockdown pantomime, *Dick Whittington*, and her post-lockdown portfolio includes everything from *My Neighbour Totoro* for the RSC (a film of which she'd been a huge fan as a child and so was beyond thrilled to be asked to light – that exuberance visible to all as she collected an Olivier Award for her work) to *Guardians of the Galaxy* for Secret Cinema. Her work now spreads beyond theatre, with an outdoor installation for the Museum of Home in 2021 followed by another at the V&A.

One of four children growing up in Essex, she discovered lighting at school and went on to study it at Rose Bruford. She started working at festivals before lighting shows on the fringe and then on from there. Her work often displays a very distinct use of colour, sometimes vivid, sometimes subtle, but always very personal. Perhaps that comes from the Chinese-Mauritian heritage, as does the distinctive surname – though even she, on her website and email signature, shortens it to just Jessica HHY.

www.jessicahhy.com

Emma What drew you to lighting design?

Jess I actually got introduced to it because I took GCSE drama. That was all down to the fact I didn't know what else to take and thought I could pass drama pretty easily, which turns out is not true, it's actually quite difficult. I couldn't act, I couldn't remember my lines. I was so wooden and terrified. There was a technician at my secondary school called Pete, and he was the person who got me into lighting. We had a really basic black box studio with a few lights. He got me to start having a little play around and explained to me what lighting can do to hold space into a narrative. I really enjoyed doing that and got really involved with it. I wasn't really academically driven, wasn't very good at art or sports. So then when it came to A-levels, I chose it because I got on with my drama teacher and the technician Pete. He was the one who said, you can go to drama school and study this. So that's what I did: studied lighting design at Rose Bruford. It was more an accident; I'd never been taken to the theatre before GCSE drama. My parents were never into the theatre or the arts in general.

Emma And are they now into the arts? Do they come and see your shows?

Jess Oh no, they still haven't been to any of my shows, but that's actually just because I never invite them. I think that they would be happy to come and see something, but it's also just not their cup of tea to go to the theatre.

Emma Did you study pure lighting design at Bruford?

Jess I studied the lighting design BA honours course. As soon as I finished A-levels, my parents were very much like, you need to go and get a degree in something. They really wanted me to go to uni. It was the year the fees were going to go up to £9K a year, the year after my year, but I was going to take a year out and go and travel. Because the fees were going up, they were like, no, you should go now, before we have to pay £9K a year. So, I went and did that. I did not really pay any attention in my first year. I was a classic uni student. It was the first time I'd lived away from home. The first time I properly had my independence.

Emma Did you get to meet other designers while you were there? And to light shows?

Jess Yeah, we had a lot of people come in and talk to us. Designers, but also manufacturers. We are had training on ETC and MA desks. They've got the Rose Theatre, the Barn and smaller studios. So, you are always doing shows. On one, you'd have to do a lighting design, and you'd also have to do a production electrician role. You got to work with a director, with a whole company. You got to experience what it would be like but in a safe environment where you were allowed to not know how certain things worked, you were allowed to ask questions. Then you'd also crew for other shows that were happening. You got good experience. Because it was a small campus, you got to know a lot of people. I really liked that because it made it a really friendly environment to learn in.

Emma What did you do after Rose Bruford?

Jess I didn't go straight into lighting design. I tried to, but I literally came out and didn't know what to do with my life. There was the whole thing of, I need to be able to pay rent, I need to be able to pay my bills. So, I went and worked in retail for two years. I tried to get into lighting design for theatre in many different ways, and nothing was working. Everyone was just like, you need more experience, and I was like, but how do I get my experience? I didn't know. I think it was also to do with my confidence: there were loads of other people in my year who were really proactive. They worked for White Light, or they shadowed other lighting designers. I wasn't confident in myself to email a lighting designer. I then did the classic thing of maybe I'll go find myself and travel. So, I went and travelled for five months, which was brilliant. I really enjoyed that. I came back and really missed doing lighting design. I missed being around that environment. So, I applied for theatre and architectural lighting. I tried getting into architectural lighting, but I didn't know any of their software like Revit or DIALux. It's a whole other world. I just needed to get back into lighting design, no matter what kind of form. I went on Arts Jobs and applied for lots of different fringe stuff, and that's kind of how it got going.

Emma What was your first show?

Jess I always remember that I was working part-time in a chocolate shop in Angel three days a week when I got my first freelance job doing an opera at the King's Head Theatre.

It's such a unique space; it has a lot of quirks to it. The show was *Tosca*; I'd also never done an opera. I remember the director, Adam, saying we want to introduce people to opera. So that was my first freelance thing. I had to quit my chocolate shop job because I couldn't get the time off. That was really scary, taking the plunge into being freelance completely and quitting my part-time job, which is stability, for this one job in lighting design. I think that's one of the most terrifying things about doing it all. I used to also freelance crew, for Urban Electric, who did a lot of fashion events, which was very different to doing theatre. I crewed for them, that was really fun. I got to meet lots of different people who came from the TV world, from events or from theatre. They taught me more about the texture of light and how tangible it can be.

Emma Do you still work in that side of the industry? Or is your work predominantly theatre, opera and dance?

Jess I'd say more theatre now, but I also used to do quite a lot of festivals. I used to do Boomtown Festival, helping to run a venue – lighting and stage management. I got a free festival ticket and was able to be in crew camping. I used to really enjoy doing that because I worked really hard for the set-up of the festival, and then when it was up and running, you could go and have fun and enjoy the festival. So, because of doing that, I started to light Cabaret Circus. From there, there was a company for which I did a show called *Becoming Sheas*, at the Vaults Festival. They did an immersive theatre and circus show all together, which bridged both worlds. Now I mainly do a lot more theatre. Dance is something that I'm also really fond of because I used to dance as a kid – ballet.

Emma Who and what influences your work, where do you find your inspiration?

Jess I'd say a lot from movies. I really love film, or even TV shows or anything like that. Photography, art, a lot of installation, a lot of light installation artists, I really enjoy their work.

Emma Are there particular people that you go to and look at their work and use as reference?

Jess There's the classics like James Turrell, Olafur Eliasson, and Steven Knapp. Then there's teamLab, a Japanese company, and there's Moment Factory. There's a lot of installation people I really love because I think their understanding of light is phenomenal because they focus really closely on a certain aspect of light. James Turrell's colour, for example, is out of this world. The same with Olafur Eliasson. It's very present in a room. I was really lucky to go and see some of these pieces in Japan and Korea. I nearly cried because I thought it was one of the most beautiful things I've ever seen. I think it's being so immersed within light and being so overcome with this visceral emotion that you can't quite describe it.

There are also architects who I really love, because of that interaction with building/light and material/light. The whole thing of natural light, artificial light and natural daylight, I think, is really interesting because we can't live without it. It's around us 24/7, whether it be from sunlight, from moonlight or from your street lamp, or now from a laptop or from a phone screen. It's constantly around us. I get a lot of inspiration from lots of different things. But I think also movies and TV I really love, because it is not just the lighting, but also the emotional response you get from it and the way that it can make you feel when you watch it, or the pace of something, if it's something where there are lots of different cross-cutting snapshots and it creates such a pace and a rhythm within a scene. The tension is rising, all of that stuff is really amazing because it's so accessible. So, it's a really great reference point for people you work with, because no matter your background or where you've come from, I feel like TV and film are something that's part of a lot of people's lives. So, it can be really relatable when you talk about certain styles.

Emma Are there particular architects you like to reference?

Jess There's a particular Japanese architect, Tadao Ando. He's an amazing architect, and his understanding of light is phenomenal. His understanding of natural daylight is out of this world. There's also an architect, Ryue Nishizawa, and artist, Rei Naito, who did an art piece on Teshima, which is an art island in Japan. It is this amazing concrete building and a circle that had been cut out, that you could go look into the sky. But then also there were trees that grew over it. So, there was sunlight coming through, and then the floor is this really smooth concrete, slightly on a slope. And if you listen really carefully, there are these tiny little water droplets that come from this concrete floor and then they drip down, and there's lots of other holes where they come from and they kind of join up to create these amazing patterns on the floor. It was light, and also the acoustic in the space was so beautiful. I remember being in there for four hours and feeling this was one of the most amazing pieces of art I'd ever experienced.

Emma How big was it?

Jess It was massive. I've never felt that feeling again since that experience. I've always tried to find it. I don't know what it was, and even just talking about it is quite emotional. It brought together this beautiful light along with nature. Then also because of these tiny little water droplets that you all of a sudden see it's going from the macro to the micro. It was also really minimal and really simple. It really made me look up and around my surroundings, but then be able to really focus down on these tiny little water droplets, creating these amazing patterns on the floor. Also having that experience of seeing people walk around and have that same feeling as you. It was phenomenal.

Emma Was it a one-off piece, or is it more permanent?

Jess It's permanent. There are two islands which are just off Japan, one of those called Naoshima and the other one's called Teshima. Teshima is the one where there was this amazing art piece, and it only has that on the island. On Naoshima, they have lots of different artists. It is amazing, you could just lose yourself.

I think it's important to take inspiration from everywhere and all around you. I think it's important to also experience life and experience the world. That will inform how your work comes out. Creativity can be from everywhere and anywhere. So, I think it is really important to go out and to hunt for it and to look for what speaks to you. That's one of the most important things. That's what will really inform your work or inform your interest, because already what we do is really niche. It's like we're trying to find even more of a niche within that of what really interests us in what we do. So much influence from a lot of different places and artists. I think also because light is culturally very different to a lot of people. The way that they perceive light and the way that they understand it is very different to how we would understand it here. That's the same with colour theory, colour is so ingrained in culture. It's really interesting to find all of that. The fact that when we see red, we think of anger and anguish, but we also think of love, we think of romance. Then in another part of the world that's luck and that's all that it's seen as. There's lots of different interest and stories to colour and how it's become really present. That's also how we see light, through colour, with colour.

Emma How does that knowledge impact on your use within a show?

Jess It's really important. I feel like I'm more aware of it in my everyday life than I used to be. I think the way colour can really psychologically change the way that you feel is really interesting when you immerse yourself in a certain colour. How I try to inject that into my work is how you can really utilize colour in a very emotional narrative.

Emma In terms of the change from gel books into the LED world of not having to pick that colour, how has that affected your process?

Jess It's weird because there's pros and cons to both, I feel like there's some gels you just can't get the same colour with LED. But then also LED is great because it gives you flexibility. You can think about colour later down the line, if a certain scene has really changed in its tone or the way that a performer's presenting it, for that LED is really great because then you can be very flexible.

Emma When you are asked to do a show, where do you start?

Jess I guess as soon as I get the script and I do my first read-through. For my process it's quite important to feel what the story is and what the narrative is and what the driving force of it is. I always jot down if it reminds me of a movie or if it reminds me of a photographer particularly. Kind of anything that it reminds me of, I jot down, because I think your gut instinct is always right and to always go with that. I find it really fun to read it. One of the most exciting things that can also happen is not being able to imagine how this could be done on stage. Then meeting the director and having that conversation about how do you see this? What were your initial thoughts? It's for them to understand you, but it's also for you to understand them and how you get a vibe of what they're like as a director if you've never worked with them before. Also, their understanding and their journey into working on this script I think is really interesting.

Then I start creating mood boards. Pinterest is always a go to, always keeping your conversations going. Even if I'm walking around and I spot something that reminds me of the show, I'll take a picture and send it to them.

Emma When you talk to a director and a set designer and you describe what you're planning to do, do you use mood boards and film references? Is that the language you talk to them in?

Jess Yeah, a lot of films and mood boards and also that thing, which is quite a weird thing, but the thing where you say when I read this part of this scene it made me feel the same emotion that I felt when I was standing on the pier in Brighton, looking out to sea and there's the sunset and it's roughly about 7pm. That kind of relationship to human life and how something that you've experienced, a group of people could have experienced multiple times in multiple different ways, I think is quite a nice thing to say, to make something really relatable.

Emma It's such a difficult medium to talk about. I guess we are more on the spot in front of a much bigger group of people when you're presenting for the first time what it's going to look like, whereas other disciplines are able to show more tangible things like model boxes.

Jess You can't be in the rehearsal room with all of your toys. So, when you get to tech you're very aware of, have we communicated in the right way to each other so we both understand it? It's always that terrifying first few hours of tech. It goes so painfully slow because I think everyone is trying to find how everyone else communicates. Everyone's trying to find how everyone likes to work. Then there's some things that could have been mis-communicated in a creative meeting, and then they turn around and go, I didn't think it was going to be like this. And then you have to try and talk it through and figure it all out together.

Emma Working with the set designer, do you like to be involved as early as possible?

Jess Definitely as early as possible, as soon as I get onto a project, I always like to talk to the set designer, get involved in what their thought process is, because they have already

Equus – ETT / Theatre Royal Stratford East, London. Directed by Ned Bennett, movement director Shelley Maxwell, designed by Georgia Lowe, lighting by Jessica Hung Han Yun, composition and sound by Giles Thomas. *Photographer: The Other Richard / ArenaPAL.*

had an amazing dramaturgical journey with the piece. After the director, and of course the writer, they know the piece inside out. Their understanding of it is really in-depth. I find it really interesting talking to them about character journeys, narratives, and then getting down to what they're thinking of and trying to marry up what both of our views on it are, or what our creative visions of it are, and to talk to them about the different materials they're thinking about using and how that interacts with light. If they have a particular interest in colour, for example, or so you can talk about light in set pieces. It's really important to get that all done as soon as possible so that it can all be considered in the design.

Emma Do you prefer to have a plotting session prior to the tech or do you prefer to light as the tech goes on? What's your process?

Jess I always like to have plotting sessions before tech. I try and fight for them. I like to get as much plotting in beforehand, before tech, and always to get everything in the book with the DSM I think is really important. Lots of little things that can just make tech go a lot quicker. I think it's really important to ask the director to come into one of the plotting sessions so we can go through some stuff. It's being ahead of the game and trying to utilize as much time as you can. You can discuss something till the cows come home, but because some directors aren't really visual, they don't understand it when you describe light, no matter how much you show them visually with boards or with movies or with different artists – they don't understand it until you actually present it. Because of that, I always like to get a director in to show them what I've been doing. There's going to be some stuff like face light that you can't really do until everyone's on stage. It's getting your basics in and working on your effects – anything that would be really time-consuming in tech I try and do beforehand. But it really pains me because I'm someone who likes to go in order of things. Sometimes I have to start at the end of the show, whereas if you go chronologically, you always feel what the pace is, you feel the rhythm of it, so sometimes it's really hard to take yourself outside that and go OK, now I've done that I'm just going to go jump five scenes ahead. But so much can happen in that time in terms of the pace, the rhythm, the narrative. Also, the performers will bring something completely different when they have the set, costume, lighting, all of the elements around them. There's just so many variables to consider.

Emma Do you keep up with technology? Do you know what every unit in the rig can do, or is the programmer able to come and support that?

Jess I am quite bad at keeping up with new technology because I'm not a very techie designer. A lot of people left uni and went and did a lot of crewing and technician work, but that really scared me because it just wasn't something I enjoyed. But then, to a certain extent, you kind of have to understand what is in your rig and how you can utilize it in new ways. I do make sure that I know what everything in the rig can do. I do a little table. I started creating little tables of all of the kit and then having key headers for each column for the things I think could be useful, especially if it's movers – then I want to know exactly what I'm playing with. I'll group things into potential face light, backlight, do little groupings of what things can be, which is quite old school, what things could be used as specials. I try not to be too structured. I want to let things flow and be more instinctive, because I always feel no matter how much you work on your rig on a plan, until you get into the space and you have everything in front of you, that's when you get to know your rig really well and get to play. And that's when you get to go, OK, yeah, this is going to work, or this is not going to work. It's an extension of you when you get to know your rig.

I do rely a lot on my programmer in terms of communicating in weird ways like, I need this effect to be like you're blowing up a beach, all of a sudden it explodes. I'm quite abstract in that way. They just translate into the desk what you mean. There are some times where you can get really stuck and your programmer has such a great fresh brain on it, and they will just go, do you mean this? And you're like, yes, that is what I mean but I couldn't get my words out. And they understand exactly how you work, and they start to see patterns in your design. Sometimes you're like, words are just not my friend today. They still understand exactly what you mean.

Emma They are so much your ally in terms of providing support in an environment which is so pressurized with everybody waiting for you.

Jess Also because they have that distance, sometimes when you work on a show, you get so close to it that you can't see the whole picture. Sometimes we can't take a step away from it because it's quite personal, whereas I feel like a programmer kind of has that two steps back which is really nice to have.

Emma Do you know what everything on your plan will do, or do you put lanterns in just in case?

Jess Definitely put loads of them for emergency use! I like to know my basics, but also at the same time, I like to try and be flexible. I never try and be, this is the plan, stick to it. I like when I'm in a focus and there's a set piece that isn't quite to the dimensions, or there's a material that is beautiful, to be able to have a light even if it means sacrificing light from other areas. I think it is important to not always stick to the script and to sometimes be like no, that would look so stunning if we did something like that.

Emma It's those happy accidents.

Jess That's happened quite a few times also. Or someone's been focusing for me and they've accidentally knocked it somewhere else, and I've gone no stay there. That's beautiful, that's exactly what I want.

Emma How was it working at the National Theatre for the first time on their panto, with their rig which is more fixed? How does that work, and how does your process change?

Jess They have a season rig which Paule Constable designed. It's brilliant because you can also add to it. It still has that flexibility. I don't think my process has been that different. I think it's still been fairly similar. But I was saying this the other day to the team, I have commitment issues to my rig plan. I'm quite indecisive in life, and that's also me with my rig plan. I'll start at version one. But there'll be so many different versions down the line because I go – what if we do this? And they make something in rehearsals, and you get really excited about it. Which is a difficult thing when obviously what the team need is a really solid plan, but you're like, what about this, what about that! Sometimes you need to reign in, but it is also important to never stop creating, to never feel restricted because you have a deadline. I think there has to be flexibility from both sides in order to create because you can't limit yourself and go, right, this is it, because there's only so much you can find in rehearsal, some things you'll still be finding in previews.

Emma I was going to ask you how you use the preview process?

Jess One hundred per cent it's play time. I don't see it as preview one, it's done. It's always preview one, let's just see how it goes. There's always stuff that comes up in tech where, for example, there are two ways we could do this. Or if a director says, can we try it this way then I will always be like, oh, let's try it for preview one, see how we feel, we can always try something else for preview two. I think it's really important in previews to experiment, and even if you go completely radical and left-field, why not just do it? You can always rein it back in.

Emma Absolutely, suddenly having an audience can change how you feel about the piece, you see emotions that maybe you've never quite seen in that way because of that response of the people around you.

Jess That's really true. For example, when I first read the script, I was howling at that, it was so funny. Then you get so used to all of the jokes and the nuances within something that you kind of become really immune to it. When you get an audience in and they have that reaction you go, yes, of course, that's why I've been stuck on what exactly the scene is. You kind of lose that emotional drive.

Emma If you were going to say something to your younger self, knowing what you know now, what would you say?

Jess Make more mistakes, it's fine to make mistakes. If it doesn't work out move on and don't get so emotionally down on yourself, don't be so harsh on yourself. There's always a new day, and you can do something new again.

Emma Can you describe a project you've been involved in that stands out as rewarding, challenging or memorable and what you learnt from it?

Jess There's two that really stick out for me. One was *Equus* I did at the Theatre Royal Stratford, and then the other was *Seven Methods of Killing Kylie Jenner*, at the Royal Court. Both of them really stand out for me because they taught me a lot about collaboration, which is really important. You can have a lot of fun and a lot of play with what you create as a team, everything is so inter-linked, everyone influences one another. There's a huge domino effect: we have to work together very closely, and we have to all collaborate really closely, because if someone takes a step to the left, we've all got to take a step to the left, we've always all got to be together as one because you will see that throughout a piece. When you go and see a piece, you can tell when people haven't communicated to each other, or not quite understood what each other are doing. It really says a lot about how people have worked.

I think it's so important because you want someone to come out of a show and go, that was an amazing production. We all have to work together in order to create something which is really true to the story.

Emma What do you think made those two productions, those two teams gel in that way?

Jess I think the communication between all of us was the thing that really clicked. I also think when you go into tech, there's so much pressure on the whole team, on everyone, but it's also how people manage their stress levels in that moment. On both shows we understood how to talk and how to communicate to each other, but also there was an openness, it was a safe environment to ask whatever you wanted to ask or to say, I want to try this really crazy thing. And people being like, yeah, just do it, and no matter how big or small the idea was, it was let's have a play, let's try it out, which I think is important because I think it's important to be in an environment where you feel safe to ask questions,

Jessica Hung Han Yun

Seven Methods of Killing Kylie Jenner at the Royal Court, London. Directed by Milli Bhatia, movement director Delphine Gaborit, designed by Rajha Shakiry, lighting by Jessica Hung Han Yun, sound by Elena Peña. *Photographer: Helen Murray / ArenaPAL.*

to be bold and to be brave with whatever you want to do and not to feel like maybe if I try and ask to do this idea, people might think it's stupid.

Emma What's been your biggest learning curve and why?

Jess It's been more of a journey, I guess my confidence in general. It's so difficult. I remember at the beginning I could be so hard on myself about everything. If anything, ever went wrong, even in the slightest, I'd think to myself, it's because you're really shit. I'd be really bad at doing stuff like that. So many times, I'd think, I've done such a bad job. I'm going to quit lighting, and I'm never going to be a lighting designer. I'm never going to succeed. I'm never going to get anywhere. It is also hard being female in an industry that can be quite male-dominated. You can feel out of place and quite lonely.

I was really lucky to have great people around me who were like, no, it's what you're really passionate about. You really give a shit about what you do. Tamykha Patterson, who is a programmer, is so brilliant, so cool, she's the person I'll go to and be like, hey Ti, does this sound really crazy? I really enjoy going to her as a programmer – she understands you so well, what your flair is, what you're trying to create.

I think the hardest thing is finding your voice. Being aware when you're not quite happy with something you've done is a really useful thing, because it means you know that something you've created is not quite you. It doesn't have your voice in it. Knowing that is OK – because it means you know you need to work on it some more, so it really becomes what you want it to be.

Emma Thank you, Jess. It has been fascinating to listen to you.

MARK JONATHAN

Photographer: Matthew Ferguson

Marko is in many ways the social hub of the UK theatre lighting industry. In 1993, while head of lighting at the National Theatre in London he founded the annual Lighting Christmas Lunch, originally for about twelve lighting managers of the UK's leading drama, opera and ballet companies. It soon expanded to include lighting designers, production electricians and programmers, managers of lighting hire companies and manufacturers and increased in size to more than 200 attendees – the perfect chance to socialize and catch up at the end of each year.

His career in lighting began with a lucky break while a member of the National Youth Theatre; having spent his formative years in the lighting team at Glyndebourne Opera, he now lights plays, musicals, ballet and opera across the world from Japan to Los Angeles and before Brexit (which causes him considerable concern) across Europe. He is waiting for an Irish passport. He has written about his adventures extensively in 87 issues of the Association for Lighting Production and Design's *Focus* magazine. When the winter comes and the snow falls, his other passion beckons, and he heads for the mountains to ski off-piste in deep powder while humming opera arias.

www.markjonathan.com

Emma I think what is very unique to lighting design in this country is the generosity of it as a discipline, the free way we share information, how social we all are. You feel like a key part of that, recounting your adventures for the ALPD magazine and, most particularly, with your famous Christmas Lighting Lunch...

Mark As a young person, I used to love reading articles about lighting, especially in Strand's old *Tabs* magazine. I would look at these drawings and hang on to every word because you just couldn't get that sort of information in any other way. There was always that sense of sharing useful knowledge, even when that was the only way of doing it. Now there are so many more ways. My agent was talking about this the other day. She said that we are completely fraternal, collegial in the way that we support each other, including supporting the next generation of lighting designers – saying to her, you should get so-and-so on your books, they're good. She said that was completely different from other design disciplines.

Emma Why do you think it is?

Mark I don't know. I think for scenic designers there's a fear in there. They don't have lighting lunches. Whereas we can ring each other up say, I've got a cyc and I've only got this much room, how should I do it? When Rick Fisher was chair of the ALD and I was the professional rep, I remember him saying to me that we had to find a way of being inclusive, not exclusive. I think we do manage that. I think that feeling is stronger than ever now.

Emma So what drew you into this inclusive world of lighting design?

Mark My attraction to theatre seemed to be pre-loaded inside me. I would always look for the proscenium arch in a room. While I was still a boy, I was always looking for a derelict church hall that I could take over and turn into a theatre. At the age of ten or eleven, I was running my own theatre company and conscripting all of my friends and kids in the neighbourhood to be involved in my shows.

Emma Were your parents in the theatre?

Mark No, they weren't. I was adopted, and everyone in my adopting family were doctors!

Emma Did they take you to see something and that's when you worked out that there was this world of theatre?

Mark I think I was totally into theatre before I even went to it, but I was taken to pantomime at a very early age, and I was completely addicted immediately. There would be hammering, and my mother would shout up the stairs, Marko, you're not building another theatre, are you? At one stage I negotiated that I could bang two six-inch nails into the wall of the spare room from which the entire theatre I was building was going to be cantilevered.

Emma So then, why ultimately lighting rather than another discipline?

Mark It's curious, isn't it? I did act, but I had this extraordinary attraction to light. I was very lucky that my parents did take me to the theatre, the opera and the ballet. My eyes would go up to try and see how a lighting state had been created, at least from the front. I was aware of the lights behind the pros – I was tantalized. I had a Pollock's toy theatre, and I built my own lighting rig, which was quite complex. I ran it through my model train transformers, which nearly went into meltdown at one point.

At the age of eleven, I was changing schools and my mother said, 'we've been to see the school, it's very nice, it has a language laboratory', which used the newly-invented tape recorder, 'there's a swimming pool, a new sports hall'. After my first day, my mother said, 'how was your new school?' Aged eleven, I said, 'it's all right, but the lighting rig's crap!'

Emma What happened between eleven and the start of your professional career?

Mark I became totally addicted to theatre, specifically to lighting. At age fifteen, the drama teacher said, 'right, we're going to do something very modern now, we're going to do a show in the round'. I remember saying to him, 'it won't work sir because all of the spotlights are hard-wired, pointing at the stage. We'll need lights all the way round, but we haven't got anything on the other side of the room'. He said, 'Could you sort it out?' So after school, unsupervised, I got the scaffold tower out. I worked at height with electricity on my own, none of which you're allowed to do now. I'd seen that everywhere else they had lights with plugs and extension cables. So I re-wired everything so that I could then have lights at the other end of the hall. And we did the show.

Then I got into the National Youth Theatre…

Emma Which led to where you are now?

Mark Which was going to change my life! Though not by plan. But the most incredible thing happened. The NYT was doing a show at the Cockpit, which was a fantastic, purpose-built, flexible space long before anybody had those. We did it in the round with this incredible director, Ron Daniels. It was going to be a show with just a few performances, with incredible youngsters, like Tim Spall, Tim McInnerny, Daniel Day-Lewis. People who were going to become outstanding actors. The show was amazing. It got reviewed by *Time Out*, and suddenly there were queues around the block. I did the lighting. Normally NYT productions were lit by a professional, but it was going to be so small. I operated it as well. It was before memory desks; my fingers flew across the switchboard on what was a cue-laden show. Then I immediately got offered a job.

Emma Whereabouts?

Mark The National Youth Theatre had its own professional company at the time and its own theatre, the Shaw Theatre near King's Cross station. I walked straight into a job. I wasn't looking for a job. In fact, I didn't tell my parents that I had run away from school. I was halfway through my A-levels. I'd got permission to come back to school late because the NYT ran on into September. So, it was only when the deputy headmistress rang my parents and said, 'when's he coming back' that they found out.

I had a place lined up at drama school. When I came to the end of that year I was going to go. On Christmas Eve, after working for three months, I was given an Equity card. That was gold dust. In those days, it was a closed shop. You needed forty weeks' work to get a full card. Thirty-nine weeks into the forty, I was due to start at drama school. So I wrote to the drama school and said, 'can I come a week late?' 'No, you can come a year late'. So, I postponed, and I was having such a good time I asked if I could postpone it another year. And they agreed I could! Anyway, after that, on the third year, I said to my theatre colleagues, I'm going to drama school now. And they said, you have your name up in lights at the Royal Court. You don't need to go now. Beware: I'm not advocating not going to drama school generally! I think it's a good idea to go.

I had an amazing apprenticeship. You had to learn very fast. I remember the stage manager saying to me, I'll show you once, I'll show you twice, but if I have to show you the third time, you're out the door. I did everything – painting, carpentry, props, lighting and sound. It was a fantastic opportunity. I was lighting shows, and I was learning from the greatest lighting designers. One of the first was Mick Hughes, and then Robert Bryan, who had been my lighting hero from the age of ten. I'd seen his lighting at the Opera House and English National Opera. Of course I thought, I've got to work for him. I've got to learn how he does it, how he makes those pictures. Then he came to my theatre, the Shaw, to light a show! I was far too shy to say to him I want to work for you at Glyndebourne, where he was the resident lighting designer.

The next year, in 1977, I bumped into Robert at Glyndebourne. He said, come for a drink afterwards. He said to me, you want to work here, don't you? Yes! So, in 1978, I did. And that was the final part, if you like. That was my master's in lighting design, working for Robert Bryan, having done many shows with Mick Hughes.

Emma What do you think were the best things you learnt from the two of them?

Mark One is the amazing pictures that they painted with light. But the other thing was how they did it. And I don't just mean technically, I mean the manner with which they did it. They were absolutely wonderful people, wonderful communicators. Both to their creative colleagues, so you'd watch how Mick Hughes managed Harold Pinter and how Robert Bryan managed Sir Peter Hall and John Bury and many others, but also then how they communicated to us. We adored them.

Emma Why were they such good communicators?

Mark They had great integrity, but they were gentle, they were full of fun, they had a sense of humour. We wanted to do anything for them. Bob Bryan attracted these amazing people who were going to go on and become amazing designers or makers – Howard Eaton, Andy Bridge, Paul Pyant, Gerry Amies, Hugh Chinnick, Keith Benson. Bob inspired all those people, and Mick inspired so many production electricians, which in those days was probably the way through to design. We didn't have assistants or associates in the way that we do now. That was part of the production electrician's job, as was programming the lighting console. By working for them, we had a very rounded education in how they made the lighting. Cutting the colour: what colour did they use? How did they focus it? How did they create those lighting states? Those were extraordinary things to learn.

Emma How did they create those lighting states? Or how do you create lighting states? What's your process from when you are sent a script?

Mark The script or the music score has clues in it. The design that the designer is formulating or the pictures that they produce have many forms of inspiration. Once we have a model of the design, I think there's an enormous number of signposts and opportunities. Also, there's a lot of things that can make it difficult. There are walls, or there's a ceiling, how will I get the light in? Or there's a window. The light has to get through the window, but there's a backcloth behind it. Have they left me enough room? So, there's a bit of negotiation going on very quickly there. Can you move this? Can I have room in order to let my atmosphere come into this designed space?

Then for me, going to rehearsals and seeing how the director is using the space. The script has lots of clues about time, place and emotion. But in rehearsal, we see where people are being placed. We start to get a feeling about the pace and the punctuation. Sometimes I think the lighting is really important in punctuating the drama. Are the lights going to snap out? Or will they blend somewhere else? By the time we get to the end of the rehearsal process in the rehearsal room, I will have very strong feelings about where the lighting is changing, and I will have notated all that. I may not know how bright the lighting is going to be or how dark, but I know that probably on this musical note or on this bit of dialogue there's going to be a shift, and I'll have a strong enough feeling to be able to put all the cues in the stage manager's prompt copy before I light. I feel comfortable having done that because I can go in with this complete framework already built.

I often have to produce a plan before I've seen a rehearsal. We now have lots of moving lights. If we put our moving lights in the right place, we can do any colour, any light, anywhere, depending on our budget and the scale. I remember 40 years ago pleading with directors to try and give me an idea of where I might need my specials. It's great we've moved on from that; that we can be much more flexible.

Emma Do you find that the expectations of directors are now greater in terms of flexibility? You have an ability to make changes quickly, but they know you have that ability…

Mark What we don't have any more is vast amounts of time. We used to work all night, doing the lighting. And in between, when you'd made the cue, the lighting designer would say, 'OK, plot that, tell me when you're plotted', and I, as the electrician, would write it down. Meanwhile, the lighting designer, the director and the designer drank red wine at the production desk and discussed the play, or the next cue. All of that's gone. I have to try and persuade directors, choreographers and designers to have any conversation that I think we can have away from the pressure of the production desk.

It's quite hard to talk about colour to a director. To you, I could say, let's put the backlight in Lee 120, for example, at full, and let's put the Lee 201 crosslight at fifty, and we could both visualize it. We've got enough knowledge and shared language to be able to do that. But with the creative colleagues you work with we can't expect that. We have to show them, but we have much less time to do that. Whereas before, we had more staff, more time if you like, and we'd say, right, let me see it in 200, and you might have ordered a number of colours and they'd have them all rolled up on the boom. Put them into the 201s and three or four electricians on each side of the stage might go and drop the colour in. Now there often isn't anybody on stage!

Emma Do you think that's affected your processes?

Mark You couldn't get away with being lazy in days gone by because you would have to specify your scroll. I remember doing big shows in the West End and the associate saying, they've really got to have your scroll, they've got to make it up now. And I would still be dithering around with colour books about what my eleven colours should be. So I like the flexibility that's afforded now. But we have to be very fast, very quick at making the right picture. We have to have very accomplished programmers to do it quickly.

Emma That relationship has changed dramatically, hasn't it?

Mark The big change that happened was when they could bring the lighting desk out of the control room to the lighting designer and we could sit close. Having the person next to you, so we're not this voice talking over a headset. I can sense when the programmer is ready for the next thing because they've stopped pressing their buttons. I can go at their pace. They can enter into the conversation that's happening on the other ear where the director's saying, a little bit more, a little bit less, they can get into where we're going with this story that we're making. That was the big change for me.

Plus, while sometimes the organization supplies the programmer, sometimes we can cast our programmer to come with us – if the management are respectful enough to pay the programmer enough money…

Emma How do you keep up with the advance of technology?

Mark By using it! I get a bit bored at demonstrations; after a while my mind is swimming about which lights I've actually seen!

It's often by talking to my young assistants and associates and saying, I want something that can do this, what can we get for this amount of money? Or the hire company will say, you can have twenty of their old bin-ends or three amazing new things, so you've got to know what your technology can do to be artful. You've got to be able to create art with whatever is available to you. There is no point in having amazing ideas that need 300 lights if you can only have three.

Sometimes I believe we encounter a prejudice about small rigs and small theatres. We don't have that prejudice about chamber music. We could put on some Mozart or Haydn, which is written for four or five or six instruments, and it's completely ethereal and transports us. I argue that we should be able to do the same with the chamber lighting rig. We may not be able to have as many orchestral colours, although now, with the rapid advance of LED, it's possible to have almost any colour with just one light. We can do amazing things with the small lighting rig vs. the big lighting rig. And sometimes you can have a more joyful, enriching experience doing something small because you maybe have time. I've done chamber opera, and we've had the lighting rig in the rehearsal room because it's the one they take with them, and we've done amazing things, against being in the most equipped opera house in the world but not maybe having the time to achieve what you'd like to achieve.

Emma Where do you get your inspiration from?

Mark I love looking at paintings. I love looking at landscape paintings. I love going to an art gallery or looking through art books. But then I love looking out of the window. I love watching sunsets and dawns and their sometimes outrageous colours, and sometimes I think, if I put that on the stage, I'd be laughed at. In London, if we stand on Waterloo Bridge, we see sixty shades of grey above St Paul's Cathedral. I was lighting a production of *Ariadne aux Naxos* for a Hollywood film director. It was in LA and he urged me to be more outrageous in my sunsets. So I started doing the most outrageous pinks and purples and blues. Breathless with the outrage of the colours, I went outside, looked down the street, that was exactly what was going on in the LA sky! I began to wonder if their taste buds were affected by what they were used to looking at and that we had a more muted taste because we don't have those outrageous colours very often in our skylines. So, I enjoy one minute seeing something that's very muted and then maybe going somewhere else and being outraged.

Emma Do you use visual imagery to explain an idea to somebody?

Mark I may do. I may actually get out something and say here's something I did before. You have to be careful because then suddenly it's in somebody else's stage design. But quite often, it's helpful. I might show it to a designer – here's a mirror thing working, or it might be the technical way we do something. I'm always a bit nervous about getting out a Caravaggio. I'd love my lighting to look like a Caravaggio painting. But once you've given them the Caravaggio… I know lighting designers do talk in pictures. The challenge would be living up to the image.

Emma If you get a set where you think, I can't get any light into this, how do you negotiate that?

Mark Do you know I've stopped getting so worried about that now. I used to freak out when I was younger, but I think I've had so many sets now that, at first, seemed unlightable. On a production of *Pelléas et Mélisande*, I didn't know the lighting department had told the designer that the set he'd designed was completely unlightable. The designer only told me later. He designed a sloping white roof, with a hole in it, and under the hole was a criss-cross gangway on which people walked. And underneath that were lots of sets that trucked in and out. Could I get the light to come through the hole, go round the staircase and get into these sets? You know, completely crazy mad design. I did manage it, but the head of lighting never spoke to me because I proved him wrong.

Emma You see it as a challenge?

Mark Yes. I love the challenge. You've really got to engage with that challenge. You've got to look for where the lighting opportunities are, or ideally be on board early enough to work with the designer to achieve the best outcome. Do that well and you can do amazing things. On the ballet *Aladdin*, I worked closely with the designer Dick Bird while he was still making the model. The result was very successful – we achieved an amazing roof punctuated by light in the bath house scene. Everyone thought the roof was angled and curved, but it was a flat, vertical piece of scenery carefully lit and beautifully painted.

The other thing I have to look at very carefully is what have I missed in the design? What is the element that I haven't lit well in my head already, that I haven't thought of? And I'm really fussy about shadows. I love doing looming shadows. But I don't want to see multiple shadows on walls unless we've got multiple light sources like candles.

Emma Do you have a set of colours that you want to use on a show in the way that you picked gel?

Aladdin for the National Ballet of Japan, also seen at Birmingham Royal Ballet and Houston Ballet. Choreographer: Sir David Bintley. Set design by Dick Bird, costume design by Sue Blane, lighting by Mark Jonathan. *Photo courtesy of Mark Jonathan.*

How the magic is made – careful planning lets light seemingly conjure three dimensions from what is actually a well-designed, but flat, item of scenery! *Photo courtesy of Mark Jonathan.*

Mark I will always be interested in something that's warm-white, tungsteny, and then those cooler shades, traditionally Lee 203, 202, 201, 200. There may be some random colours that are bold. I might say give me a red. I might then say that blue is too green or that blue is too purple. We're doing much more live colour changing now, especially now we've got colour paths. So, we're not only looking at what colour we're in here and what colour we are arriving at, but how we get there. And that's become very interesting, particularly on things like cycs, because in the early days of LEDs you'd go from colour to colour, and it would go through some ghastly shades of green or purple in between, which didn't work.

Emma When you sit at the production desk and you've got a blank stage, where do you start?

Mark You start probably with the most important element. Sometimes people call it the key light. So, it could just be a person standing, and they're going to be in a beautiful backlight or toplight or crosslight. It could be that the scenery has some elements in it that need lighting. It could be there's a cyc, in which case I'd probably start at the back and work forwards. Create the sky. If there's a window, the light through the window, or if it's night-time and there's a candle alight, then it may just be the candle light and then beyond.

Emma Do you like to have a plotting session, or do you prefer to light with the cast?

Mark It's horrendous lighting without the cast. However, it very much depends on your situation. You've got to have a programmer who can keep up. Opera is always tough. In one European opera house they won't do any modifications during a rehearsal. So you have to write everything down, and then when they're not rehearsing, you're maybe given a day to do your lighting notes with stand-ins. Whereas at the Royal Opera House in London, there's none of that time so you've got to do it fast, over rehearsals. You might get fifteen minutes before act one, and you might get fifteen minutes after act three. If you've got any lighting time, light the act in the middle!

So, it is nice to have some private time. I quite like before we have a lighting session or a rehearsal to say to the director and the designer, if they're interested, would you like me to show you what my paintbox can do? Then we can have a more enlightened conversation with the director, who can join in the making of the picture. We just have a better conversation and a quicker conversation because we help them to be able to join in our vocabulary. You also get a steer when the designer or the director goes, I like that – or not!

Emma When do you work out your cue times?

Mark The longer flowing cues, I might have a stopwatch in the rehearsal room. And if I've had the luxury of getting the cues in the book already, in the rehearsal room I might get the stage manager to nudge me, run the cue and see with my stopwatch how much time I've got before you get to the place where I need the light to be. If it's fifteen or twenty seconds, I say that's great. But if it was only ten, I might say move that cue back ten.

The thing that never changes is my cue synopsis. Regardless of the scale of the production and whether it's drama, dance, or opera or musical, I have a system for notating cues, times and action. It will gain columns depending on how many followspots there are. I add a column for notes during rehearsals and previews. So I don't need a desk light or notebook or pen anymore.

In one opera, the director asked, did I mind if he gave me the cue list? He'd known me for a very long time. I said, I didn't mind. He said, 'because the younger lighting designer I worked with last objected strongly to being given the cue list'. Well, of course, he sent me the cue list and every cue was five seconds too close to where it needed to happen. So generally, all the cues needed to move five seconds earlier and be five seconds longer.

Emma You've worked abroad often. Can we talk about what that process is like?

Mark There's three different sorts of working abroad, I think. One is, you pick up your show and you take it on tour or it transfers. Two, abroad decides they're going to do a new show and employ you. Three, you've done the show, not a touring show, and they suddenly go, we want to take this abroad.

I've had some very successful examples of doing operas at Scottish Opera and at Welsh National Opera. In both cases, we knew that they were going to go to the Danish National Opera. The Danish staff arrived. They measured everything. They notated everything. They photographed everything. They did everything. Knowing in advance, for example, that the Danish National Opera didn't have as many moving lights as Scottish Opera, I carefully designed it not to use every moving light in the Scottish Opera rig. I used some of them as a fixed focus. I was really careful and disciplined myself so that they could translate that. The frustration for me is when, unexpectedly, two years later, Barcelona says, 'can we have that opera?' Now you feel the doors are shut a bit, and you are on your own because the originating company isn't very interested, and the company that's taking it hasn't turned up to see the show, and you're there with your tea-stained old ground plan wondering if you fully updated it. That's all a bit of a headache, especially when it's a completely different rig and a different type of control desk.

Then there's the productions abroad which are brand new. I've done quite a lot of those, both opera, ballet and drama. Then we have to understand capability of the staff, capability of the equipment and timetable available to us. Though actually that isn't just about working abroad. You have to achieve the production in the time that they've got for you. It's really important we find a way of getting the broad brush out. My advice to every lighting designer is, put your broad brush strokes in for the whole piece. Now, I've worked very successfully with one director who will not allow me to do that, and some of my finest work has been done with him, but it's pant-wettingly scary because he won't let me light act two until he thinks I have finished act one. So, you've got to look at your timetable. What are they going to do tomorrow? We've done act one today. They're going to do act two tomorrow. So, what will you light tonight? You got nothing in the desk for act two. You've got lots of notes for act one. What will you do?

Emma Light act two...?

Mark Yes. But not with that director!

Occasionally I've seen the stamping of feet. I stamp my feet very, very rarely. But I did stamp them recently, and I got a bit of extra time. I felt they, the management, were being completely unreasonable. The production manager said to me, they won't pay the overtime. And I said, well, we're going to have carnage. And indeed we did. And then after the horse had bolted, I got the time...

Emma The thing I found difficult in Europe is the change of board-op.

Mark They change shift. The French shift system is incredible. These things can be deeply frustrating. In Barcelona, there are five operators, two at a time on an Eos, and they ask each other which button to press. In the morning, we program in French. In the afternoon we program in Catalan. That's fine. I learned Catalan. I think it's helpful if you can try and speak their language, then they can't say I'm finding it very tiring because I'm having to work the lighting desk and translate. I quite enjoy the challenge of speaking their language. In Johannesburg, I tried to learn a bit of Zulu, but I couldn't get the clicking right. They just laughed at me.

It's really important, of course, when you're working abroad that you find out what left and right are because, of course, we work stage right and stage left, and most other countries apart from America go audience left and audience right. Many places have their own words for right and left, like we have prompt side and OP. They have city and farmyard in Florence; in Barcelona they have court and jardin, but they're the other side to the court and jardin that you have in France. So your head's spinning before you've even brought up a channel number by simply saying, put your moving light on this side.

It is surprising the theatres that have moving lights and yet have very little experience in how to program. They still focus them like a generic. So, you say, put the moving light down the front and make me a strip of light, and they overshoot and back again and then bring in all the wrong shutters. They've got no boxes or oblongs or macros to give you the mirror image of the one you've just done. Whereas a UK programmer would just press a button and you'd get the opposite and things like that.

Emma When your shows move from one country to another, how do you cope with the differences in kit? And in the spaces?

Mark You have to almost analyse every single light and go, what was this doing? Can I duplicate that or is it going to be twenty foot higher up? If so, let's not have it as a Fresnel, let's make it a profile. At the same time, you have their equipment list to work to, which is different to the gear at the original theatre. So, it's a whole game of chess that you play – only slightly more complicated. And through all of that, you're wondering, did that light

Mark Jonathan

Sleeping Beauty for the Royal Ballet at the Royal Opera House, London. Choreographer: Marius Petipa. Set design by Oliver Messel, lighting by Mark Jonathan. *Photographer: Johan Persson / ArenaPAL.*

really work from there in the first place, or should it be somewhere else? And there may be other things, like the production now has to play in rep.

I suppose one of the aids that's really becoming useful is to have a video recording of the work. Actually, in my process now, I like to have one of a run in the rehearsal room – because cameras now often have a wide angle lens, you can put it on the centre line not just in the furthest corner of the room. That's really good for working out your cue times and where the cues go and being able to replay it with the stage manager. And then having videos of dress rehearsals or previews is fantastic for reviewing them and doing notes efficiently.

Emma And now, very often shows, particularly opera, are broadcast...

Mark A few years ago, on a Sunday, the phone rang. It was Dame Monica Mason from the Royal Ballet: 'we're going to broadcast your *Sleeping Beauty* at the cinema and it looks dreadful. Any chance you could go to the Odeon in Shaftesbury Avenue tomorrow and have a look at it?' They were going to show the test recording of it. So I turn up. As it's a big opera house with not much time, I've used the followspots on the principals. So they then rack down the cameras to stop the spots burning out the picture – and the scenery and all the corps de ballet disappear. The result is you have to take the followspots right down. So now what I say is, OK, if it's going to be recorded for cinema I want a big TV monitor on the production desk, and I will look at both the TV image and the stage image at once. Then they go, 'we'll give you that on the general'. I say, no, I want it from when I first light. They expect theatre lighting designers to light it acceptably for cinema without having the camera's view. A television lighting director won't do that.

Emma How would you describe your lighting style?

Mark I quite like the fact that I don't really think I work in one style. People think I do. But they don't see all the different work I do.

Emma What do you think allows you to be that free?

Mark Well, the design, of course, the story, the approach. But I suppose I have certain tricks. Quite often, I might have a light at the end of the bar that's probably focused to centre, then another one that's going to far side with the same coming the other way. I'll be comfortable if I feel the moving lights can achieve that or I've got that in my generic rig. So that's a constant in my work, I suppose. But the end result will look different each time.

Emma Do you see lighting design as an art, as a science, as a mixture of the two?

Mark I absolutely love the idea that it's a creative art achieved through a technical scientific medium. But it's absolutely painting. Painting with light, or are we creating music with light? I'm really interested in the speed of the cue. Interestingly, Scottish Opera take a photograph of each lighting cue as it completes for their records. But for me, it's the journey the light takes to get there that's interesting. As a cue completes there might be another one starting. So the light undulates as required as the story progresses. Fundamentally we are telling and punctuating the story.

Emma If you were to give a young lighting designer some tips, what would you say to them?

Mark You have got to completely visualize what your equipment can do in the space provided. Sometimes I may want to do the most fantastic shafts of light, fingers of light in a sunrise. But I have to know in advance how I can do that in the minimal space that I probably have. You've got to think about whether your stunning backlight can get through the set or if it's going to hit a border and die in the back three foot of the stage. Woe betide you if you haven't thought about the capability of your equipment and where it is and of course, the capability of your programmer to do it in the time. There's no point in putting up 300 lights if you haven't got time to focus them. You must make sure the lights you put up are the right ones.

Emma And if you were able to tell your younger self something, what would you say?

Mark I'll tell you one thing. There are things that I was not ready to do one day sooner than when I did them. The first time I lit for the Royal Ballet, a massive production of *Cinderella* in 2003, I had been working in theatre for thirty years. I was not ready to do that job one day sooner. You cannot fast track getting the experience. To be able to cope with the scale of something, but also the lack of time and the quickness with which you have to work.

Mark Jonathan

I decided one day to not waste any more energy on being nervous. That was the day I arrived at the Met in New York. And there was no time to put the show on. The joy was I was working with really amazing people from American Ballet Theatre who weren't going to let me sink. I turned up on Monday. We lit, focused and ran the show on Tuesday. We got Wednesday off because it was a matinee. We focused, lit and ran on Thursday. We focused, lit, dress rehearsed and opened on Friday. Then I made a couple of mods on Saturday. You know, when I made those mods on Saturday they said, 'we come in at half past one, the show is at two'. So don't waste time on being nervous. But do spend time on double-checking everything and whatever you forget to check, or you think, that'll be all right, is what's going to screw you up. Always check your section. Can the light get round the border? Double-check the masking because they think they can put the masking up later. No, no, no!

Emma That is good advice – really, all of this has been good advice! Thank you, Marko, for sharing it with us.

AMY MAE

Lighting a show can be stressful; the only chance to deliver your work being after everyone else, in the theatre, often with everyone else watching. Different designers have different ways of coping with this, of balancing those periods with calmer times away from work. For Amy Mae, the counter-balance is yoga: as well as holding a BA in stage management and performing arts from the University of Winchester and a postgraduate diploma in stage electrics and lighting design from RADA, she is a qualified yoga teacher. She says she tries to bring this experience and mindset to the productions she helps to create.

Those productions have been many and varied since she jumped into the public eye as the lighting designer for the acclaimed production of the musical *Sweeney Todd*, set in a pie shop and here staged in an actual meat pie shop in south London before its success led it into the West End and on to New York. Amy received a Knight of Illumination sword for the show in London, and two award nominations in New York.

If the original venue presented practical challenges from a lighting point of view, it also presented another more personal one to a lighting designer who is a committed vegan…

www.amymaelighting.com

Emma What drew you to lighting?

Amy I did art at GCSE, and drama. I helped out backstage, and I guess I was really drawn to the lighting side because it looked really interesting. The technician at my school was really nice. He helped me light one of the shows there – terrible, by the way, when you look back at the first stuff you did! I found it really interesting how you were painting with light in a way, and then it was gone, straight away. After spending all my time at GCSE or A-level doing paintings that would take days, sometimes I would just hate how they looked. But with light, it was so refreshing: you could make these amazing images and feelings, and then they were gone, and you'd never see them again. It was like an art form, but very visceral. That was really interesting to me.

Emma What influences your work?

Amy It really depends on what the show is, because I try to research around that particular show and go from there. There's no set thing I go to for inspiration. I remember when I was studying some of the feedback I received was, Amy needs to go out and look at light in nature more. I really took it to heart, and I did: that really helped. I'd say as I'm walking around, I do try and notice the light in everyday things.

I did a show about an artist, Isadora Duncan. I researched her life. Her autobiography gave me the inspiration for a lot of the colours because in her book she references fire a lot, and the fire within herself. Or it's listening to music, like the music of *Sweeney*, that really helped me shape how I wanted each moment to feel.

I also try and imagine how I would do son-et-lumières in loads of different places. So, on the tube. I imagine if it was like a blank tube, and you could completely gut it out and do your own light show in there. That's good to do when you're bored!

Emma How do you talk to a director about light?

Amy Oh, I find it so difficult. I feel like some directors I can talk to and we're on the same page straight away, and others, we just don't know how to talk about light to each other. I find it useful to show images. I feel like that's a pretty surefire way of explaining what I mean. But I do find it really difficult to talk about light because I think until you're finally in that tech and you see it, everyone imagines it differently.

Emma You've had amazing experiences with *Sweeney Todd* of putting a show into a building which isn't a theatre and then of taking a show from the UK to the States. What was the starting point of this *Sweeney Todd*?

Amy I actually got the job because a friend of mine couldn't do it. I didn't know what to expect. All I really knew was they were doing *Sweeney Todd*, and it was in a pie shop. I didn't know where the pie shop was or what sort of state it was in. I turned up, and it was this East London pie shop in Tooting that sat 32 people. I remember walking in and sitting down with everyone on the first meeting and looking around thinking, what have I got myself into? Because I'd never done anything like that before. It was really scary. I'd just turned down another job, a really well-paid one, to do this, because I was of that mindset of, once you've said yes, you should stick at it. Obviously, I'm so glad I've done it now.

When I first looked at the space, I thought it was impossible, I had a total mind blank. On the other hand, it was like walking into a pre-made set. We could walk around with the director and say, we could put light here, or this will work really well for this bit. When else do you ever get to do that? Literally walk around your set and it's done – the paint job's done, all the texture on the walls is done. You can see where all the power is straight away. That was actually something that I first thought about because it was just me on the lighting team to start with, because there was no money. I knew I was going to have to be the production electrician, the programmer and everything. I was looking for all the power sources, and I remember seeing the little 13-amp sockets in the wall and thinking, OK. At that point, I didn't really have any idea about power. I've never really studied it, even when at university, I just focused on the design side. So now I was, oh gosh, I'm just going to have to go off 13-amp power and hope for the best.

Emma The pie shop was running?

Amy Oh, yeah. The idea was it would run in the day with customers, selling and serving food. Then you'd get to six o'clock and you'd shut the doors and it would become the theatre.

Emma And all your equipment?

Amy It would all have to be set up and stay there. We did discuss taking it down and putting it up every day, but because of the money and minimal staff, it would have been impossible.

The first thing we had to do was to get Dave, the owner, on side – to build that relationship. Luckily, he was lovely, and thank goodness they were planning a refurb of the shop after we'd finished, because I was already thinking, I'm going to need to screw into these walls. He said, just do what you want, it's all going to be painted over anyway. He also said, make sure you don't use that plug, that plug or that plug – there wasn't actually as much power as I thought. He said, the kettle makes that one blow up. That one sparks every so often . . .

I also asked him, do you do any vegan pies – I'm a vegan, and that felt really important if we were going to be spending a lot of time there. He said, we don't sell that crap in here, smiling. He's a really lovely guy. He just had that kind of East London humour.

Emma How did you go about designing a rig?

Amy It came from a safety point of view, which is probably the least creative answer. However, it was a mix of two things. I went in for a day with one of those machines that you put against the wall to check if there's any metal behind it – and it turned out there were wires and metal everywhere. So, I felt really limited – there were just a few positions I could put things, some useful, some awful. I also knew that, because the shop was so small and you could see everything, I wanted to pick small things. I wanted to clump them all together – I didn't want loads of stuff dotted around because I thought it would

Sweeney Todd at Harringtons Pie Shop, Tooting for Tooting Arts Club. Directed by Bill Buckhurst, designed by Simon Kenny, lighting by Amy Mae, sound by Josh Richardson, with Siobhán McCarthy as Mrs Lovett and Jeremy Secomb as Sweeney Todd. *Photographer: Bronwen Sharp.*

look messy. So, I found the safe points in the wall, and then it was a lot about trying to add in more side positions rather than front positions because the shop is quite wide, so I thought I'd get the most out of units coming in doing a long beam rather than a short beam.

Emma And this was using practical sources, or using birdies?

Amy A mix. I chose birdies because of their low power and because they're cheap. I wanted to use chrome birdies because I thought they'd look nicer during daytime and might blend in a bit more. But because the budget was so low, we were really stuck beyond that. It was birdies, it was 500W floods, we ended up getting some mini profiles.

I did consider LED because of the power and the colour options, but it felt so wrong in that space, and because of the budget I think we would have had low-quality LED lights that would have made it look terrible, with really poor fades. It wouldn't have fitted in with the Victorian period, the feeling of it. I knew the director was really keen to use candles, and that became a massive part of the design. You can never match an LED light source with a candle and make it look right, especially in that space where everyone was so close.

Emma Do you think the budget being so small was a positive when you look back? How did it change the way you designed?

Amy It massively changed the design. It was a positive, looking back, because it made me use really simple things that normally, I guess, I wouldn't use so much. I'd never used that many birdies on a show before, but it just had to happen because that was all we could get.

Emma What is your process in terms of reading the script and coming up with ideas?

Amy I'll always read it three times minimum. I'll read it first just to enjoy it and take it in. Second time to note, it's day or night, or there's moonlight or something. Third time I'll go through and note little bits where there might be an atmosphere change, or we might need to close down on a certain moment. Then I try not to get too into that and try not to read any more before rehearsals start, because I feel like everything will change. It was weird with *Sweeney* because normally, I'll also wait until I see the model box, but I'd already seen it. That was great.

Emma It was Simon Kenny who designed it. How did that work in terms of how he designed in the pie shop? How did the collaboration work?

Amy He was really good. He added a lot of bits that really supported the story and didn't take over the shop. It was something really simple, like a sheet that got hung up by the actors. And the costumes that were really interesting, to me. He was very keen from the start on keeping units hidden as much as possible, which I totally agreed with.

Emma How did you work with colour?

Amy Colour is so interesting, it's such a personal thing. I really enjoyed working with colour on this because I thought, well, I'm not going down the LED route, and I've got limited units that I need to make work really hard, so I'm going to pick natural tones to start with, because I know from a very basic level, we've got day scenes, we've got night scenes. Then, of course, we've got the killing scenes – though we weren't yet sure how they were going to be lit or even staged, because normally the chair would disappear or they'd fall down a shoot, and we couldn't do that.

For the natural tones, I picked ones that I'd used before and really liked, like Lee 200 and Lee 366. But I wanted to do it in a way that I wasn't using the same colour from both sides because I wanted a bit of depth. So, from one side, having L200 and L201 a bit lower down, but the other side you'd have L366 and L202 just to try and get a bit of difference, because I thought then we can play with the levels in the space and change how it feels and mix them together in different ways.

There are so many different locations in *Sweeney Todd* – how was I going to separate those with a basic warm-cold cover? So, for the song 'By The Sea', we had our one gobo, a ripply break-up gobo focused just off-sharp. I wanted to link it somehow to the pie shop, so I picked Lee 241 because it felt like it would link to the fluorescent strip that we started our pre-show in – that was already in the shop. The shop also had this china pendant light that was beautiful but obviously hadn't been used for years. We cleaned it out and put a bulb in, and used it for the interval and one of the other scenes. It was great – and it was really lovely seeing Dave, the pie shop owner, walk by and go, oh my God! you made it work! We did try and use what was already there, making a feature of it rather than hiding it.

Emma Because it was kind of one set, lighting obviously has a major role to play in changing the environment. How do you think that enhanced the story?

Amy I think it helped a lot. Haze also massively helped. I really pushed for haze at the start because I wanted the beams to shape the space. It makes such a big difference if you see beams in the air, especially in a space that small. It can really help close down the space or help separate off different areas.

And just going back to colour, I found something on that show that I'd never thought about before. In one scene, a night scene, we had quite a lot of colds in. Then for the big judge killing scene, we ended up using a flood in red, backlighting them from a low, waist-high level for that moment, with some red from the front as well. Normally for the killings you'd have the red on for a second, and then it would fade back out again as they drag the body off. That was our language. But for the last killing, because it was such a momentous kill for Sweeney, his big moment, we left the red on for twenty seconds. Which doesn't sound like a lot, but when you're sitting there just watching it, it did feel like a long time. But it was so funny how it made the blues already in the rig go greener when the red faded back down. Lee 200 suddenly looked totally different; it was the same lights, but a whole new state.

Emma Your perception of colour changes.

Amy Yes! It was crazy. I wasn't expecting it, but I thought, this is useful, I can use this again. It was a happy accident, but it was great.

Emma Where do you find inspiration from for your lighting in general?

Amy Pinterest. I love making Pinterest boards for shows and seeing what other people have done, but also searching for things. For *Sweeney*, I remember searching for blood splatters; that gave me a really strong inspiration for some gobos I could use. Also, stills of the film and how they use shadows on people's faces.

I also remember while I was drawing the rig plan, I would stick on the score and just listen to it, because when you were thinking about designing a certain scene, just to have that in the background helped me get in the mindset of what I wanted it to feel like.

Emma How important is it to do research and development on a site-specific show, and how do you go about doing that?

Amy Honestly, I think it's different for every space. We did some lighting tests, which turned out to be so useful. We were still thinking about how to do the killing moment. In rehearsals, they were practicing with sheets and backlighting sheets to make a silhouette. They asked me to bring in some lights to test with. Originally, I was like, oh, it'll be fine, I'll get a short nose par can. Or maybe I'll get a half-k Fresnel that'll do the job really well.

Jack Williams, when he was at the Royal Court, let me come in and borrow some lights and thank goodness he did because he said, take this Fresnel, take this par can and do you want to just try a flood as well. That turned out to be the best thing for the job. We ended up cutting the sheet, and we never tested anything else for that moment. I was relieved we'd tried that flood, or it would have been a disaster in tech. The flood was under a shelf, then Simon added hooks to hang tea towels on, and there was choreography for the actors to take them off at just the right moment so you didn't see the flood before it was turned on. It was a big collaboration to get that moment to work.

Emma That's the beauty of collaboration, isn't it.

Amy With the candles as well. Sometimes a moment would be lit with one candle. Then we'd have moments with the actors where I'd say, try moving it a different way. And as a lighting designer, I'd never felt like I'd been able to do that before, where you could talk to the actors in that way.

Emma What do you think using a real source gives you?

Amy It's just magic. I don't think you can beat it, especially being in a space that close: you can see it's real. It makes it more authentic. I've never seen a source that matches a candle on an actor's face.

Candles in *Sweeney Todd* at Harringtons Pie Shop, Tooting for Tooting Arts Club. Directed by Bill Buckhurst, designed by Simon Kenny, lighting by Amy Mae, sound by Josh Richardson, with Siobhán McCarthy as Mrs Lovett. *Photographer: Bronwen Sharp.*

It was really lovely to be able to use candles in the shop. They became a backlight system because we put a lot of them against the back wall. I was actually really worried when I was rigging because after all my tests, there was no way I could put any backlight in. For me, as a designer just coming out of drama school and being taught how important it was in relation to everything else, I was concerned the show was going to look so flat, which is probably why I over-compensated and put loads of side positions in. But having the candles, that really gave a shape and a silhouette to people in front of them.

Emma Are there things that you feel you learnt there which have been useful going forward?

Amy Oh, my, yes, many things. I think about staying calmer, about putting your mental health first over working too many hours. I guess it goes back to doing site-specific shows and just diving in, because if you've done that, when you work on a show that gets a bit tougher, you feel it's OK because you've already worked in an unusual situation like a pie shop, so you have the confidence to do this. I think it was a good lesson in communication and making people want to help you. You need everyone to come together to make it work.

Emma From its really successful first run, what happened next?

Amy Cameron Mackintosh came and saw it. Stephen Sondheim came and saw it. It was crazy, it just took off. We got this space on Shaftesbury Avenue. It used to be a restaurant, and it was about to become a different restaurant. They had this gap in the middle where we could come in. Simon redesigned the shop but made it a lot wider and quite a bit higher. And it had an alcove. The shape changed completely.

Emma How did you go about taking that design, which was so particular, to Shaftesbury Avenue?

Amy I met up with Paule Constable. Because I'd never transferred a show before, I wanted her advice on it. Her advice was, just keep the feel the same as much as you possibly can. I really needed to hear that because at the time I was really excited about going to the West End and the possibility of adding in loads of stuff. I could add in all this LED and have all the colour changing options. But obviously, it wouldn't have been right, it wouldn't have felt the same, the feel of the show would have been completely off.

In terms of positions, I tried to keep as much of the original design as I could. I wanted to keep the side light. I could have added in backlight, but I chose not to – I thought the candles do it, let's not fix it, it's not broken! We did have some upgrades: we had actual Source Fours instead of our mini profiles, so we got some of the brightness back, and I added in another gobo that was inspired by the Pinterest blood spatters – though we kept a lot of the birdies because, again, the budget wasn't great.

But now we were building our own walls. We could go further with hiding the lights. The set designer and the director were very keen on hiding more lights. We had all these conversations about cutting holes in the walls and putting grills in. That really freaked me out as I was worried we were going to get a grill pattern – I didn't know how the light was going to react, whether it would reduce the light output from the birdies that are already not that bright, and in a bigger space. A grill arrived, and it was just so dense that I just had to say no, that's not going to work. I've never had to make that call before. It was a really tough moment because they'd already ordered those grills. But I thought, if I don't speak up now, we're going to get to tech and it's going to be the dimmest show of all time. Looking back, I'm really glad it happened – it taught me how important it is to speak up when you know something is not going to work.

Beyond that, there was a window at the back where we hid some birdies then covered them with a blind. We kept the floodlight; we upgraded it to 1 kW instead of 500 W, but it was the same system with the same tones of cool and warm. We added in a lot more red from the front for the end killing moment because the space was so much bigger to fill. And we had similar problems to before, such as the ongoing saga of flour getting all over the lights under the counter...

Emma When the audience entered in the original pie shop, you had fluorescents...

Amy We added our own fluorescents for the new pie shop, wired straight down to a switch on the wall that an actor controlled.

Emma Then from Shaftesbury Avenue, you went to New York, but this time into a theatre?

Amy It was the Barrow Street Theatre, but they stripped it all out inside. It was a big empty black box. And then we did the same thing as we did in Shaftesbury Avenue, where the walls of the theatre were remade for the pie shop, which meant we could do the grill system again.

Emma What are the fundamental differences between working in the UK and working in New York?

Amy I've only done the one show, but from what I noticed, the organization was a lot more intense. There was a lot more paperwork. The lighting team structure was quite different. As someone from the UK coming in, there were things I couldn't do. I couldn't go up a ladder, which I found really strange – great, but really strange! I couldn't touch the lighting desk. I feel like we could learn a lot from the American way of working in terms of the way people get paid and the breaks they take. It made for a nicer working atmosphere. However, I think there are also things they could learn from us – sometimes I felt like the paperwork was just too much! The original plan for Tooting I just drew in a notebook...

Emma Who did the paperwork?

Amy I had an associate on it, which was great.

Emma Who was American?

Amy Who was American. Jessica Creager. I'd never worked with her before, Rick Fisher suggested her. I was really grateful that he suggested someone. I'd give her my one plan, and she then separated it into five different plans. In the focus, it was really interesting because she would sit and say, OK Amy, this is channel 15 and it's in Lee 506 and it's doing a cross-shot. Just having that person took half the thought away from my brain. I was almost on autopilot because she was just telling me all this information, whereas normally you know your own channel number and you'd know exactly what it was doing straight away. It did feel like the difference was the hierarchical thing of the associate being over the production electrician. They worked together quite closely. I felt like I wasn't working that closely with the production electrician where normally I would.

Emma Because the associate was filtering?

Amy Exactly. She filtered everything and dispersed it out to the rest of the department. Though that was lovely in a way because it did let me think more about the design side of it and less about the practical side.

And interestingly, even with so much paperwork, there were still things that got lost in translation. When I got there, some holes which had already been cut into the walls were completely off. They weren't going to do the shot at all. I had to be the bad guy coming over and saying, actually that's not how I've drawn it, you're about two metres off…

Emma How did the rig differ; did you keep the same units going from Shaftesbury Avenue to New York?

Amy Kind of, and actually it was a big mistake, because I'd gone out there for a visit before for a day or two to have a look at the new model box and to meet the team. I'd done some tests with some birdies because I just felt they might be different over there, so I just wanted to check them out. At the time I thought they were fine. But when we were focusing, they seemed really dim. I was like, actually I think I've made a big mistake here, I should have gone for punchier units. Luckily because we were going into a theatre – we were building a theatre in a theatre – they had lighting stock, so I was able to swap out the side light that was usually a birdie to a profile. You could tell that really threw the American team. They'd be, but the paperwork says it's a birdie. I had to explain that it didn't work as a birdie, so we were going to have to change it.

I remember the production electrician said to me, but you've done the show two times before, how come it's not a copy-and-paste? I had to explain that the shape of the shop had changed, the size had changed. I remember in Tooting, one light would do three different jobs – it could three-quarter backlight someone behind the counter, or side light then sitting on the end of the counter or catch someone on the stairs in a different way. With the shape changing slightly each time, it had such a knock-on effect. Suddenly that light would only do half a job, and so you had to rethink it.

Emma What would you tell somebody taking a show abroad from this country?

Amy Well – the birdies. We couldn't work out the issue. We'd put on two fifty-degree lamps and they'd look completely different in colour temperature and brightness, because they turned out to be from different manufacturers. That's something I'd never thought to specify – but now I do.

I would also say, be really wary of the health and safety regulations. We had a really horrible moment where we'd pretty much plotted the whole show, and one of the producers said, we need to boost those aisle lights. The show relies so much on darkness and shadow and the mystery of it. Suddenly we have these bright aisle lights come in, and with the haze, it was these horrible, ugly beams. It was terrible. We had a lot of previews where we had to try different gels and different levels. It was a whole layer of stress that we didn't need – not a good creative atmosphere, and hard to make the show what we knew it could be. So, I'd say check out how bright your aisle lights need to be, where your exit lights need to be, because that can all have a massive impact.

Emma Did you do the same thing with putting the fluorescents in as the houselights?

Amy Yeah, same thing. We found it worked really well in the first place because when the actor would turn it off, it was just such a satisfying snap blackout, it was such a good start, and then you'd light a candle and that would be the start of the whole thing. It would be a nice transition from these ugly fluorescent lights into this soft, warm, small pool of light. I felt like it was a really good way of separating out the space from the pre-show to the world. We were out of that shop now, and we were in the magical musical world.

Emma Was there anything you felt you lost by not being site-specific?

Amy I definitely thought we lost the intimacy and the magic of the first show. Simon did an incredible job; he made that pie shop exactly as it was, but I think because I had the luxury of seeing the first one and being in the shop where it only sat 32 people, nothing will ever compare to that. It eventually sat about 200, it had a mezzanine level, which was a new thing to think about for the lighting, because it had always been so low and front on, and suddenly, we had this higher level to think about.

Emma How do you think light can help with telling the story?

Amy It's so important. It shapes mood; it shapes the location. It's the atmosphere. You can relate a light to a character. In *Sweeney*, there was a happy accident: I found that whenever Sweeney got out his razor, he was talking about killing or revenge, and he'd always have some Lee 200 on him, glinting off the razor. It just followed him through the story. At first it was unintentional because I used it in the first song when he first gets the razor out. But then it would always appear: when he was at the top of a staircase or when he was about to kill someone, we'd boost the Lee 200. I find that really exciting how you can link a certain colour or feel with a character.

Emma When you look at a piece now, do you see it as a whole arc, or do you break it down? How do you map the lighting across the show?

Amy I find it easier to break it down into manageable chunks. I think if I looked at it as too much of a whole, I'd freak myself out. I'm a big fan of lists. I like making lists about exactly what I'm going to need – I'm definitely going to need a front cover in this area. I'm definitely going to need a special here. Or, I'd really like to add some texture in for this scene. I'll make a big list and then check things off as I'm drawing my plan.

Emma And in terms of colour?

Amy I really love adding in colours that I've never used before, because how else are you going to learn about them and how they react on skin tones? It is so interesting to sit in a dark room with a model box, a birdie and a swatch book and just look at how it reacts on the model, on your skin. I used to spend hours at drama school doing that. Unless someone creates a mini body with a Lustr LED engine, I just don't know how people are going to explore colour in the same way.

Emma Do you think the ability to change colour in the way that LED allows has created a difference in how you work with a director?

Amy Massively. I feel like directors are getting more into that technology, and they can say, oh, can you just try that in a red or something? Is that a moving light – can that go over there? I think they're becoming more clued up on what lights can do. Depending on your relationship with them, that can be great, or it can be a massive hindrance – when they give you specific orders to try something, and it slows down the process. I try not to let it be insulting – but why not let me show you something first rather than just assuming you know what to do. Otherwise, why have you employed me?

With LED, I think having directors know they can have any colour in the world is really not helpful: I feel shows are more effective when you have a set quantity of colours. It makes the design feel concise, like it's a whole thing with a structure.

Emma What do you think's been the best piece of advice you've been given?

Amy There's two bits of advice. One was from Paule, when I was talking to her about taking the show to America, and she said, you have to grab the bull by the horns. That was the phrase. I think it's so true, like the grill's not working or we're swapping the light out, you just have to go in and say if something's not going to work and be confident about it and not be too shy or worried. You have to stand up for yourself and your design. Before I got that advice, I'd always be, I'll make it work, it'll be fine. That pushed me to speak up a bit more.

The other one was from Ben Ormerod, about whether you should take a job or not when you're starting out. It's the three things you should think about. Is it going to fulfil you creatively? Is it going to help you pay your bills? And, is it going to introduce you to new and exciting people and help you further your career? If you can answer two out of the three, you should probably do it. That's really stuck with me – I think about it every time a job comes through.

Emma Thank you. This has been an amazing conversation.

Amy You're welcome.

BEN ORMEROD

There are many mentors in the theatre lighting business, known as it is for everyone being willing to help others. But it can surely be no coincidence that so many leading lighting designers – including a number in this book – worked with and learnt from Ben early in their careers. He's not just a fantastic mentor but almost a guru, extraordinarily knowledgeable about the science behind lighting and the person to go to with questions relating to, in particular, colour perception.

He applies that knowledge to his own lighting work, across genres ranging from the *Ring* Cycle to *Oedipus* to *Zorro: The Musical*, across countries from the UK to Holland to Tokyo to Greece, and far beyond theatre – he is the head of lighting at the Calico Museum of Textiles in Ahmedabad in India.

www.benormerod.com

Emma Is there one particular influence that drives how you go about designing the lighting rig for a show?

Ben I remember Andy Phillips saying that you should never find yourself drawing the same rig for two plays, so I've always had this little guilty voice in my head when I reach for a set of solutions that I know are incredibly powerful. At the same time, I think of the flexibility of those solutions we have available for us now.

But I've never been wedded to the idea of the rig as an expression of the show. I think that partly comes from touring so much, which is really where I started. I left drama school and joined a touring company, and within a year was touring Europe doing British Council shows. I was doing the same design day after day in theatres where they didn't expect you to turn up with a lighting plan: one-night stands, theatre after theatre, everywhere from number-one houses in Holland to the Young Vic Studio. So, the idea that there was this rig that was the expression of the show didn't make any sense, because there was no way you would take a rig from the Young Vic Studio and put it up in a big theatre in Holland.

Emma So shows where you were using kit you found in each venue?

Ben Completely. You were thinking in terms of ideas and qualities of light right from the beginning. I worked out a way of notating the way the show was lit by saying this element, high priority, this element, medium. There were some jobs that only profile spots could do – hard circles of light – but otherwise, you'd look at their list of gear and go from there.

Emma So when you analyse a show, what do you do? This is after you've lit it for the first time?

Ben Yes – you go through each cue. You can see just from the printout what's going on, or you put the state up, see what each light is doing. Then you list them in order of brightness. You're trying to list them in the order you would plot them, and that's usually brightness.

Emma So to go back to before that: when you start to create a state, where do you begin?

Ben I struggle slightly with this question, because there are so many different things which happen when I'm going to make a state. Sometimes I have a very, very clear idea of how a state is going to be made. Sometimes I don't – so the approach can be very different. And also the order is important – if you are lighting something midway through a scene, your process is going to be very different from starting from lights-up.

But taking a few steps back: I have a cue list. That came from a conversation I had with Bruno Poet, which took me years to understand and put into practice, fumbling my way towards what he'd been doing for years, which is to make up a cue list with times on it, in its entirety, before you go into tech. I don't do it necessarily for plays because often you really don't know where the cues are going to happen until you are in there and somebody goes and sits on a chair, and they are too bright or too dark. But with an opera, I will mark every cue. I'll mark in probably three times as many cues as I'm likely to need, so every time I hear the music telling me to put a cue there.

Some cues are there because there is a moment where something needs to start happening. Some cues are there because at this point something needs to have happened by. Building a chair is a good example. It's much easier to build a chair if there is a little bit of music for thirty seconds before you need to build the chair, as it implies something is happening.

Emma It's based on the timing of the music…

Ben Yup, and actually, all my cues are based on that. With anything music-based, all the cues are driven by the music.

As an example, a few years ago, I lit the *Ring* Cycle at Longborough Festival Opera, where we did it all in one go – which is unusual.

We had the most amazing time, particularly one really memorable day when we had problems with the scenic solution for the rainbow bridge. It just wasn't working – partly because it was in a country house grounds with no fly tower. This delegation came to the production desk after the stage and orchestra rehearsal and said, we're cutting the rainbow bridge, and we want you to give us a solution instead. Well, I'd been thinking about lighting the rainbow bridge for about thirty years, from as soon as I knew I was going to be a lighting designer. I'd sort of come to an idea – so I'd actually already booked the equipment to do it!

In opera, you get days off while the singers rest their voices, which is great because you can get lots of work done. So, we had a day to ourselves in the theatre where we worked with a video of the rehearsal and lit the last ten minutes of the opera – it took ten hours because it's a massive section and you have to do something amazing, create a rainbow on stage. It was ten of the most enjoyable hours I've ever spent, and it was actually one of those rare occasions when I was actually doing a plotting session, which I normally hate: I almost only ever plot in tech – I'll volunteer at production meetings to give an extra session of tech time, because I just find plotting sessions on the whole a terrible waste of time.

We were using very lovely LED battens, and they could shoot right the way across the space and get an image of the spectrum through masses and masses of haze. But the thing about the rainbow bridge is that it appears about seven minutes before the end of the opera; it's a massive reveal, but then you've got seven more minutes of music. But Wagner has the same problem and he solved it, so all you have to do is listen to the music and do as you're told!

So we just worked our way through, drawing on all of the musical references that appear – almost everything you have already heard before in the opera. All but one of the musical references in the final scene of *Rhinegold* are drawn from earlier scenes, so our imagery was drawn from those scenes, following the music phrase by phrase. From having listened to Wagner since I was a teenager, I try to create visual images that connect

Theatre Lighting Design: Conversations on the Art, Craft and Life

Der Ring Des Nibelungen at Longborough Festival Opera. Conductor Anthony Negus, directed by Alan Privett, choreographed by Suzanne Frith, designed by Kjell Torriset, lighting by Ben Ormerod. *Photographer: Ben Ormerod, webcam footage for notes purposes.*

144

with ideas, then let the ideas drive what you see and when you see it. Wagner does the same, linking musical material to ideas in the libretto, which he also wrote. This idea is at the heart of everything I do – I've based my lighting on the *Ring* Cycle for thirty years, treating most of the work I do as if it had been written by Wagner and lighting it accordingly. When I got the chance to actually light the *Ring* Cycle, it was terribly exciting – but rather daunting!

Emma Since you are usually plotting in tech, in terms of moving light technology and finding time to focus those moving lights into position palettes, are you then doing that within your focus time?

Ben I think the big transformation in moving light technology is the programmers, who are so fast now. The big difference is that we don't plot shows any more, we program them!

Emma How has your relationship with the programmer changed as that role has evolved?

Ben It's interesting. For a long time, my primary relationship with a programmer was with Andi Davis. He is very meticulous about not wanting to have any influence on the design. He wants to achieve exactly what you want, thinking ahead of me but not for me.

Then I worked a lot with Anthony Arblaster. I met him at RADA when he was a student and was immediately really impressed by him; he lit a show there which was gorgeous. We started working together; I booked him to program that *Ring* Cycle with me in order for him to get to know the way I thought. Then Antonia, my wife, got pregnant, and the baby was going to be born while I was in the middle of three shows! So I booked Anthony to programme those three shows on the basis that he would take over when the phone rang. Later, we were doing Britten's *Midsummer Night's Dream* together, set in a 1970s disco. There was no in-house kit, just a budget, which is marvellous. We got some K10 moving lights, and with all the amazing eye-candy stuff they do, they were perfect – pixels half in green, half in white, shards of light like they were leaves, but with that disco look. One day I said to Anthony, is there any more level on that K10? And he said, it's at twenty-five per cent. I had no idea – and I realized Anthony had been setting the levels. Anthony had been setting the levels for months and I had not noticed – but actually he had taken on a big chunk of the design.

Emma And that was because you were talking in ideas?

Ben No, not quite. I've always asked programmers to wheel channels up rather than setting levels, but Anthony took that a step further.

In *Zorro*, I just had stuff at full, and it was very much that kind of painter thing of going, that one there, that one there. But you were always at full. There was a lot of tungsten in *Zorro* as well, so you needed to be at full, partly because you were working against Mac 700s and partly because of the colour. When you are doing a highly coloured show, if your kit isn't at full, it gets complicated. It was a balanced rig, and you wanted things to be at full for balance.

Zorro: The Musical at the Garrick Theatre, London. Directed by Christopher Renshaw, choreographed by Rafael Amargo, designed by Tom Piper, lighting by Ben Ormerod, sound by Mick Potter. *Photographer: Elliott Franks / ArenaPAL.*

Here is an interesting analogy. There was a very great conductor called Frans Brüggen, who did a lot of period music. He experimented a lot with orchestral seating layouts – he needed to see what happened if they sat as he believed the orchestra would have at the time – and they'd re-seat themselves between pieces in a concert. By doing this, they never had any balance problems, and the musicians were always able to hear everyone they needed to hear.

I think a well-designed rig is like that. It's something I know I'm good at and I have no idea how I do it, but I draw a rig and it's balanced. You turn a light on and you can see it, and you turn another light on and you can still see it, and things don't get swamped. It's to do with the right unit in the right position, such a cliché, but just in the same way as putting the right musician in the right seat for Schubert then moving them into a different seat for Beethoven, it's like that.

Emma So if you were going to tell someone who was just coming out of drama school your key points about quality of light, what would they be?

Ben There aren't many of them, actually; it's a short list which gives us such a fantastic raw palette, but they multiply up against themselves.

Take colour. There's one big thing you need to know about colour: colour only exists in its relation to other colours. That's it. There is no such thing as the colour as it actually is. There is its relationship to the other colours you are using and nothing else. When you put a system of Lee 161 up on the stage because you want to do a cold moonlight scene, and the director looks at you and says, I was thinking this scene should be blue rather than white, and you are going, it IS blue and if I go much bluer there is going to be no light coming out of the lights. That is because you think that because it says slate blue in the swatch book and because you can see blue when you look at it in your studio that it is going to be blue up on stage. But if it doesn't have another colour to relate to on the stage, it's not going to have a colour in itself – what it 'really' looks like is what it is in relation to other colours because that is how we perceive colour, as a set of relationships.

Let's take Lee 161 in its relation to my favourite straw, Gam 365; you light one side of the face in G365 and the other side of the face in L161, and you see the L161 you get when you oppose it with G365. Then you light the other side of the face with a pink, and you get a different L161, so if you have a palette of five colours set up, you already have twenty-five colours for that show. And that's when you're only using them opposite to each other. You could be using them on top of each other as well, of course. And if you're using a tungsten light, you could take the G365 down in level, and you have another L161 in relation to it.

So the qualities of light? There's the softness of the edge and the softness of the shadow. There's the intensity. There's the angle. There's the size of the light on stage – is it a spot or is it a large area. There's the colour. You know, it's not a very long list. But you start putting them next to each other, so you start saying it's a small, steep, cool – that's only three qualities that we've already mentioned, but you've created a fourth quality with the combination of them. So that's the first thing I would say: there are not that many qualities of light you need to get your head around, which means you can now spend a lot of time getting your head around them and really drilling down into them, seeing them everywhere and understanding how they behave.

Then the next thing is that qualities of light are a means to an end, and the end is telling a story or supporting a story. And I have my own way of doing that, which is attaching qualities of light to ideas and then allowing the structure of the narrative to dictate what happens in lighting terms – as in that *Ring* Cycle.

Emma So when you are reading a script for the first time, or you are looking at a modelbox for the first time, how are you generating those ideas?

Ben The first thing I'd do is read the script. The first reading is for pleasure, then I'm obviously on the look-out for qualities of light within the text, even things like times of day…

Emma The practicalities?

Ben Yes, because it's very embarrassing to go into a lighting meeting with an idea and have the director go, but it's raining in that scene. That might be from looking at the modelbox too much – huge great windows down the side, so you just get excited by the idea of sunset and miss that someone mentions that it's raining! But in that search for the let's-not-make-a-fool-of-ourselves-at-the-lighting-meeting thing, I might spot that light has quite an important role to play and if that happens then I will trawl through the show, pull out all of the references and print them out separately.

Emma What sort of references would you pull out?

Ben It could be someone says 'fair lady'. It could be someone saying, 'ill met by moonlight proud Titania'. It could be a play set in the nineteenth century where someone had just installed electric lighting. It's an interesting exercise. In *Macbeth* you pull out a huge chunk of the play when you do that, and in *Hamlet*, almost nothing – that tells you something about the two plays.

Then I use that list in a variety of ways. Sometimes, to actually build a structure of the design. Or I did a play, Goethe's *Iphigenia*, that had a lot of imagery of light in it, but it didn't quite provide me with the structure I needed. But there was definitely a sense it was important. So I printed out the light references of each scene as a separate piece and treated them like poems as a way of uncovering a secret narrative within the play. I would just read that 'poem' in the tech while they were sorting out the scene change, and then in quite a non-intellectual way go on and light that scene – but I'd just read all of those lines.

Emma When you speak to a director about light, how do you approach that?

Ben It's quite tricky, I think. I still, even after all these years, am trying to work out how to do that, because I've sort of waded so deep into light I don't know how to talk about it anymore. Directors I have worked with for a long time, for instance Laurence Boswell, who did the *Iphigenia* – we've been working together for years, but I didn't tell him that I had these poems. But one of the actors found out about it and asked if she could have a copy, and I said absolutely. So Laurence became interested in what I had been doing, and I was very happy for him to see it – but this isn't something I would generally talk about as I think it can lead to misunderstandings.

I remember talking to the director and designer about attaching images to musical ideas on an opera. The director was totally up to speed on Wagner's leitmotivic structure, and he understood what I was getting at, but the designer was totally freaked out and just said, it sounds really busy to me – which of course it did. But I did it anyway; the director said I think we should follow this, I think it is going to work – and it did. The designer was completely delighted with the result because I gave her what she wanted but using a technique that if she'd been in control she wouldn't have used. But I can't talk to many directors about how I think about light and how I work technically.

Emma When you pick your colours, do you have particular colours you like to use?

Ben I have a repertoire. If we are talking about filters for tungsten, I have a list of colours that I add maybe one colour to a year. I feel very comfortable with colour, very at home now I know a lot about it. I feel a bit like those nineteenth-century music-hall artists who add a song to their act at a rate of one every two years – they'd work on it at home, pop it in one night to see how it works, take it away again, work on it a bit more.

Emma What draws you to the colours in your repertoire?

Ben Need. So for instance, when I started out in the business there were three straws – I was using Cinemoid 52 – a pinky, straw-type colour, then Lee came along, and there was Lee 205, which was better than Lee 103, but I didn't feel I had anything as gorgeous as a Patt 743 at 50%, there was nothing as good as that. And then I went to see a show lit by Peter Mumford, *Cosi Fan Tutti*, and it was set on a beach, and the lights came up and I thought, wow, that's the most amazing straw. I looked up at the roof, and there were loads of par cans, and someone had chinagraphed the number on the front – it was 608, an obscure Rosco Cinegel. It was a colour you'd find in the swatch for film use, in front of HMIs; it was a CTO with this extra pink tinge to it, the minus green, that just made the face come to life. It just made everything look fantastic. That was it, I used it from then on.

Emma So your choice of colour is about what picks out skin tone, what makes someone look beautiful on stage?

Ben It's not just that. It's about how good a team player it is. It's like casting, like building up a repertoire of actors that you want to spend the rest of your life working with. This is all changing of course, because now I have gone through shows where I have talked about Gam 365 all the time, but there is not a single piece of gel in the rig, and it's actually 25% magenta, 25% yellow in a TW1 – but it's like you know you've got this company of actors, and then you need a new one to play the irascible old man. You don't just get the best irascible old man; you get the one who is going to get on with everyone else. And because colours are defined in relationship to each other, for a new colour to enter the repertoire, it has to play ball with all the other colours in the way you want it to.

Emma How do you work out which one does that?

Ben You can actually do that by looking at the swatch and looking at the little graph and imagining how it's going to work. But you ultimately have to try it for a bit.

Emma In terms of LED coming in – that reference that we've got isn't going to be there maybe even in just five years' time. How do you imagine dealing with that?

Ben It depends what you mean by LED. There are three groups of LED lights: white LEDs with coloured flags on top. There are four colour LED fixtures – red/green/blue/white where you take a white LED, and then you kind of punch in one of three monochromatic colours to make it resemble the colour you want. Or there's seven colour LED fixtures, like the Lustrs or the cyc battens Robert Juliat make – these are very impressive. I think that with the seven colours, we are kind of there in terms of being able to dial up the colours that we want.

Emma So are you excited by it?

Ben Yes, massively. It's the way forward. I was pretty anti-LED for a long time, but I'm not going to be one of the people who wants to use tungsten only. But I am going to miss par cans.

Emma How have LEDs and moving lights changed your process?

Ben It hasn't actually changed it very much in that I've always thought in terms of qualities of light rather than lanterns. It's made drawing the plan a little easier in some respects. There aren't that many good places to put a light, and the lights are all competing for those choice positions. I use the end two metres on every bar a lot, and sometimes lights will be on one bar because the other bar has no room in that choice position. So, moving lights have kind of solved that problem because I would just put a moving light on the end of each bar – that helps. But I think you need to be very careful when you design with lots of moving lights that you don't just kick the can down the road in terms of decision-making. I do a lot of rehearsal attendance; during rehearsals, I light the show in my head, then I draw a plan that will give me what I saw in rehearsals.

Emma Do you start with lighting the actors?

Ben Yep, absolutely. I rarely light the scenery first. Musicals are a bit different; in a number you are often using followspots, you are often able to say, let's make the set look like this and then the followspots will do the work, but that's different. Nine times out of ten, light the actor and then if the set needs some help, give it some help. But usually it doesn't.

Emma One of the big things I learnt from you was crosslight – the joy of it, so different from the traditional 45 degree from FOH you might have learnt in college...

Ben They still teach that? That if we don't light like that, the lighting police will come...

The thing about crosslight is that it's very easy and very difficult. It lights the actors without lighting the floor, you have what looks like an enormous dark stage, and an actor comes on and is brightly lit. It's marvellous. It sculpts the face in an interesting way. Then you hit the problems, which is that generally speaking, you want the sense of the light to be emanating from the centre line, not from the wing because that is where the actors spend most of their time looking, looking at each other across the centre line. If you can get the sense of light emanating from the centre line, then the actors are sharing the light source. You don't want them getting brighter as they go towards the wings, and you don't want them lit brighter on the side of the face as they face away from each other unless you are making a particular point, I think.

And then it's difficult for them – it's uncomfortable for the actors, and they start casting shadows on each other, and you have to take responsibility for all those things. At the beginning of tech, I actually tell the actors not to try to avoid shadowing each other until

I ask – not allowing myself the luxury of actors having to restage the entire production just because I am using crosslight. Crosslight is of huge benefit to the actor in that it makes them very, very visible, very see-able – we can see their eyes, and we can see what they are thinking, but you can't just slap up dance booms and put a gobo backlight on the floor and think your job is delivered.

Emma When you talk about light emanating from the centre, how do you achieve that?

Ben With crosslight there is a very simple technique, which is that you rig your crosslight at three metres, and then you cut it off the floor so that you do a kind of letterbox into the opposite wing, which means that your face is going out of the crosslight as you cross the centre line. If you like, you can then have a lower crosslight that maybe cuts off the floor or touches the floor at the centreline, depending on what you need. That can be almost at body height, so that when you are on the opposite side to the boom you're lit by two lights, and when you are on the boom's side you're lit by one. That's one way.

The other is not to use crosslight by itself, so you put in a pipe-end system, lighting from the centre line to the opposite side. So again, as you walk across the centre line, you go out of that system and go into the system from the other side. That really, really helps – it's rare for me to use crosslight by itself, I would supplement it with a couple of other systems. It's much easier for the actors, and it's a much richer look.

Emma So what are those systems?

Ben There's an area cover, which is dividing the stage on the plan into square areas and then lighting the person standing in that square. That's a Stanley McCandless invention. He was talking about areas of 2.5m to 3m in size; I find more than 2m too big on the floor and less than 1.5m being smaller than an actor, so quite hard to handle. So somewhere between 1.5m and 2m in size. Area cover means various things. It can mean something very simple like a Fresnel from each side coming in from somewhere downstage, in front of the area – it may not be very far downstage of it, so like a sidelight, or it may be very far downstage depending on what I need. These might be in what I would call the base white, which might be Lee 202 or 203. The advantage of the area cover is that you are splitting your stage up into smaller stages, and you are able to light as many or as few of those as you want, so you can have one and you have a special, or you've got five and you have a strip of light along the front edge of the stage.

Emma So it's about working the lights harder?

Ben Yes, so you don't have a general cover and specials. You can extend that and then really design lots and lots of little stages, so you could have a backlight in each area, a toplight in each area, a gobo in each area and so on. And then you've really got something interesting to play with where you treat it as a collection of stages, each one of which is made up in the same way. If someone re-blocks a scene it's fine because you just move the look over.

Then I've got a pipe-end, an American expression for a system of par cans, one on each end of a bar, CP62s with scrollers on, you put the filament vertical, across the stage, and you touch the centre line with the bottom of the beam and let the top of the beam go into the wing, and you work at 45 degrees to the head on centreline. That's an incredibly powerful system, you space them 1.5 metres apart, and you've lit the stage with twelve par cans. That's a system I use a lot. I'm now replacing it with the Desire LED fixtures.

Then another element that I use a lot is a three-quarter backlight into each area. It could be a par can, it might be white, or it might have a bit of straw in it. And then the crosslight system, which tends to be quite fronty in theatre. I like a crosslight system not to go straight across but to go upstage, so a lot of it will be rigged in the FOH boxes. It will get me through lots of shows, that system.

Maybe I'd add a full stage backlight, but that would now tend to be handled by moving lights. If I'm on a budget I rig movers asymmetrically: say you've got four moving lights, the temptation is to put two on the number one bar and two as backlights, but it's much more fun to have one on the number one bar, one on the number three bar but on the other side, one on the number five bar on the other side again, and one at the back. Then you've got a light on the back bar, a light on the front bar and two mid-stage, plus the unit on bar 3 can do a lot of the same jobs as the one on bar 1. It's great, you've got moving lights everywhere you need them. It works.

Emma When you use practicals on stage, how do you approach them?

Ben I do think the human brain is constantly in search of meaning. Part of the job of a lighting designer is as you light a scene to ask, am I generating meaning here and if I am, is it the right meaning? If it is, great, let's follow that. If it isn't, let's knock it on the head now before we lose control of the situation. Practicals are a really good example of that, where you can inadvertently set a narrative going which should not be there, and so you've just got to take control and go, no this is just about the fact that we're in a room with an oil lamp, it is nothing to do with his relationship to her, the way he's lit and the way she's lit.

On the other hand, they are an incredible lever. The wonderful thing about lighting in a natural-driven way is that natural light is very extreme in the kinds of things that it does, and that allows you to light in a much more expressionist and extreme way than expressionism itself gives you licence to do. I lit one scene which became progressively darker and then culminated in a spectacularly violent fight. Midway through that fight, the better fighter switched on the lights so he could see what he was doing, giving me a huge cue that would be impossible to justify on purely aesthetic terms. In another play about a young woman dying of cancer, I noticed that the effect of light from a table lamp by the sofa evoked a sunset, so I took control of that look: as her husband sat next to his dying wife, his face was lit by the setting sun.

Emma Would you just talk a little bit about the collaboration with the rest of the team?

Ben One thing I learnt from Paul Pyant was the idea of asking them about the golden moments. Paul would ask, are there any golden moments – the moments when they turn round to you in the tech and say, by the way, this is the moment that we need this person to disappear in a shaft of golden sunlight or something like that. So those are things you know you have to do, and as a coherent part of the picture, not just kind of add-ons.

Nine times out of ten, when a director or anyone gives you a note they tell you how to solve the problem, but they don't tell you what the problem actually is. So, they say, could we use that blue light that we used in the other scene. The question then is, we could, but what is it…? Oh, well, in this other scene when there is this sense of… And then you go, ah yes, I know exactly what it is, it's not because of that blue light, leave it with me. And then you go off and do something, and they go, that's exactly it! That's the sort of conversation you have again and again, and you have to sort of reverse engineer from the note to the problem. Notes are like symptoms: they are always indicative of a problem, but they are often very, very different from the actual problem.

Emma When you work through previews, how do you think an audience informs your work?

Ben A lot! I think working through previews is an important thing to talk about because there are some directors who regard previews as the time when they do the real work with lighting.

Emma As if it's the first time they've really looked at it?

Ben As if the tech is the time to sketch things in, and then you fix it in previews. I like to be ready for the first preview by the end of the tech, and then the dress rehearsal is about cleaning up. And then the previews are the time where I take it up to another level. Sometimes you make discoveries about scenes. Previews are important for a lighting designer for lots of reasons. One of them is you have to sit in the middle of the audience. People have paid money, and you have to sit there and suck it up because you have to take responsibility for what you have done. There is nothing like sitting amongst people who have paid for their ticket and they can't see.

Note-taking is key to this. Eighty per cent of the challenge of note-taking is identifying the moment when you took the note …

Emma …which is hard when you are trying to write the note down too.

Ben Yes. I've solved this problem in tech and dress rehearsals with a little AppleScript I wrote years ago. I set up a webcam that goes into my laptop so when I take a note, it marks that point on the video. With a musical, I might sometimes actually speak the note rather than writing it. I just tap the button and it puts the note right into the dropdown menu in the video, then when I go back, I can read the note at the point of the show when I made it. That's quite life-changing. It means I don't take my eyes off the stage – a big branch of my working practice, of my technique as a lighting designer, is not looking away from the stage. So I don't even have a lighting plan with me.

Emma Even when you are plotting?

Ben No lighting plan, no monitor.

Emma So you memorize?

Ben I memorize the rig. I put a lot of time into numbering the plan, so that makes a difference. Once you know the numbering system, you only need to learn about six numbers to know the whole rig, and that's the starting number of each system. If I'm using an area cover, I tend to go across in five, and that's handy because it works in 10s, so DSC would be 5 from SR and 6 from SL, and then 15 and 16, 25 and 26 all the way up the centre line.

Emma If you are working on a thrust stage or an in-the-round stage, how does your process for lighting the space change?

Ben I don't think you need, or in fact want, to be as coherent with light sources and directions of light as when you are end-on. I talked about light emanating from the centreline, so I think when you are in-the-round, the light emanates from the centre point. So, you divide the stage into areas, and you light each area in a way that is consistent with the area adjoining it and following the rule of the motivating light that crosses the centre point.

There are two disadvantages to working in the round or on three sides: it's incredibly constraining because of not lighting the audience, and it's impossible to be pictorial because people have such different views of the stage. The advantage is that the audiences are close and so visibility is much less of an issue, and the solution to not being able to be pictorial is to not try to be pictorial on a big scale but to be pictorial on a small scale.

I lit a show recently with the audience on three sides and I wanted an incredibly sunlit day but I didn't want to have one-half of the audience to be looking at backlight the entire time and the other half looking at front light the whole time, so I divided the stage up into areas with a par can in each area, but I changed the angle it was coming from by thirty degrees, so the light kind of curved around the space. But because you never look at more than one bit of the stage at one time, you don't see the inconsistencies – it's a more cubist approach to lighting. If you look at a cubist painting, at first you might ask, what can I learn about lighting from cubism, and then you look closely and the paintings are extremely lit, it is just that every fragment of them is lit from a different angle, perhaps the best angle to suit each particular element.

You know the experience when you are sitting on a hill in the sunlight talking to someone else, you have different visual experiences, but you both experience, one way or another, sunlight, even if one of you has the sun on the back of the head and the other has the sun in their eyes – so you don't need to be coherent.

Emma And combining the light from different directions?

Ben I talk a lot about motivating light and opposition rather than overheads and front-of-house. Opposition is a light that opposes the motivating light, and it opposes it in as many respects as you like – the obvious way is intensity, where it's less bright than the motivating light. But it is also an opposing angle – so if the motivating light comes from upstage left, then the opposition light comes from downstage right. The great joy of this is that things are defined off each other, one light is brighter because another one is dimmer, one light is warm because the other light is cold, the more the opposing light opposes the motivating light, the more the motivating light is allowed to be itself.

The beauty of using motivating light and opposition is that the opposition light makes the motivating light look even better. And working in the round or on three sides, the motivating light and opposing light can actually be at 180 degrees to each other, and that's enough – you don't need anything else because the audience are so close. You can't necessarily get away with that end-on when the audience are further away.

Using opposition, you don't get that problem of a beautiful lighting state where you can't see people, and when you turn up the front-of-house so you can see everyone, you've lost the beauty. The opposition doesn't wash out the motivating light, it defines it.

Emma Thank you, Ben. This has been a fascinating conversation.

BRUNO POET

While many lighting designers stick to one field – theatre say – and sometimes even just to a few genres within that field (dance, or opera), Bruno happily strides across them all; anywhere light is called for, he'll be there. He's lit plays, opera, dance, musicals but also concert touring music acts, ice shows, spectacles. The fascination is what light can do to help the show, irrespective of what the show is. He freely admits that the lessons learnt in one genre fuel his work in the next – the big ideas opera requires transferring to, say, the thousands of light bulbs he used as part of his design for the play *Frankenstein*, the rhythm and pacing from concerts for Sigur Rós or Björk or the Pet Shop Boys feeding into shows like *Tina: The Tina Turner Musical*. Such is his control of light that he seems almost to achieve the scientifically impossible and make it curve in his outdoor light shows for the UAE National Day.

Between-times, he escapes, back to his family and to the beaches and, in his sailing dinghy, the seas of Cornwall where he lives. And from where, during lockdown, he and fellow lighting designer James Farncombe started their own series of fascinating conversations about lighting and theatre-making at their *Making Theatre* podcast.

www.brunopoet.com

Emma There's a big debate, isn't there, about lighting and whether it's a science or whether it's an art form…

Bruno I always think it's more of a craft than an art, because I think you're making something that exists in the context of the show rather than something that exists purely in its own right.

Emma Because it's working in that collaboration with everybody else…

Bruno Yeah. I think that most of the lighting we do in theatre, in opera, in live performance shows is relevant because of the show. It doesn't have any meaning without the show that it's for, whereas the great pieces of art stand up on their own.

Emma What drew you to lighting design?

Bruno Just having a go at it, really. I did a bit at school because I didn't like acting but quite liked being part of putting on a show. School theatre with four lights wasn't anything, really, literally just fading up and fading down. But being part of a team to make it happen was fun.

Then when I went to university, there were loads of shows being made, and I very quickly got involved with that, and I very quickly got in demand. Then suddenly I found that every week I was lighting another show somewhere around the university.

So, I volunteered to help out, then got drawn into it – and I haven't stopped yet.

Emma I think we're all aware that lighting is a massive community, where people are very generous about sharing information and helping the next generation. Is there anything you were told when you were starting out that has been useful?

Bruno I think I learned how to do what I do by being nurtured by some great people. Starting with Linda Clayton, who was the chief electrician at the Oxford Playhouse when I was there, giving me a hard time about being a student who knew nothing. But she taught me the basic stuff, how to dead bars, how to draw a section and to work out where borders go and where lights go and that sort of thing that I hadn't even thought about beforehand.

Then I did a lot of work assisting Ben Ormerod and Paule Constable and other lighting designers. Their generosity of explaining their techniques and how they think about things definitely rubbed off on me going forward. But I think you are right. I think it's a generous community. I think we all generally share information and support each other as much as we can.

Emma Who or what influences or inspires your work now?

Bruno I think nature inspires me, although I don't know if it's directly connected to what I do. But I spend a lot of time outdoors in Cornwall, where I live. And that world is definitely a world of light – the colours, the possibilities, the magic of sun bursting through cloud. That's very influential.

I think for some of the more abstract things I've done – contemporary dance, pop shows – looking at what contemporary artists do, installations of various sorts when light is used to stand up on its own, I think that can be quite useful and inspirational as well.

And then you know, references, photos. You can just scour books and the internet for references and things which you can use as language for conversation. I recently did a show involving riots – so just news footage of ambulance lights and police lights and sodium street lights and fire and all those things was useful. I'm often very tempted to keep everything on monochrome, and I think sometimes you just need to go, actually the world is quite colourful sometimes. Those references let you feel confident in doing bolder things.

But on a particular show, I think the biggest influence is the creative team I'm working with at that time. I think the context of the set design, of the environment you're working within, and how the director is staging the play. So, within a particular show, I think I'm mostly influenced by the team I'm working with and the show itself.

Emma In terms of working with a creative team, when do you get involved?

Bruno It varies massively. Sometimes it's right at the very beginning. I'm working on a project now where the model hasn't been made yet, and we are talking about building lights into the scenery, because the practical lights will be doing a lot of work to tell the story of the show. But sometimes you turn up and the set is basically designed, and then you work around it.

Emma But if you went into a modelbox showing and you thought, crikey, that's got a ceiling there, and that's going to... how would you approach that?

Bruno You talk about it. I mean, I think I've quite often had that situation where you need to try and persuade them to some kind of compromise. There normally is one. Our job is to make the lighting work. Maybe the designer hasn't thought about it in the same way. So, you do have to have a conversation about that. Sometimes you go and see a set and you go yeeesss, that's fantastic, can't wait to get started. But other times you go, well actually, how are we going to get light into this room; what can we do to help? Then you talk about it and work out how to solve things. Is it a bunch of practical lights? Do you hide lights somewhere? Do you cut a hole in the ceiling, out of view, or whatever? Or do you accept that the point of the show is that it's only going to be front-lit, and that's OK. There are lots of different ways to approach things like that.

I do think that in terms of discussing things beforehand, I almost have more conversations with the designer than the director because a lot of it is about looking over the modelbox, and how do you build lights into the sets, or what can you do to enhance the set or tell a story, or practical lights and angles. Colour as well, and fabric and materials and finishes. I find it really useful to talk about what light can do. Quite often I will play with some colour on the modelbox and look at paint finishes and things and show the designer what warm or cool or whatever does to the paint finish so they get a sense of what's going to happen when it is twenty-five times bigger. It's nothing very sophisticated – a torch or a birdie and a bit of gel. But it just gives a sense of what colour can do.

Emma When you talk about lighting within a team – how would you talk about light to a director who you don't already have a relationship with?

Bruno Sometimes reference material is useful. I find quite often I have very few conversations with directors about it – I literally just turn up and do it. The best conversations are the two-minute conversation you have in the rehearsal room, in a break after they've rehearsed the scene, and you go, oh I'm thinking this, and you get these snippets of things. I sometimes find that when you sit down and have a lighting meeting it's very hard to talk about it in words. I think a lot of what I do is watch rehearsals and kind of light the show in my head. I imagine how the pictures will look by looking at the people, where people are standing on stage, think about the angles and shapes I might make with light and then, hopefully, translate that onto the stage.

I go into the tech with an idea of how I imagine each scene is going to look, and sometimes it ends up being like that, and sometimes something happens and you go off in a different direction, reacting to what's in front of you. There are loads of directors who just want you to get on with it, I think, and then talk about what they see, rather than plan it massively in advance.

Emma When you sit in rehearsal, how do you record your thoughts about what you're going to do?

Bruno I scribble in the script. Normally I draw little rectangles, which are the shape of the stage, and arrows – keylight from this corner or whatever, just little aide-memoires. I always put cues in during rehearsals, and I always plan, before I start the tech, to put a cue structure in the book and a cue structure in the lighting desk, and I label it all up, and then I just follow along – sort of building blocks. The cue labels are an aide memoire for me about what each point of the show is, so I don't need to look in the script for anything else – those few words in front of me remind me what I'm trying to do. So, a lot of it is in my head, I think, until we sit there and plot it.

Emma Do you think technology, particularly LEDs and moving lights, has changed how you work – even how you design a rig?

Bruno It's interesting. I remember when we did English Touring Theatre shows together – then you could design the plan very late in the process. You could have seen a run-through in the rehearsal room and then draw the plan and then it gets rigged that weekend. So, you're very confident that the lights you're drawing have clear purposes in the show. I think for small shows there's a pleasure and efficiency in that, the feeling that every light is for a reason and you know what each is there for, and that's come out of what you've seen in front of you in the rehearsal room. But for operas and big shows where you have to do a lighting plan six months before rehearsals start, you have to approach it in a very different way. You have to design possibilities, I suppose. To have things up your sleeve that you can then work out how to use to deliver the things I imagine when I eventually sit in that rehearsal room.

Emma Does your design process change between genres and between spaces?

Bruno It changes quite a lot, actually. There's a big difference between rep work and non-rep work, because with non-rep work you have a blank piece of paper with a set design drawn on it, then you can basically put lights wherever you want to try and deliver the show. So, you have much more flexibility – you're designing what you think is going to be the ideal rig for that show.

Whereas with rep work, you have to work backwards because the majority of the lights are fixed. They're there. You get to pick which ones you use. Sometimes they're moving lights, sometimes they're not, but you're then trying to shoehorn the rep rig to do the things you're imagining. If we go back to that thing of watching rehearsals and imagining the show – if it's a blank piece of paper I'm thinking I can stick a light over there and it'll do that shot which would be really great for this moment. If it's a rep rig, you're going, what's going to be the most appropriate bit of the rig to do this? So, it's a very different way of working.

I found it really hard when I first started doing opera rep. All of the student shows I did were basically a blank piece of paper so I could put lights wherever I wanted. I always drew lights for specific purposes – I could build up my toolbox to deliver the things I needed. But when I first did a rep show, which I think was probably Opera North which was not then a moving light rig: they had four overhead bars you could refocus, but they weren't necessarily the lights I would want to put in those places for that show. You couldn't add much else, so you had to try to work out how you'd use what's there to make the show happen. I think it's easier in a way now – reps often have moving lights which gives you that flexibility. But I still find it a slightly backwards way of working compared to starting from scratch.

Emma Do you use pre-visualization tools to help with this?

Bruno I've used pre-viz a few times, in different ways. The Royal Opera House has a WYSIWYG suite, which I find useful because you get to sit with your programmer and get to know them a bit. If it's a complex three-dimensional set, it's a good tool for checking your angles work as you'd imagined.

And I've used it for pop concerts and musicals to make a first pass. With musicals you can spend hours teching a scene of dialogue, and then you get a five-minute number with about two hundred cues and a whole load of dancing that you run once, and then they move on while you go aarrgghh! So for some of the big numbers in *Saigon* and

Tina: The Tina Turner Musical at the Aldwych Theatre, London. Directed by Phyllida Lloyd, choreographed by Anthony Van Laast, designed by Mark Thompson, lighting by Bruno Poet, projection by Jeff Sugg, sound by Nevin Steinberg, music supervision by Nick Skilbeck, orchestration by Ethan Popp, wigs, hair and make-up designed by Campbell Young Associates. Photographer: Manuel Harlan.

Tina and Sigur Rós and other music stuff, I've used WYSIWYG to build cue structures and building blocks. And for moving lights – if you want to have moving light effects in the air, it's fantastically useful for that.

Emma And how do you work with a budget?

Bruno By negotiation! But yes, you have to work with a budget, so you design a fantasy rig and then get it costed. The problem is you don't really know what anything costs because there are so many parameters in terms of the deals hire companies want to offer, whether the producer is paying cash up front or not, how long the show is running for – it's hard. You know roughly what you can get for a certain scale of show, but you don't know exactly. Is it a bunch of lights that have fallen from favour so they're sitting on the shelf and you can get them cheaper? There are a lot of different ways of doing it. I think you have to design the rig you want, then negotiate. Then sometimes you have to persuade the producer to put a bit more money in the pot. And sometimes you have to cut things.

I think initially you try to give yourself all the possibilities you might want, but as you're forced to reduce it that makes you focus more on what you really need. It's not necessarily a bad process.

Emma Once you get on stage, how do you then start to construct a state?

Bruno I start with whatever is going to shape the space, whether that be a particular direction of light – it might be a bunch of lights in one direction, it might be a single light in one direction. But I think you have to have a sense of what the most dominant light source in the picture is going to be. I tend to start with that and then add as little as possible to it. But it's difficult to generalize because there are other things, things like big musical numbers, where you start to take a different approach. You think about beams in the air and chases and flashes and colour bumps and all those sorts of things. But even that, I suppose, is about what's going to make the main shape of the picture.

Emma Do you like to have a plotting session before you go in to tech?

Bruno I do. I quite like a plotting session with the director before tech, because it's quite a useful time – it's one of those funny times when you're slightly nervously putting ideas forward and sort of testing to see how they react to it, and whether you're on the right track or whether you have to rethink. I think having some rough looks in the desk before you get to tech is really great because it makes the tech more efficient – you can then hone it with the cast on stage.

Emma In terms of your programming time, do you then put all these focus groups in to make them the equivalents of what your generics would once have done?

Bruno Yes and no. I do that less than I used to because programmers are so quick now. But I always do the sort of, cross-wash, big backlight, certain kinds of key looks that you know you're going to use. I tend not to do things like grids of specials or those very specific things, because I know that if I want to stick a special on the table then the programmer can do that in seconds.

I do think that for colour choice, moving lights and LED give you an incredible freedom to not decide anything too soon – but I also think you have to be careful, because if you just do a spot-wash-spot-wash-spot-wash rig you're not necessarily shaping the show. I think you still have to think about it. *Tina* has got a hundred and twenty or so moving lights overhead – every light overhead is a moving light. But they're designed in a shape to, hopefully, deliver considered looks, even though I designed the rig without knowing exactly how I was going to use it, because I had to design it a long time before rehearsals started and the show was still changing, still being written even.

Emma Do you have a colour palette that you put into the desk?

Bruno Yes. I still think in terms of Lee and Rosco filter numbers, so we'll do building blocks of colours based on old favourites, but then constantly tweak them. Quite often in my shows, you've got a palette Lee 200 but then a palette 200.1, 200.2, 200.3 – slightly different versions of the same colour, a bit bluer or whatever. It's a way of making it a relatable colour. But obviously beyond that, you can mix new stuff if necessary.

Emma Can we talk about the language of colour, because we've grown up with gel books – but in ten years' time, will anyone know what Lee 201 is?

Bruno It's extraordinary, isn't it? I can say a three-digit number to you and you will know exactly what I'm talking about. And we probably know exactly what two or three hundred colours from a swatch book look like because we've used them, we've looked at them. It's a very clear, definitive reference.

Desk manufacturers go, you need to talk about hue and saturation – but for me, right now, those numbers mean nothing, particularly with the complex seven-colour LED fixtures. I know I can say stick in 204 and, certainly if it's an Eos with a Lustr, I'll get the colour I imagined.

Maybe swatch books will become like Pantone charts in graphic design – a language of reference, because how do you describe a colour?

Emma Working with programmers you've mentioned – has that relationship changed over time, now that it's a very specialized role? When we worked together I remember you saying, could you try to use two fingers rather than. . .

Bruno *(laughs)* – oh God, did I?

Emma And it was totally right. But now, there wouldn't be the chance for that, because you'd have a dedicated programmer.

Bruno I've always found I work with programmers as collaborators. I enjoy the banter. I enjoy the conversation. I enjoy people suggesting things and offering things up and questioning things. I like it being a team thing rather than just an individual dictating numbers. I like having another person in the room. I like to be able to ask them to offer things up, especially if you're making effects and chases. Having someone just do something which you can then react to is great.

I think lighting design has got way more sophisticated, way busier, more cues, more lights doing more things. I think the speed at which you can programme now is extraordinary – the amount you can expect to achieve over a three-hour tech session. And the desks – they're just fantastic tools. You feel much less limited now. It just opens up more possibilities.

Emma In terms of working with the rest of the technical team, do you have a particular process you go through in terms of explaining a plan and how you want it to work?

Bruno I think you'd have a conversation about the plan once you'd drawn it. What the lights are for. It's really helpful if the people rigging the lights, so the production electrician and their team, have an idea of what you're trying to achieve so they can maybe suggest better ways of achieving it. Problem-solving is great. And they're normally brilliant, creative people who find solutions – impossible ways of rigging lights in impossible places.

Emma What do you think are useful skills – beyond lighting – for a lighting designer to have?

Bruno Lighting design is more than just lighting design. Quite often, the lighting designer is the person in the middle of all the tech. You've got cans on, but you're also talking to the creative time. You know what's happening technically, you know what the creative team are talking about. You're in the middle of everything, juggling all that. Understanding the technical side of it as well as the creative side is fun, and a role that you often have as a lighting designer.

I do think you have to be pretty confident. Experience helps confidence grow. But the scariest bit of lighting design is the first day of tech when you're basically hanging out your ideas for the whole room to see before you've even really seen the reality of what you've been thinking for yourself. You have to be confident to try it and not get freaked out when, as often happens, you get bombarded by notes. It's that thing of somehow trying to stay true to your ideas while also reacting to the details you're constantly being told about. Somehow you have to connect those things together and make something that's elegant and flows and that's connected, all while under massive time pressure with the whole team waiting for you.

I do think that's fun – the best bit of the job. Terrifying and fun. And every show you do is still terrifying, but it's a buzz – taking an idea and seeing how it turns out, reacting to whatever's happening around you.

Emma But if you have a moment when you realize that you've got a different vision to the one the director had in their head at that moment at the beginning of tech – isn't that kind of a nightmare?

Bruno That definitely happens. It can be all kinds of things, colour, taste... I find it's good not to hold on to things if someone feels they're not working, but I also find that the trick is to take the note rather than the solution. The thing I've offered up isn't working, so how can I offer up something different that will deliver what everyone's asking for but stay true to what I'm trying to do.

Directors generally are storytellers, they've got ideas of how the story should be told. And it may be different from how I imagine I'll tell the story. I think it's good to listen. I think there's no point being at loggerheads and saying, I'm doing this while they're doing that – you have to try other things. The chances are the things you try aren't what you thought of and aren't what they thought of as the original idea. But maybe it's something better that solved both problems. I think you have to be able to go with the flow, really. That probably then affects the next scene or the one after. Because lighting is all about contrast, if you've done one scene in a certain way that's different from what you had planned, that probably means the next scene or next cue is going to be different as well. So, you do have to be quite fleet-of-foot about it. You have to be able to negotiate with yourself and with everybody else and see where it takes you.

Emma Have the advances in technology helped you do that?

Bruno Yes, because you can obviously change colour very quickly now. You don't have to send someone up a ladder. And I think directors now expect lighting to change instantly. It used to be that if you wanted to re-colour a rig they'd have to wait for a tea break, and then you send someone up to change a gel, or if you wanted a special on the sofa then you had to wait until someone had a chance to go focus a light. Now it can be instant. I think that means there's much more flexibility to re-stage things during a tech; we can just react to it. You have to be very careful not to just put blobs of light everywhere – you still have to try and work out what the overall picture is. But moving lights give you more flexibility and choice – as long as you've got the rig in the right place in the first place.

Emma How do you keep up with what's coming onto the market?

Bruno I'm really interested in that. I do try and keep up with what's happening. Manufacturers talk to me about products that are coming out. I've been really excited about the latest wave of LED, because I've always found discharge moving light sources to be slightly unsatisfying – you get a great punchy white, but they don't really deliver anything warm. Whereas tungsten sources give you a lovely tungsten glow but don't do anything cold. Now we've suddenly hit a point where LED moving lights are coming that can deliver a really beautiful warm and a really strong cold. It gives us a whole new world of possibility and flexibility with less need to compromise.

Emma Can you describe a project you've been involved in which stands out as rewarding or challenging or memorable?

Bruno I'd say probably the most rewarding, challenging and memorable projects I've been involved with have been working with the Icelandic band Sigur Rós, lighting their concert tours, because it's a very different world from the theatre and opera worlds that I grew up in. It's non-narrative, even more so than contemporary dance, so you're making light that is purely a reaction to music. You get to make pictures. Their music is extraordinary and really inspiring. It's a gift for lighting because you can hear music and imagine what you might do.

They gave me ten days in a warehouse with the full lighting rig to build the show. We sat there, twenty hours a day, with my programmer, and played the music and tweaked things and honed things and played with it. There's not a director. The band come in and have a look and have opinions, then you discuss things, then they go away. There's a creative director who's involved in video content and things. It's a really lovely kind of bubble, of people making something special and very connected to a piece of music. It's different from a play with a story. I found it really hard because there are no rules. You don't have to set a context, there's no time of day, you're not saying a sunset or night-time or look at this person in the corner over here – all the things that we often do in theatre to make the show work. It's a bunch of guys on stage who don't really want to be lit, playing instruments. But you've got to fill an arena full of light and emotion.

Emma Do you find that when you've done something like that, it affects your other work?

Bruno Yes, definitely. I think the big opera-ey stage pictures I've done – they helped me with the concerts; I think bringing the theatre knowledge into that world, that we can be really delicate, really detailed, have a lot of variation, was really useful. But then going back – I don't think I'd have been so bold with a lot of my ideas on *Miss Saigon*, and probably on *Tina*, if I hadn't done the pure rock concerts. It's great – it informs all the possibilities.

Emma Do you think the audience affects what you do as a lighting designer during previews?

Bruno I think the audience affects how I see the show. I think I hear and see the show differently when there's an audience in. There's a focus you get from being in an audience. The performers perform differently with an audience as well – so I think you only really know what the show is when you see it with an audience. Sometimes it's as simple as your cleverest, most beautiful lighting state is great – but actually, they're missing a plot point because they can't see them at a particular moment. It's a chance to sit back and look at the show. In tech, you're constantly putting out fires, constantly adjusting. In previews, you can't do that – you have to take notes and fix it later. I think that gives you a bit more perspective on the show.

Emma How does your relationship with stage management fit into your work?

Bruno Stage management is so important. A good DSM is worth their weight in gold. It's really great when you've got a rapport with a DSM who understands what cues are for and understands where to call them. I just did a ballet at the Opera House where I hadn't been in that many rehearsals, and the DSM had been in lots of them. She just wrote down when the choreographer was talking about stuff, where she thought, that'll be useful. She was almost like an assistant lighting designer to some extent. So yeah, they're a crucial part of the team, and they're brilliant.

Emma How do you balance light and dark on stage?

Bruno Carefully? I think it's very easy to start off with a scene that looks great because it's really beautifully sculpted, and you go, yeah, I'm really happy. And then in a preview you add a little bit, then in preview two, you add another little bit, then they stand in the corner so you build the corner, then they stand by the sofa, so you build the special there, then you go, oh that bloke over there is a bit dark so let's just put more front to fill him in. Then you suddenly realize that incrementally you've killed the whole thing.

So, I think I start from, what is the strong shape of this scene? It doesn't necessarily have to be a keylight. It could be footlights, it could be all kinds of things. But basically, you have to try and keep true to that.

Ultimately how do you balance light and dark? It's about taste, I guess. It's about what's important. Is it supposed to be a dark and mysterious scene and therefore you can tolerate not seeing people as well as you might if it was supposed to be a bright, sunny day, or actually is seeing the actor's eyes totally crucial and therefore you work with that as the main thing and then balance the shape of the scene around that.

It's very normal to find I start previews with people probably slightly under-lit, because you've been concentrating on the big picture. Then when you see it with an audience, you often realize you need to get more light on the story and on the people. Then it's about being sophisticated about how you add that, about how you fill in the detail. And that's often about having lots of cues that just catch people in certain places when they need to be caught.

Emma Using practicals in a show, which is something you do brilliantly with shows like *Frankenstein*: how do you create that world with practicals?

Bruno That's nearly always a collaboration with the set designer. I think practicals are incredibly useful because it's a source that the audience sees, so it's a way of making people understand the light, what the light's doing. It can be really magical having a lot of practical lights.

On *Frankenstein* it started as a reference that the set designer had seen, of a man sitting in a room full of light bulbs which weren't on. Originally it was a bunch of plastic spheres we were going to hang, and the idea was we would have a few lights dotted around, LEDs, or light them from the outside. Then we went through the process of going, it'd be great if we could make them into actual light bulbs that can light up. As we started looking into that, Danny Boyle, the director, was really keen on doing it with LEDs. And I was feeling that wasn't quite the right period feel for *Frankenstein*. I felt that it needed to be a bit rawer, glass and tungsten and electricity – that it had to be more elemental and less digital. So, we did a test with a bunch of LED bulbs and a bunch of tungsten bulbs, and I think everyone immediately fell in love with the tungsten bulbs. There was something about the organic-ness of them and the early technology of them that felt appropriate for our story.

Mark Tildesley, the designer, had always had the mirrored ceiling. So, then it was really about how many bulbs can we get, how many dimmers can we get, how do we build it up? The National Theatre were a massive part of that – Sacha Milroy, the production manager, and all the electricians who were on it. It's amazing going into a building like that and saying, we want to hang three thousand light bulbs over the audience's head, is that OK? And instead of saying no, they really went for it and were really supportive of the idea.

We did a lot of testing, worked out different ways of achieving it, and it ended up as something spectacular. Something that was really, really exciting. While the glowing bulbs were a beautiful thing, when the creature was born and opened his eyes for the first time we wanted that sense of shockingly bright light which of course three thousand light bulbs with a mirror above delivers. But there was a side effect that we didn't expect, didn't think about, though it was obvious in retrospect: the heat that came off them! You bump them up to full, and you suddenly feel a real heat coming off the ceiling, and then it goes away again – a real, visceral thing in terms of feeling the light as well as seeing the light.

Frankenstein at the National Theatre – Olivier, London. Directed by Danny Boyle, director of movement Toby Sedgwick, set design by Mark Tildelsey, costume design by Suttirat Anne Larlarb, lighting by Bruno Poet, sound by Underworld & Ed Clarke. *Photographer: Catherine Ashmore*.

Quite a lot of the time the ceiling wasn't on. It was used for very particular moments. We used a few bulbs as the glow of stars. It had a role in electrical pulses for the birth of the creature. It sometimes did much more lyrical things for dance moments. Sometimes it was just trying to be a night sky. It was also very beautiful when they went to the North Pole and we lit the bulbs with lights from outside, so they were like icicles. The bulbs themselves were very beautiful, just lit by cold light.

Emma What are the pros and cons of using actual sources versus replicating the behaviour of a particular source?

Bruno Actual sources have their own beauty. We're never going to have fake tungsten lightbulbs that really look and feel like real tungsten light bulbs. A lot of the time we have other tools that do an equally good job, but there's a very particular organic thing you often want. I'm working on an opera where we'll have a whole load of chandeliers which have to be warm LED bulbs instead of tungsten bulbs for a whole load of boring reasons. We did tests. We found the best we can probably find. But I just know that it won't warm up when you dim it, it won't have such a nice curve. All that subtle detail is very hard to replicate.

And then equally, the other way. Having a real sodium streetlight gives you that very particular monochrome look that, although you can mix a yellow that looks a very similar colour, it doesn't do the same thing to the other colours on stage because it's actually got more colour in it. Fluorescent lights, neon, all of it, you can get pretty close with other things, but there's a really pleasing trueness to the actual source.

I do think that right now we're at a really lucky and exciting time because we've got all of the old tools, and we've got a whole load of new tools. We have a massive box of possibilities for lighting. But who knows where it's going in the future – how many of the old tools will be taken away from us. It will be a loss if we can't pick from as many things as we can right now.

Emma Where do you think the next technological changes might be?

Bruno Recently I've been using automated performer tracking systems for some shows, sometimes sharing the system so it works for both sound and light. That opens fascinating new possibilities for design.

And WYSIWYG-style visualizers are getting better and better, but I wish they understood reflected light and bounced light more effectively.

Emma Can we talk a little bit about the working life of a lighting designer?

Bruno It is hard, this life. I think I'm not at home enough. I hit the point where I'd got my first show, *Tina*, that was paying a royalty, and suddenly I went, OK, so actually I could probably work less – but I was booked up for the entire next year because I didn't know that was going to happen. You have to earn money. Plus, this is quite different from the opera revival world I have been in, where you do a show and two years later they phone up saying, it's going somewhere else and they've basically sold your design to go with the show. They want to pay you half the money they paid you the first time because it's a revival, even though for lighting, it's a different rig and you'll have to unpick the show you made and put it all back together again for a totally different rig. I'd much rather be paid more money to go and do a new show!

It's interesting, looking at this in different countries. In America, they have the strength of the unions. As a British team, that can be very frustrating when you can't split a break, and everything seems very inflexible – but they do look after their people and pay them very well, which we're not good at here. Work in Scandinavia, and everyone finishes rehearsals at half past three on a Friday so they can pick up their kids from school and spend the weekend with them. We need to find ways to allow people to balance work and life outside work. I would love to ban Saturday rehearsals, for example, and we should open the possibility of job shares. Surely on a long-running show, you should be able to have roles that could job share?

Emma Do you think lighting designers could do a job share? Could you have two lighting designers doing a job?

Bruno Yes. I've done it a few times now. If it's set up well, it can be a really positive and collaborative experience. I've mainly done it in the concert or event world, but also in opera. I think it's different from working with an associate; while an associate is there when you first make a show, if they were lighting it, they'd be the lighting designer rather than the associate, though of course they step more into that role when reviving a show.

But making a show for the first time with someone else, that I'd call a co-design. It would have to be with someone with whom you shared taste and style and judgement. Making a show for the first time – at the speed you have to do it – you haven't got time for a conversation. You just have to go at it. It's your instincts, it's your pride, it's your taste, it's your work.

Emma Thank you, Bruno. This has been so interesting.

JACKIE SHEMESH

Photographer: Chisato Shemesh

Jackie began lighting for dance, going on to study art and design for performance at the School of Visual Theatre in Jerusalem before becoming chief electrician at the Tel Aviv Opera House, a chance to learn from the work of other designers. In 1995 he started creating his own work, with *La Crimosa* for the Batsheva Ensemble. Lighting for dance filled much of his early career and took him around Europe before he settled on London as his base.

His résumé shows that his work now encompasses far more than dance, crossing regularly into drama, music, opera, visual art and light installations – and that many, particularly Ben Duke, Omar Elerian and Jamila Johnson-Small, choose to collaborate with him time and time again.

He was one of the first LDs back to work post-lockdown, with *Death of England: Delroy* at the National Theatre, as well as his first ever online design, *Changing Destiny* at the Young Vic.

He enjoys spending time with his family, travelling, and cooking or eating a good meal anytime, anywhere.

www.jackieshemesh.com

Emma What drew you to lighting design?

Jackie I guess it is related to cinema. When I was a child, I used to go watch movies with my father once a week. I think that was the beginning of it – watching westerns and historical films. Of course, I hadn't realized that as a kid, but at some point, I understood that this was the source of my interest in drama and visuals.

Emma Did your parents work in the arts?

Jackie No, not at all; my father just loved to watch movies in a cinema. There weren't many theatres where we lived, so not many live performances to go to when I was young. It was mainly cinema. It was only later when I started to see live performances.

Emma From watching the movies, what happened next?

Jackie It's interesting, because there isn't just one thing, it's always a combination of several things that make up why you do something. I think one of them would be going to see a live performance of a band playing live music, something really simple and basic. I remember seeing the beams of the lights glowing in the smoke and thinking to myself, this is really beautiful. At that point, I didn't think that was what I wanted to do – but the memory of it was very vivid.

Emma Did you train in technical theatre?

Jackie I started to work in the arts when I was a teenager. I asked people in the business if there was something I could do; I did anything I could get my hands on, and they let me do it. The peak was operating a followspot! That was before college. I felt very lucky. Later on, I was out of the business for a few years, travelling, doing all kinds of things. Then I went to study at The School of Visual Theatre in Jerusalem. My focus at the school was primarily studying art and aspects of design for performance.

Like most of us, I started as a lighting technician, then I became chief electrician at the Tel Aviv Opera House, and then I started to design myself. Slowly, slowly I became focused only on design. I meet young designers today and it seems that they are doing the same thing, leaving college and starting to work as technicians so they can build up their style, navigating their way to become designers.

Emma Who would you say are the key practitioners in lighting, and how have they influenced the development of your work?

Jackie I don't really follow any special practitioner. I have a lot of respect for the pioneers and inventors of our practice. People like Jean Rosenthal and Josef Svoboda, to mention a few. The fact that we are all still using their ideas and elements is magical to me.

There are so many artists and lighting designers whose work and brilliant approaches I appreciate and have been inspired by. A brief list would include artists like

Laurie Anderson, Stanley Kubrick, Mark Rothko, Romeo Castellucci and Jim Campbell, and lighting designers Heather Carson and Paul Pyant, amongst many others.

Emma What has been your biggest learning curve, and why?

Jackie There is no need to do more of the same – there is enough of that. You have to come up with your own voice and your own ideas.

Emma Who and what influences your work?

Jackie There are so many answers to that question! I am very influenced by the visual arts – from painting, sculpture, performing arts, photography, to cinema and video art. If I need to choose two particular works, one would be quite classic, the other would be more recent.

When I worked as Chief Electrician at the Opera House in Tel Aviv, we had Pina Bausch performing *The Rite of Spring*. When it was created back in 1975, it was one of the most important and breakthrough contemporary dance works. Here I am, sitting in the theatre with my headset, standing by for any issues that may come up from the stage during dress rehearsal. The piece is about half an hour. At the end of that dress rehearsal I felt as if I woke up from a dream; I realized I was totally still throughout the piece and had forgotten where I was or what was happening around me. I didn't see or hear anything, I was completely immersed in this work, it was very powerful.

Our producer, who was sitting next to me, said, isn't it amazing? I said yes, and she said she felt exactly like me when she saw it for the first time twenty years before. So, the piece was already twenty years old – but it was incredible. Not particularly the lights or the design, but the whole work together. Even though I'd walked the set, focused the lights on my own and knew the stage design very well by the time I saw the work, I was still totally taken by it – that's the power of live performance to me.

The other work is David Byrne's 2018 *American Utopia* tour. I actually never saw it live; my dear friend Andy Pink saw it and told me that it was one of the best rock concerts he had ever experienced, and that I should see it. The only way I could watch it was through a YouTube recording made on a mobile phone. It is a wonderful lighting design by Rob Sinclair. The amazing thing about it is that you are watching a rock concert, yet there are none of the usual effects and tricks – you have David Byrne as the lead singer, all the musicians and the dancers/singers with him are on a bare stage, the set design has only three walls, two side walls and a back wall made out of steel chains, streaks of long metal chains that have movement, when they touch them they move. A grey dance floor. That's pretty much the whole design. They are all barefoot, mics and instruments are wireless – there are absolutely no cables or monitors on stage. It's all about the staging and the choreography of the musicians and dancers. It is perfectly made. Rob created one of the most precise and minimalistic lighting designs, which worked brilliantly. He reduced the design to its bare elements.

Emma What spaces inspire you, and why?

Jackie Do you know this theory that when you meet a person you know immediately whether you like them or not? It happens in a split second. When you think about it, it is right, there is an immediate feeling of: I like this person, or this person feels a bit awkward. I believe it's the same with spaces, when you step into a space or a room, whether it's a gallery or a new house. You immediately have a feeling about whether you like the space or not. Of course, we as lighting designers understand that light has a lot to do with this feeling. Sometimes you step into a space, and you don't know why you feel uncomfortable, it takes some time to understand it. I'm attracted to spaces that make me feel welcome and comfortable. The immediate spaces which come to mind are galleries and art exhibition spaces, which have this generous wide space and a neutral feeling to it so you can enjoy what it is you have come to see. The experience is almost like starting to work on a white canvas.

I remember seeing an exhibition in Vienna at the Albertina Museum, a fabulous retrospective of Egon Schiele, and as you go through the rooms and spaces of the exhibition, in every room, the walls are painted in a different, strong, saturated colour. So, you look at Egon Schiele's iconic drawings, paintings and sketches, which we are all so familiar with, and they are mounted against dark green, mixed blue or turquoise. It's absolutely stunning. These kinds of spaces are so exciting!

Emma To you, what is the role of a lighting designer?

Jackie I don't know! When you need to talk about it to someone who doesn't know your job, you can talk about the practical sides of your role as a lighting designer. When I talk to theatre professionals, it's more about how you're the last person to put the picture together. As a lighting designer, you are actually in charge of weaving all the other design and dramaturgic elements together. That's part of your role.

So, you need to design, you need to be artistic, to contribute with your own input and vision into the play. But, you are also the last person to come into the creative process. Everyone else is done by the time you start working, and they're waiting for you to stitch the whole thing into one coherent piece. Usually you're also being asked to rush as there is no time.

Emma You're totally right; it is about weaving things together and connecting them…

Jackie Of course, others are fine-tuning; you find the set and sound designers tweaking their work, but you actually need to create and pull the work of the other members of the creative team together at the same time. There isn't much time to wonder when opening night is around the corner. It is a very tough role, requiring focused work under pressure. When you talk to people outside of the industry, it sounds a bit romantic. You can't really describe this kind of stress.

Emma How do you approach a new collaboration?

Jackie It is always quite hard for me to work with new people. You are invited to work on a new production, and you go to meetings with new teams where you have no idea who they are. You are going into the unknown. It's not scary, but you know it can go in any direction.

My first aim is to get to know the people and what the environment is that the production is allowing. The other thing is to have a bit of research about the artistic team if you don't know them. Trying to find information about their work online. Finally, it would be observing what actually happens to the core design and how it evolves, digesting as much information as possible from everyone. Then come up with thoughts, ideas and suggestions.

Emma Your long-term collaborations: how have they changed?

Jackie I think we are all changing in our own ways.

I have all kinds of collaborations. For example, I've been collaborating with choreographer Ben Duke for the last fifteen years. We keep working and enjoying our creations together, creating new approaches to our stories. There are collaborations which stop after the fourth or fifth production, you just feel this is going in a different direction which isn't necessarily interesting for me; I can allow myself to let go, Sometimes it is me who changes direction and become interested in different styles, different sizes of production, different lighting sources.

Misty at the Bush Theatre, London. Directed by one of Jackie's regular collaborators, Omar Elerian, designed by Rajha Shakiry, lighting by Jackie Shemesh, video by Daniel Denton, sound by Elena Peña. *Photographer: Tristram Kenton*.

I'm happy with the vast variation of collaborations I have. This is part of our work – dynamics. We are working in a very dynamic environment. You crave being around good people. That's the beauty of it.

Emma What methods do you use to express your ideas to the wider creative team?

Jackie Conversations are the base of it all. I like to use visuals. I will collect visuals if I know I'm going to work on a production which will be dealing with a very particular subject. I always have a few visuals on my desktop ready to share for the next meeting with the artistic team. Another useful tool is images of shows I've done before, to show a colour or an effect from my portfolio. It could be also sending a link to a particular reference website or a video clip to present motion or timing concepts.

Emma What is your process in the rehearsal room?

Jackie In the rehearsals, I sit with the text and follow the actions, taking notes. The notes are mainly topographic, what happens where. Sometimes as you write it you realize you can shoot a light from a specific direction, so I add this as a note on the text. Sometimes there is a strong feeling of an effect which needs to come either from the spacing or positions of the characters or from the director's vision or from the sun. This all goes as notes into the text alongside where I think those effects happen, where the cue point might happen. All these notes and sketches are with me when I'm drawing the plan. Once I have the first sketch of the plan and after my first visit to the theatre, I take all this information back to the theatre and look at everything again to hone it as much as I can.

Emma When you work with a deputy stage manager or show caller, do you give them a cue structure before the tech?

Jackie Only if I have one. There is not one system for me. It can be ready for the weekend before the tech – or not. There are productions which I don't have a cue structure to pass across, but I do always have a conversation with stage management to discuss what my plans are.

Emma What is your process for then taking all of the inspiration and all the conversations that you've had and translating them into a lighting plan?

Jackie There are a couple of things about drawing a lighting plan. You draw the lighting plan before the end of the process; it is a race to try and get as much information as you can from the artistic team, the director, the set designer and from the work at the rehearsal room. There is a lot of information to collect. Then when we're talking about theatre, there is the text. The aim is to know the set design by heart, the colours, the shapes, the textures and how it evolves during the show. The rehearsal room where things are happening and developing, the sound design, the costume design. All this information is already there, and by the time I start to draw the plan, I have an idea of what I need. I now need to translate it into what light fixture I want where.

Another thing which is very important to me is spending time in the theatre. I always ask to sit in the theatre before the production time on stage. I might draw some of the plan there. I'll have at least two visits to the theatre, usually by myself. I find myself just wandering and looking at the space. It's mainly for the practical things like finding the best positions I can for the lights, to see how much I can learn about the space in terms of height, colours, architectural shapes and how these elements might influence my work. You can of course see most of this information on the building's plans, but I find spending time in the space helps with the practical decisions even if you know the space very well. The first visit is to learn and understand my positions. The second, after having drawn a draft of the plan, is to see and find the things that might not work and relocate them before handing the final plan over to the theatre.

Emma Do you know what every fixture on the plan will do, or do you put some in as backups?

Jackie If you are in a position that you need to put lights as a backup, you are in trouble already. You need to know what you are going to do. There is this thing in horse riding where the horse knows exactly whether you know how to ride or not. It's the same with

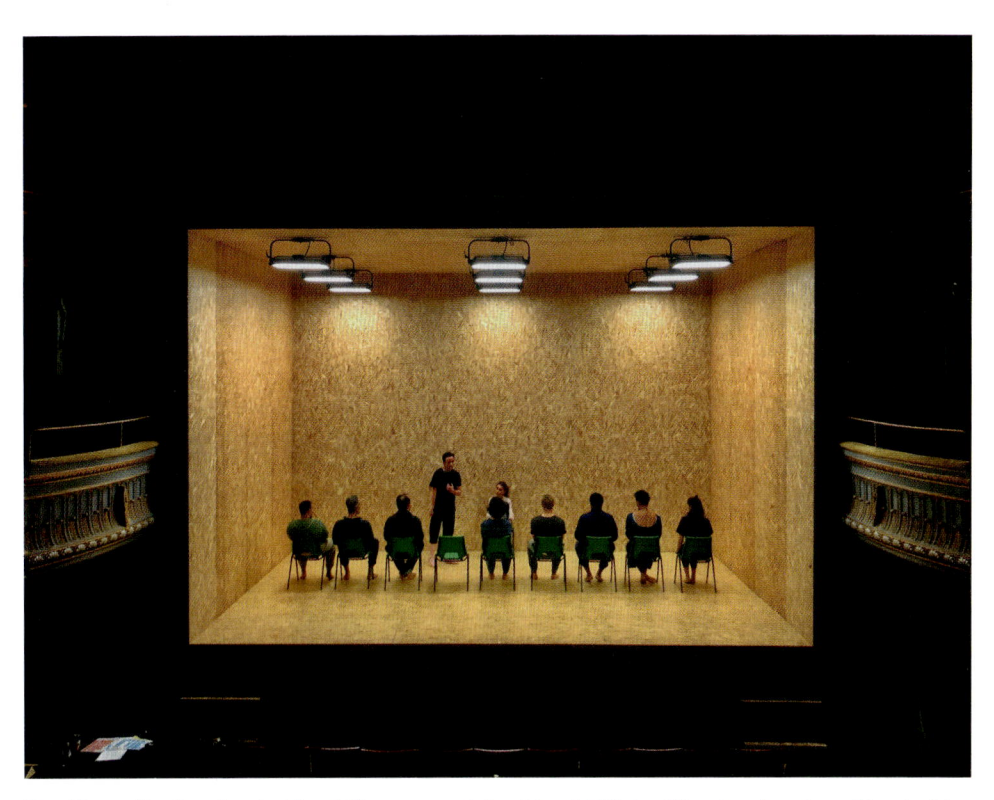

The Seagull – the Jamie Lloyd Company at the Harold Pinter Theatre, London. Directed by Jamie Lloyd, designed by Soutra Gilmour, lighting by Jackie Shemesh, sound and composition by George Dennis. *Photographer: Jackie Shemesh*.

your LX team – they know exactly if you know how to ride or not. You can't really cheat, and you need to be honest if you don't know what you are going to do rather than try to cheat!

For at least ninety per cent of what I have drawn on the plan, I know exactly what I want to do. Sometimes there would be a position that the stage designer or the director isn't clear about, like the table might be more towards upstage or downstage so I put a couple of lights for both options. I'm more often reducing lights rather than adding lights – where you realize you don't need the full set of front lights or don't need the side lights. On *The Seagull*, I managed to reduce the kit from around 60 lights to just 28. This is of course also due to the production changes and due to LED technology.

Emma How do you balance light and dark?

Jackie Dark is one of the strongest tools we have. It's almost as if the blackout is the zero point on a scale. Plus equals light up, minus equals dark down. From this way of looking at it, I find it very rewarding creating with dark. Not only how dark we can allow ourselves to light a scene but trying simple things such as the duration of holding a blackout. A build-up from pitch black into a scene. The contrast between a total dark area of space to relatively bright parts of the same space, chiaroscuro. In more than one production I have designed, we have used the dark as a political statement.

Emma I've heard you talk beautifully about old masters starting from black and modern-day artists often starting from a white canvas. Can you tell me more about that?

Jackie Back in the sixteenth century, painters used hemp-made canvases for their painting for the first time. This material was more of a dark brown colour. For most of the painters the canvas was first layered by a base of dark brownish/blackish colour before starting to work on the painting itself. There are many reasons why they did it, but I'm interested in the fact that they started their work from a dark base colour and created their paintings by adding layers of different colours on the dark canvas. This way, they created a new world of images we know now as the old masters paintings.

Now, if we take a giant leap to the beginning of the twentieth century and look at the canvas again, it is made of cotton, and the colour is off-white or white if bleached. This is a whole new way of starting a painting! The painters now start to create their works from a white canvas as a base. What they need to do to create their own images is to reduce the base white colour of the canvas. In other words, what they did is actually totally different than the method of the old masters. We can see it quite vividly on the Russian avant-garde paintings from the beginning of the twentieth century.

I see similarities in these techniques and in our methods as lighting designers. There are lighting designers who work from blackout, then create their images by adding light into the dark. On the other hand, there are lighting designers who flood the stage with lights to start their work and then reduce lights and levels to create their images.

Since I discovered these two options, I'm adapting myself and using one or the other in relation to the set colours, the rig size and to the lighting elements that I'm using.

Emma When you light, do you like to have a plotting session first to discover things on your own, or do you prefer to plot during a technical rehearsal?

Jackie It really depends on the production, whether you have time, whether the build-up of the set at the beginning of the tech week went well. It's often the situation that there is limited time before tech. It also depends on the process of the production. Sometimes you have enough information and enough ideas from the rest of the creative team, like the sound designer, for example; I might have all of the information I need from him before tech. Sometimes you work with a director and set designer who leave it to you to do what you want and don't have much input into what you might want or need to do. In these cases, it's helpful to have plotting time for you to see how your ideas work.

Emma Can you describe where you start when you light?

Jackie It really depends on the set design, the stage size and the production's ambitions. At an early stage of rehearsals, you understand where you are and what is the style of the work. In dance productions, while you watch the rehearsals you sometimes feel that there is not much room for manipulation with the light design. You feel like this work would probably require a very subtle work of washes, for example. There are choreographers who like to see a massive rig of lights and heavy haze all over. They want to see the beams; the lighting turns into another show that happens alongside the dance piece. There are choreographers who just want to see the dance and the dancers and the choreography they created, they aren't really interested in all those effects and scenery. When you light contemporary dance, the stage is usually empty, there is not much scenery at all. In these cases, you become the set designer with your lighting design.

As such, one of the first questions I tend to ask choreographers is: what is the colour of the dance floor for you? This is the base of the conversation. When they are emerging choreographers, younger and less experienced, I explain that these questions are the base of their choreography. Usually we are in a studio where there is often a grey dance floor, so they are watching the rehearsals and creating the work on a grey floor, they see something very particular. Sometimes they are creating the work on a black dance floor and then again they see something different. I just start to sort of wake up their awareness to the base of the whole thing. That is the beginning of it. You definitely are designing the space with your light. Lucy Carter does it brilliantly with Wayne McGregor. It feels like she is the designer of the entire production. With light, you definitely design the space for contemporary dance.

Emma How do you work with a programmer?

Jackie The main thing is, I always want to meet the programmer before we go into tech rehearsal. I always hope my programmer can see the last run-through in the rehearsal room. Usually, I give them a general view of what I'm planning to do, including colours and timing methods, the way I work and how I communicate with stage management. For the first day of the technical rehearsal, I will have prepared a list of groups and positions I need, and I hand it to the programmer for their input. Usually, they are quick and get exactly what I am talking about. There is always this base palette of ideas in the desk ready for us both before we start.

Emma The role of the programmer feels like it's changed so much as technology has advanced – they've become like your right-hand person…

Jackie Totally. I find myself more and more talking to programmers about moving lights and new LED technologies. Matching the colours between the fixtures; balancing the colour. When I'm talking to programmers about open white, it's also about temperature of the light, which I'm calling in Kelvins. Programmer Miguel Figueiredo and I enjoy talking Kelvins rather than colours while working together, though managing white, especially across a variety of LED lights, is a hard job.

Emma How does light aid storytelling?

Jackie Light can do a lot. There is the usual pattern with the text and the scenery and the story they are telling, and you can follow the story. I work as collaboratively as I can with that. For example, if there is a window and there is light coming through the window you try to make it as natural as you can to enhance the story.

But, I also try to have my own story, my own dramaturgical thread if you like, which you might see or you might not see. It is usually the people who work with light who can see it. You go and see the work of a lighting designer and you can read the information, it's almost like we have a secret code that not everyone can read. It's not necessarily created to work against the storytelling of the main work, it is just another layer. I love to see those things.

Back to the window light: you can bring the light through the window and it can be as precise as possible, but you can add a twist to the story by adding another layer of light to this window which distorts it a little bit, providing a contrast. Sometimes only through the contrast of the situation can you understand exactly where you are. If the light needs to come from the window and it's daylight, it might also be paired with another light which is coming from another direction that can suggest something a little bit different. This can also make the light coming through the window even richer.

Emma Do you value constraints on a project, or do you prefer a blank canvas? For example, if the set has a ceiling…?

Jackie Most of the time in theatre, when a lighting designer joins a project the set is already designed. It has been decided. Of course, you see a white card presentation of the design and you can share your notes and say what you think, but you are not the designer. There is a vision of another artist, and I find myself taking it as it is. I might have a couple of notes here and there which would be more practical than design based, maybe about a position, like I might need a specific element to be a bit more downstage so I can shoot through it a bit better. If I can spot a tricky texture somewhere, I say that we might struggle with the texture of a wall, so maybe they want to think about it. I mainly take the design as it is and try and work with what is there, and enjoy it, of course. It's always a challenge! The designers are not there to make a design which would be easy for a lighting designer, it's usually the other way around. They do their job, and we should do ours.

Emma What would your top tip be to a designer taking a show from the UK to Europe for the first time?

Jackie I guess the basic thing is to respect whatever the rules are within the house you are working in. By instinct, when you go to a foreign country your mind is already set to be open to anything that might happen. My top tip would be to lower your expectations – you can go only higher from that. The other thing is to prepare as much as you can by undertaking maximum research. Do the research of the space you are going to work with. Today you find online images of every theatre in every configuration, you can find technical information and plans. Try to talk to other people who have worked abroad. There are a lot of lighting designers and technicians who work all around; contact them and ask if there is anything you should know before working in that house. Do your homework.

Emma Moving on to colour: how do you pick your colour palette?

Jackie That's a very hard question. The whole idea of colours is a tricky one for me. Sometimes you see designs which are either over-using colour or using it in a way that doesn't complement the production, and this makes you think very carefully about colour. The main thing about colour is that a colour represents a feeling. It could be a feeling that is very personal and right for the moment. It could be a feeling that comes from the action on stage. The colour suggested by the text might not necessarily be the right colour for this feeling. I don't think there is a definition for colour. The colour is the right colour at the right time and at the right moment to do magic by delivering the information in the best way. It can be any colour.

We learn a lot about colours and what they represent by looking at the works of painters, the old masters. You learn a lot about colour so you understand how it works, where to use it, how to use it. The truth about colour is that colours literally contain cultural knowledge. The colours as we know them in Western society will be seen and understood quite differently in a different society. The meaning of a colour in a different country is not the same meaning as it is in this country. It is a cultural thing.

There is this simple question of what is daylight. Daylight as we know it here, the Northern European daylight, doesn't look like the daylight across Türkiye. Southern European daylight looks completely different, a totally different story, a totally different colour. Here in the UK, we have a daylight which is mainly soft and blurred. The clouds make it soft and cold-tinted. If we had this conversation in Cairo on a sunny day, the colour of the daylight is warm and the light is harsh, plus there are shadows all around. That's two different looks for the same time, same conversation, just different colours and different visuals.

I think that countries in the northern part of the globe, where we are now, we as visual practitioners usually look at the sky as there are always visuals and scenery in the sky. You see the clouds in so many variations, and you mainly look at the sky. It is not sunny, so you are able to look at the sky. It's quite open and your vision spans 360 degrees. When you walk in the countries in the south side of the globe, it is usually very sunny and the sun hits quite strongly straight above you. You can't really look at the sky or the sun, it's impossible, the sun and heat are harsh. You find yourself looking down. By looking down you see shadows, you see far more shadows than you do in the Northern Hemisphere. It is similar to talking about the white or black canvas, but in a different way.

Emma So people's experience changes the context, so their ability to translate what is onstage is going to be influenced by their experience of the world?

Jackie Yes. If you do *Arabian Nights*, you might want to be thinking about shadows and strong beams of light to start with. You don't need to be literal of course, but this is the place you might want to start. If you are doing Ibsen, you might want to think of it differently as it is set in a Northern country, it's colder and darker. The same applies for colour: India would be an amazing example, the saturated vibrant colours you see in India are not seen as much in other countries. That is why I find it hard to talk about colours without relating to a specific culture and a specific geographic position. There is so much depth in it.

Emma So do you have some favourite colours that you tend to put into a rig, or is it very open in terms of everything being within context?

Jackie I want to say it is very open, but that would be a lie because it's not, there are trends. You have trends with colours. Sometimes you use very little colour, which is where I am at the moment. Sometimes there are one or two colours that you really like, and you use them again and again and enjoy using them. Sometimes I just want to challenge myself: there are colours that I don't like, so I choose to work with them and see what happens.

Of course, it's true that if you put a strong colour on stage for a particular scene during the tech rehearsal you either hear an appreciation or a horrified response around you. Immediately the reaction is so emotional, and you can feel whether it's right or wrong. I love those moments where you go for something really bold; sometimes, you have the right people around you to appreciate it.

Emma How do you balance colour to focus an audience's attention?

Jackie That has to happen in a very subtle way, but having said that, we shouldn't confuse it with working on a specific tint colour to light faces in a particular scene. I don't believe this works as much; I don't believe that in a big theatre you can see the intricacies of that. Of course, people might claim that this is a subliminal thing which works on your mind. I believe in a radical change of colour while a scene happens, so we can start with one colour and slowly, slowly slip into another colour so by the end of the scene you find yourself in a totally different colour or tint of the colour. It doesn't necessarily need to be a different colour, but it just changes the mood that goes together with whatever happens with text, movement, music, whatever it is. There is a journey. I find this has great potential. I just did this sort of thing with *The Seagull* for the Jamie Lloyd Company.

It is a bit like a dance piece which I designed not long ago, where I used just the three primary colours plus open white. The design was just shifting from one colour to the other, about fifteen minutes between two primaries. That was, of course, an effect, but the way that the colours slowly changed and took over, the journey of the colour through its colour path is what I was interested in.

Emma How do you work out how a piece of scenery or costume will react to colour?

Jackie The set designers work very carefully on the set and on the colour schemes. When you see it on the model and in the workshops, and you see all the painters and the artists working on the texture and colour, it's incredible. I have so much respect for that. My instinct is not to add another colour from the rig. The scenery usually doesn't need colour, it just needs a bit of light to bring it out and accentuate its presence. I might use a colour correction to it. Often the set is painted with more than one colour, it might be a mixture of a few colours. In this case, you just want to bring it out rather than change it with another colour from the rig. It is a very delicate job. You have to have a lot of respect for the artwork that is in front of you. There are some stage designs which are magical. You look at them and want this texture in your house! So I treat the scenery very carefully.

Less is more.

Emma Thank you, Jackie. This has been a fascinating conversation.

JOHANNA TOWN

Photographer: Colin Grenfell

Johanna is the UK's appointed leader of lighting at the moment, in her tenure as Chair of the Association for Lighting Production and Design – the first chair of the organization under that new name, having helped lead its transition from being just the Association of Lighting Designers to an organization representing the full remit of lighting roles because she felt it better reflects the wide range of skills and people it takes to deliver lighting to the stage.

That awareness is perhaps because of her own career path, a route that is increasingly being lost, as a resident head of lighting for building-based theatre companies, including the Liverpool Playhouse and London's Royal Court. Since moving into the freelance world she's lit countless shows, including *My Name is Rachel Corrie* at the Court and in New York. She's also lit many shows at Guildhall, leading, to her delight, to receiving a Fellowship from the School.

Her escapes? Walks on the beach with her wife and their dog. Driving her classic car. And golf – perhaps a hangover of growing up surrounded by the game in Lytham St Annes.

www.johannatown.co.uk

Emma What drew you to lighting design?

Jo I was drawn into it really young – nine or ten. I had problems reading and writing; I couldn't express myself, and got very frustrated. My mum did amateur dramatics, and then my father died, so my mum used to take me to rehearsals. I got messing about with the lighting there – it was great fun. I'd do all the dimmers and operate all the shows, and suddenly I felt able to express what was always sort of stuck inside of me that I couldn't quite get out verbally, because for a long time my language was quite limited, and because of my dyslexia my drawing is terrible and I have no co-ordination. Here I didn't have to read or write – suddenly I was going, I can change this, you see it, and I'm expressing myself through light. That was that. I never wanted to do anything else.

Emma What was your career path from there?

Jo I didn't have much fun at school. The lighting, I kept being told that's what boys do – we are talking the 1970s. My Mum didn't want me to start working at sixteen, so I managed to wangle myself into a boys' sixth form college by picking subjects that I didn't have to have any qualifications in – computer science and law. So having failed all my O-levels, I studied those two at A-level.

But I'm in this boys' school which has its own theatre, and who's doing all the lighting – I am! I'm up the ladders and teaching all the boys how to put the lights up. That was quite a change – from being in this comprehensive school where they were saying, no, the boys do that, you need to sweep the stage, to being in a boys' school teaching them how to make the lighting desk work.

Because my Mum was passionate about the theatre, we used to go to the theatre all the time, so another thing that really made me want to go into theatre was going to the Royal Exchange in Manchester, one of our local theatres. It had just opened. We'd sit in the top balcony. We watched an Athol Fugard play, these people's lives in Africa and the traumas of apartheid, and I was so moved that the theatre could teach me so much. I knew I wanted to light and use light, and then theatre was added on to that by watching that play. Years later, I met Athol Fugard at the Royal Court and he told me a story about how he sat in the upper circle at the Court, and that's what made him want to be a playwright, so I shared with him my story of watching his play at the Royal Exchange.

Emma How old were you then?

Jo I would have been a teenager, fourteen or fifteen. By sixteen, I definitely knew what my career path was going to be. We looked up all the drama schools, but I had no qualifications, and they only did stage management courses. I knew that was never going to be what I wanted to do.

By this time, my mum had started booking the same two seats for every show at the Royal Exchange, right next to the lighting desk. The lighting control room at the Exchange is open to the audience – less so now, which is a bit sad – but I could have reached across and pressed the go button in those days. I plucked up enough courage to say, I've been trying to work out how to get a job in theatre, what can you advise me? The operator said, well they do this apprenticeship scheme here and this year is finishing so the next placement is coming up – why don't you apply for it? That was Jackie Lee, who is now an amazing production manager; she went and got me all the paperwork, and I applied and got it.

So, at eighteen I left school with no qualifications and started the apprenticeship at the Royal Exchange. As part of that, I had to go to college once a week, to do an electrical qualification – suddenly, I was having to learn something that was really important to me, and I was always top of the class. I got distinctions in all my electrical qualifications because I could suddenly relate to how it all worked together, whereas everything else I'd been taught just went in one side of my head and out the other. Even today, I don't retain very much unless I'm engaged and interested – that's just the way my brain works.

That's why I'm a big advocate of apprenticeships – the education system is just not right for some people. I've been so lucky in this industry – I've had a good job, a good career, I've sustained myself because of that break after everyone had written me off and said you're uneducated, you're severely dyslexic, you're going to be working in a supermarket for the rest of your life. My mum said, no, this isn't happening, I'm going to find you something you're passionate about, and it's been fantastic. When I got my fellowship at Guildhall a few years ago, Mum was so proud.

Emma Who and what influences your work?

Jo What I want to say is, a lot of the older lighting designers. As an apprentice, I was able to watch some great craftsmen at work. I think I have been most influenced by Mick Hughes and his work and how he worked as a team with his creatives and his director, cast, script. Even though I didn't work with him very often, maybe a dozen times, his way of working really touched me and that's how I've wanted to continue to work.

Emma What was different about the way he worked compared to other people?

Jo At the time I was working with him, you either lit a show in order for it to be illuminated, or you grabbed something that was emotionally evocative within the script, whether it was through the performance or through what the writer was trying to get across. Mick always managed to blend that into his lighting and channel the words through light. The mood would sing up and down, but it was never about him, it was never about lighting – it was all about the script and supporting that story and who was speaking and what they were saying. I sort of miss it a bit these days. I'm as bad as everyone else – it can go red, let's do red. It's great that everyone is visually aware of lighting now, I think that's fantastic, but sometimes when we didn't see it, it was more interesting.

Theatre Lighting Design: Conversations on the Art, Craft and Life

Orfeo ed Euridice at The Grange Festival. Conductor: Harry Christophers. Directed by Daniel Slater, choreographed by Tim Clayton, designed by Robert Innes Hopkins, lighting by Johanna Town, video by Nina Dunn. *Photographer: Craig Fuller.*

Emma Do you also draw inspiration from outside the theatre?

Jo I draw inspiration from life; everywhere I go, I'm looking at what light is doing in the environment. While we've been here, I've been looking at the angle of light hitting your face and the shadow. I get told off all the time by my partner, who goes, you're staring at them; no, I'm looking at how the light is falling on them … Everything around me is what I take light from, more than art or film. I feel I am absorbing the world around me the whole time. Whether I am ever able to re-create it, I don't know.

Emma What environments or spaces inspire you the most?

Jo I think when I want to be inspired, I go out into the countryside. I go into the light of day more than lit interiors. If I'm stuck in a theatre struggling to light something, I'll go up to the roof and watch the light in the sky. It's one of the reasons I go and play golf if I'm stuck at my drawing board. I love sitting on a beach in winter and watching the sky for hours and hours, how it changes. It's the slight, ten per cent shift as opposed to a film or a concert that gives you lighting boom, boom, boom. How do we create that shift that's just made my heart grow a little bit sadder? The sun is just popping out over there now whilst rising…that's what I love. That's why I sometimes say I don't understand what I do because it just comes from here – I'm not trained in any way, no one ever told me what to do, I only did what I saw.

Emma When you talk to a director, how do you talk about light?

Jo I try and talk from the heart, because I always think if you can be emotive about the script and what they're working on, then they'll trust you because you are being as emotionally engaged as they are in the product they are trying to produce.

Depending on the script and where I think we are going from I either use a lot of art references to try and explain what and where I think emotionally it's coming from, or I have an awful lot of nature books at home – light in Australia, light in North America, light on the North Pole. I might go in with a whole lot of ice book pictures because I don't think they understand when I say I want it to be cold and warm; I don't think they can picture what that really means, so I try to be as descriptive as possible, then I know we are on the same journey together.

Emma Do you use go-to books, or do you research everything from fresh?

Jo I do research afresh. I do less research than I used to, partly because I now have to earn a living as a lighting designer whereas the last ten years it had been a bit of a hobby, so now I don't have the time.

By the time I get into discussions where I sit down with the creative team as a whole, the set designer's often done a lot of research, so I trawl through all their research and take out bits I like and then add to that, use that to start describing what I want to do.

I also work with an awful lot of directors who employ me because they know and like what I do; they don't want to talk to me or get involved in any of that, and that's fine. They're doing their job and I'm hopefully doing mine and once we get to the tech I'll get yes and no, I like that, I saw you did quite a bit of that, let's have more of that, and that's about as much input as I get.

Emma What do you think makes a collaboration really work?

Jo When everyone is talking together. It doesn't have to be the most exciting show, it's about all the designers sitting in a room together, in rehearsals, not working in isolation, not drawing that plan in isolation, not being presented with a model, not being ignored in the rehearsal room. I've travelled half the country to go to a run and the director spends his whole time on the phone, and you, go can we have a conversation . . . ? Those are the ones that don't work. The ones where you can pick up the phone and go, I've had an idea, what do you think about this, collaborating right up to press night as a team together, those are the ones that really work.

Emma What about new collaborations?

Jo I try to share as much information as possible and take as much to the room as possible and really open those doors, have conversations. I think portfolios are still pretty good, even an electronic portfolio. When I meet a new director for the first time, I always ask them what they like, what theatre they like, what designers they like, why they've chosen me. I try and talk through my portfolio. And if I'm sort of engaged and I've got the script, even though we haven't met yet, I try to take things in that are relevant to that work so we can talk about something – you've got to open that dialogue up. I do a lot from the heart. I try to be as emotive as possible. I'm not a great word person, I don't have those words, so you have to find something else to get that across.

Emma And when you then discover the set has a ceiling – how do you approach that?

Jo You have to tell them what is going to happen. On a show where exactly that happened I had a conversation with the set designer before I met the director; I saw the modelbox, which was already signed off, and said, you do realize that this little room isn't going to be isolated, can we not make the ceiling a little smaller so I've got one more angle in there. They said it wouldn't look like a proper room if we make the ceiling smaller, so you have to explain what's going to happen, and I did do drawings with angles showing the shadow and what that would actually mean, how I couldn't light someone standing in the doorway of that little room, just so the director really understood what I could and couldn't do within that space while giving them solutions within that. I think that's really important – you have to go in with a positive solution.

I've also started using Capture visualization a lot more. I can't do it myself; I have to pay for someone to do it. But on that show, we also had a spaceship; the set designer said, I've given up with how to achieve this spaceship within budget, over to you. So it was a thirty-second moment where a spaceship comes down and zooms somebody up. We'd decided it was going to be a ring of lights over the audience like a real traditional spaceship with beams underneath, and that's all the audience saw. But I didn't actually know whether that was CP61 or CP62 Pars, I didn't know what to choose, and I wasn't one hundred per cent sure the director actually knew what it was going to look like. So we Captured the whole thing up, which gave us different beam angles to show him – we ended up with ACLs. Literally, when we switched it on in tech it looked just like it had done on the Capture. Since I'd spent most of my hire budget on those 48 lights and had a special bar made for this thirty-second moment, it was good to know this in advance. I'll do it again in the future for special effects. I wish I could do it myself – maybe if there were enough hours in the day to learn it.

Emma How do you come to your vision for a show?

Jo I don't know; it just happens. What my vision is at the beginning can be so altered by what happens when you see the set, what the director does with the piece. Quite often, we still work so independently of each other; you end up in the rehearsal room on the last run-through going, what, that's not what we talked about. Then you've got to be flexible – the director's made a change from what was discussed, and they are probably right as it's developed over those four weeks in rehearsal, so how do you adapt? You've got to be completely malleable all the time for the good of the production.

Emma With the advance of LED and the ability to have any colour and with moving lights any direction, how does that affect how you plan your rig?

Jo It makes us a little bit lazier! But I did a show recently where our leading lady was Afro-Caribbean, and I could always just shift the Lustr facing her to a slightly different tone to the one facing the other direction. What a joy to be able to do that; it's such a beautiful tool to have.

Emma When you go into a production, do you set a colour palette for that production?

Jo Oh yeah, I love colour. I do have a lot of favourites, and again I like to keep experimenting. I love the different shades and all the different blues and warms. I use a lot of green tinges and lavender tinges. I'm not afraid of using colour in things that you wouldn't expect, places you wouldn't expect. It's really interesting how colour works, it's my favourite part of the design. Some designers are all about angles and shafts and directions. I'm all about colour.

Emma The effect of colour on visual perception, how colour affects space, perception and emotion?

Jo Totally. I mean, emotionally we play with those tones all the time to shift an audiences' emotion, and that's the beauty of LED – you can do that without anyone noticing at all because you're not shifting the angle, you are literally just changing what's happening on stage, cranking it. I absolutely love it.

Emma How do you choose your colours?

Jo I see it linked to emotion. When I read a play the first time, I write down what that colour is – so a page might say this is red, this is purple, this is green. Slightly extreme, and it doesn't mean I'm going to do that in the show, it's just the colour that comes into my heart, not into my head, as I'm going through the script. It's my emotional response to what I'm reading.

Then I usually get into conversations with the director, with the set designer and see how they are going to play this, and that's when I adjust those colours, to go: what have we got, what am I going to do with those emotions, then all the colour palettes change again, and then I decide on the reality of the room or the space. This reality is actually daylight, so how can I tinge that daylight with that emotional colour for that scene. Is it going to be Lee 711 or to be no colour pink, or is it going to be L169 or no colour lavender or Rosco 373? So, my daylight can be five or six different versions of something that the audience probably just sees as daylight. I think colour is an incredibly useful tool and I just don't think people understand what colour does to them, so therefore, the less they understand, the more manipulative we can be because they don't register what we are doing to them.

Emma And does the type of light source play a part in this?

Jo I hate arc – because it only does green. I try to avoid it and only use it for a very specific reason. It's not good with colour. Tungsten – I don't necessarily love it, I appreciate what it does emotionally, but I'm not wedded to it. I think you can create that warmth in other ways, although others say you can't. Good LED, bad LED, that's the issue. You can choose how it dims colour-wise. I think what's frightening is that I knew what a piece of colour did in a Patt 743, and then I had to learn what it did in a Source Four – it doesn't go as warm as a Patt 743 as it dims down, so I have to choose a warmer colour to give me more options these days.

Emma In terms of colour and set finishes and costume, how do you work out whether a colour is going to work?

Jo I do look at all the costume designs, and I do use that to influence those decisions I've made in the script because there is no point being dogmatic about something when they think everybody should be wearing green frocks and I think that emotionally it's mauve or violet – it's not going to work, so then what is the colour choice you are going to make to allow that frock colour to really work? I think we are the element which is constantly floating and adaptable.

Emma Now that directors are learning that any light can go any colour anywhere in the room, how does that affect your decision-making?

Jo Everyone thinks this technology means we've got more time, but we've got less time because sometimes we will spend sessions before previews instead of doing the notes just making sure the preview is safe to go out that night with all the technology doing what it's supposed to. I think my production weeks have got longer: I'm always there now because it takes so long to do that programming in the morning to be ready for the actors in the afternoon, tidy it up, watch it again. You used to be able to do most of that work in the afternoon, perhaps come in and do a bit of rigging in the morning, now it's all about the programming.

Emma And rehearsals, how do you approach those?

Jo Loads of notes. I draw. I write. I write what I'm feeling. I keep going back to my colour, I keep going back to what it is feeling like. Often the director will say to you, don't bother coming in today, we're not doing anything, but then they'll say something to an actor and I'll go, oh, that's what this is about, and that can completely transform what you thought you were going to do in that scene. I'd love to be paid enough to sit in rehearsals all the time.

I very rarely take my laptop into rehearsals. I will print off my cue sheet if it's in that sort of shape, print off my A3 plan in whatever stage it's at and I'll scribble on it and move things around – actually, I need to flip the whole sun that way because that's how they've decided to do it. Or I'll have a conversation with the director, can we put them over there as it would be really lovely if the light came through that window that they've forgotten is there. I love wandering around the rehearsal room looking at all the stuff they've put on the walls, all the conversations, all the research they've done. Those little conversations are so important. It all feeds into the whole thing; I just love hanging around in a rehearsal room.

Emma And in terms of putting the cue structure together, when do you do that?

Jo Straight after I've done the colour! I read the script, do the colour, do the cue structure. The first cue sheet might read scene 1 – autumn day, scene 2 – winter night, scene 3 … I then I go to the read-through and go, oh, I missed that they switch the lights on, OK. And then I go to rehearsals and go, oh, they are doing that. I try and leave my plan for as long as possible, until I really have to hand it in, so the cue sheet builds and builds, and then I draw the plan from the cue sheet.

Emma When you've got a cue structure together, how do you share it with the DSM?

Jo I always give the DSM a cue sheet, sometimes without numbers on it, and just say park this in your book. I'll usually give it after the first run, then they might get some more stuff added later. From giving them the cue sheet, I know what sort of DSM they are, how much work I'm going to have to do myself or whether I can just trust them to get on with it.

I'll give my cue sheet to the director, always, even if they don't want to read it. I'll always say it's written in lighting speak, read through the shorthand. Some of them love it, read it, come back to me, no, that's not right, I don't want something to happen there, or, I'm going to add something that you haven't seen in rehearsals yet. It's interesting as they've obviously read it. I did once have a director who sent a cue sheet back spell-checked, and I thought, I'm never working with you again!

Emma Do you like a plotting session before tech?

Jo I do. I like to have two focus sessions on a standard size rig, and a lighting session. That doesn't necessarily mean that I get any cues into the desk, it can be for me to just look at things. I always go through all my groups – I'm big on groups – and go, that needs refocusing, I've messed that up. I hate starting the tech not knowing what the rig is doing because I think you can lose track when you are focusing. If I can get cues in, even if it's the beginning of scene 1, scene 2, scene 3, so we've got something to build from, great. I like being able to hit go and then say, OK, let's fix that.

Emma A starting point…

Jo I think the actors get really frustrated when you constantly go, 'just building this lighting state'. You are constantly jerking them all through the tech. They don't notice if it's not looking good.

But I would say, if you don't get your focus right, you can't get anything right. So always spend your time focusing. That's where your craft starts and ends, and if you are doing something really traditional and everyone is going, we don't know where we are going to put the furniture, put it somewhere, mark it, focus it and then you say to the director, well that's what it will look like, now you can move it where you want, and then you can go back and refocus it, but that's what the scene will look like, and you know it's right because you focused it properly.

Emma When you are putting a state together, where do you start?

Jo I build up from the set I have around me. I work quite strongly with colour but in a soft way; I think how colour is in a room is really important, and I'll tint it slightly one way or another depending where I think we are emotionally in the script. That's the strong balance I have to get, then I have to light the words. I do think lighting what's coming out of the actors' mouths is really important; I have a real bug-bear about not being able to see faces, eyes and mouths, and therefore, for me, it's layering it in order that you create the environment and the space and can then layer the actor on top.

Emma What is your ideal working relationship with your team?

Jo People who can second guess what I'm trying to achieve. I think a programmer can make or break a show. Sometimes you only go so far as you know that's the only way the show can be solid, that's all they can achieve. I sometimes wish I knew more to help them grow more; I don't think there is enough training given. I think your programmer really has to know who you are. I did say to a programmer I worked with quite a lot recently, don't you get fed up with me going, can you twirl over there, maybe just a bump over there – aren't you doing my job? He said no, because I can do all that, and then you tell me whether that's what you want. I know how to make a bump and swirl, but you're the one who goes, that blue's not right. He said, you make all those decisions, and that's really important because the difference is your eye is feeling it from somewhere else, because I'm always feeling it from the back of the machine.

Emma What makes a production sing?

Jo It sings when all of it sits together. Every bit of it: sound, lighting, acting, set, choreography just work as one, you don't know why that scene was amazing because you can't quite pinpoint who was responsible for making it. That's when it really works.

Emma Can you describe a project that you have been involved in which stands out as rewarding or challenging or memorable?

Jo They're nearly all Royal Exchange shows, and it's because that space is all about lighting, so I suppose I couldn't have started at a better theatre, where lighting becomes visual scenery and you have to shape the lights around the actors. I found it really hard going to a pros arch theatre after that.

People say lighting in the round you've got to light them from four sides, but you're not lighting them the same from four sides, you're going – I've decided the sun is going to be up there and the moon is coming up there, but if they are going to get the sunlight over there for that scene and they're going to get the moonlight from over there for that scene, you're giving everyone a chance of something. But you're then going, if that's doing that from this side of the face, then it's going to look like this, and that's natural and that's real. If the director's decided to have the actor's face behind the sun the whole time, his back to the sun, then he's going to have a greyer face than if he was turning the other way, but of course, that all has to be worked together. It's not about lighting the same all the way round, it's about taking that space and going, that's what this is, and that's what's exciting about it.

I did *Frankenstein* there, and that's all about light and shade, fear and darkness and not darkness. So much of the script was set in a cabin on a ship with no light, or a single light swinging. There were storms, ice, an attic room, the monster appearing. That probably is the most exciting production I've done, where I had to create light by creating darkness.

Emma And how do you do that?

Jo I broke up the light as much as possible. I had worked with the set designer a lot; the director had seen my work at the Royal Exchange, but I'd never worked with him before. We had a chat where he said, I can tell you the one thing I really hate is gobos. Of course, everything at the Exchange hits the floor – to light an actor you have to light the floor, there is no crosslight, no magic, no mystery. Doing it in a pros-arch theatre would be a completely different ball game.

I made my general cover very high so the theatre space that the audience were in stayed as dark as possible. We put nearly everything on the top level and a little bit on the next level down, keeping the lower levels off apart from when we tried to do a little bit of sneaky crosslight, so the space remained as dark as possible. Then I went, I've got 24 Lustrs and I'm going to put gobos in every one, so it will be totally broken up. And of course, the space was going to be full of smoke. The audience were not going to be able to see across the space. We constantly used this break-up general cover, soft focus – I kept saying to the crew as we were focusing, either I'm going to be killed for this or it's going to work. Not once did I get told off for having a gobo on stage. But what was really interesting was how breaking up the light gave it a completely different character and really did create a lot of light and shade on the stage, so in the end it was always broken darkness in the haze, and then we could be dynamic through it. I was really pleased with that.

Emma And to be brave enough to do the opposite of what you'd been told to do…

Jo I really had to trust why I was doing it and why I needed to. One of the things I love about the Royal Exchange is everything is accessible, so I always push the boat out there: I always do one thing I haven't done before because I know I can change it. The crew are amazing. If we don't constantly push the boundaries we never really create. I find the pros arch a bit scary, and what I hate working in commercial theatre are the time restraints we now have on everything, and how that stops us being creative because we have to sort of do the one thing we've learnt. We are never able to just play, look at stuff, let's just try this for half an hour, oh, I'd never have imagined that, that's amazing. We've lost that chance.

Emma Because we are the one discipline where we are not showing something before we get a hundred people watching us.

Jo Yes, so you make sure you don't make an idiot of yourself. I think I was very lucky working at the Royal Court, doing stuff in the studio space in the days when I had the front door key and knew I could stay all night and experiment. We are put under too much pressure now, and young designers don't have that opportunity to work in rep for a while

Theatre Lighting Design: Conversations on the Art, Craft and Life

Frankenstein at the Royal Exchange, Manchester. Directed by Matthew Xia, movement director Angela Gasparetto, designed by Ben Stones, lighting by Johanna Town, composer and sound designer Mark Melville. *Photographer: Johan Persson / ArenaPAL.*

and light a studio show. I even used to light the youth theatre shows and just mess about to fail.

More recently, I did sixteen shows in one year. I did it to find out what that felt like and to find out whether it was possible. It was – but the last two shows were quite tough! I went to the last venue having drawn the plan over several different production periods. When I looked up, I went, what have I done – this is never going to work! I didn't put any lights through the window, how did that happen? But then, OK, let's get those lights rigged. And I realized I could be put in a theatre with a rig and just told to get on with it, and I could create something. I wouldn't want to put myself in that position again, but I think you get to a stage when you know your craft well enough that you can get yourself out of anything, should you need to. I think it was like when I went skiing and got to the point when I knew I could get down any mountain.

But it does feel like nobody's allowed to fail any more. You learn amazing things by making mistakes.

Emma What do you think the key skills to being a lighting designer are?

Jo Patience! Communication – getting your ideas across to everybody. You've got to get everybody engaged in the project. I think too many of us go in thinking it's all about me – but I think because I grew up in a theatre environment working in a building, I realized that lighting design wasn't my be-all-and-end-all. I actually loved making theatre and loved being part of a team and loved us all working together to a goal that at 7.30pm the show went up on time, and that was the most important thing. I take that into all my technical rehearsals, and I will sacrifice my design for the show to be right, and will do everything in my power to help that show be what the director wants. Of course, I'll do my best within that, but I'm never going to let my work sacrifice getting that show on, the responsibility of that show on press night being good, solid work. Sometimes that work can be amazing for everybody, sometimes you are lucky we've got it there.

I will stand there and defend my time, though – you are all going away and this is my focus session, I am having my eight hours now; you've had your time and you, production management, are going to tell the director why there are no doors on the set not why there's no lighting. Of course, things happen in theatre all the time where you have to just go, OK, you can have that time. But I'm not a soft touch; I believe everyone pushes lighting designers too much anyway.

Emma If you were going to say something to your younger self, what would you say?

Jo I think I would say read more, see more, go out more, explore more. It opens doors to your imagination. Now, I don't know how anyone gets anything done – I seem to spend my whole time feeling tired and overwhelmed, and I really wish I had more opportunities to spend an afternoon in an art gallery or at the cinema.

I don't think we need to be more technically savvy because there are always people who can do that for you, but you have to be really appreciative of the art that's around you. I would go for the art more than the science or technology because if you can't feel emotion about all of that, it doesn't matter. I sometimes think because I came up through the school of being a chief electrician, I worry about the technology too much. I'm always very conscious about how many hours it takes to move that bar and how tricky it is. I've put eight lights on that boom, it would be easier if I just put six; I do a lot of that, I should do less – but if that gives me a bit more focusing time… That knowledge means I can be savvy about stuff when I need to. I do think every young designer should have a time being a practicing technician to understand what they are asking because sometimes it's possible, and sometimes it's not.

But: what I really loved about theatre is that it embraces everyone. That's what I really love about it. I have just been me all my life – aren't we lucky to be able to do that? I do think sometimes now it's getting a little bit career-ey – I'm supposed to be like this, I'm supposed to be like that. Some people can talk the talk. I go, I don't know how to communicate this, trust me, it's just in here, I can't say anything about it. I'm allowed to just be me, and people employ me because I am me.

Emma I wholeheartedly agree. Thank you, Jo, for sharing so much.

TEAM CONVERSATION: *BILLY ELLIOT*

Billy Elliot began life as a non-musical film written by Lee Hall and directed by Stephen Daldry, about a coal-miner's son living during the 1980s miners' strike who dreams of being a dancer. Elton John fell in love with it, and suggested it become a stage musical for which he would write the score and Lee Hall the lyrics. Stephen Daldry again directed, bringing in his collaborators from *An Inspector Calls* and *Machinal*, designer Ian MacNeil and lighting designer Rick Fisher.

The show opened at London's Victoria Palace Theatre on 11th May 2005, establishing the principle of three performers sharing the demanding role of Billy that has continued ever since. From there, it set off around the world – to Sydney, to New York (winning ten Tony Awards, including all of the design categories), to Holland, touring the USA, the UK and Australia and still making regular appearances in Korea and Japan. In London the show ran until 9th April 2016, a total of 4600 performances, with the production filmed before it closed and so now with an ongoing life on television.

This conversation is a group conversation, with the show's lighting designer, Rick Fisher, and members of the lighting team who helped make the show, then maintain it and re-create it around the world.

Rick Fisher – lighting designer, whose history features earlier.

Vic Pyne – associate lighting designer and programmer; Vic started working with Rick Fisher on *Jerry Springer: The Opera* at the Edinburgh Festival and they just kept going from there, along the way Vic becoming the first associate/programmer to get billing on the front of a Broadway theatre on *Billy*, until she left the freelance world to join English National Opera and to become a Mum. She is now head of lighting at Glyndebourne.

Paul Franklin – production electrician; Paul had previously been chief electrician at the Yvonne Arnaud in Guildford and at the Old Vic in London. At the time of *Billy*, he was a freelance production electrician and project engineer. He went on to become a theatre consultant, first with Carr & Angier and now with Charcoalblue.

James Nowell – head of lighting, *Billy* London; James joined *Billy* from *Matilda*; from there, he also moved to theatre consultants Charcoalblue, where he is now a director designing and leading on projects in the UK and internationally.

Rob Halliday – associate lighting designer and programmer; Rob took over looking after *Billy* from the 2011 American tour on. He was wearing two hats during this interview since he's also a co-creator of this book!

Rick It's funny. I don't ever really remember being asked to light *Billy Elliot*. I think somehow it was just assumed that I was going to do it. I'd worked with both Stephen Daldry and Ian MacNeil a long time. At one point I did finally confront Stephen and say, do you want me to do this show? I'd love to do it. We had started talking about it, but it never turned into anything. They did some workshops, which I wasn't involved in. My memory is they actually staged the 'Solidarity' number in a pre-workshop, and that's where they had the idea that perhaps the show could work because of the way that number, which went on to be the anchor of act one, developed.

Then they did do a workshop at the American Church on Tottenham Court Road, where they didn't have any scenery, but they just kind of told the story. One of the things I remember is that they used all the doors into the big hall there: eleven doors. And if you look at the set of *Billy Elliot*, I think there are eleven doors, including a secret door or two.

One of the challenges and one of the brilliant things about the show is the way it moves along so beautifully and the stage is full of people and scenery and then all of a sudden, the stage is not full of people and scenery and it never really stops to reset, which musicals often do. I think there is only one blackout during the course of the show, at the end of 'Born to Boogie'.

Like a lot of big musicals, the lead-in time was very long. I remember endless meetings and looking at set models. But it also meant time to put together a brilliant team – Vic as my associate and programmer, although at that time she was just called programmer since they wouldn't pay for an associate or assistant lighting designer. And Paul as the production electrician.

The actual production period was also very long. They needed to dig a big hole in the stage of the Victoria Palace, for the two big stage lifts, which they did before we even loaded in the show.

Paul We got a window in the theatre before panto where we dug the hole; it had to be dug by hand because they wouldn't allow us to use mechanical diggers because of all the tube lines that run just beneath the theatre, and the services aren't mapped, and you're very close to the royal sewer.

Rick We went back in after panto season. We loaded in the lights and you bagged them up and sent them up in the air while the rest of the set got installed.

Paul From the day we loaded in to the first sort of lighting session was six weeks.

Rick It was a big install. It's funny, because it's a show that doesn't look like it has a lot of scenery.

I never was given a proper budget for the show. I told our production manager, Steve Rebbeck, that I thought it was a £5,000 a week show. It was just my gut feeling of what I thought, from knowing what things cost in 2004–5.

The rig was being designed the previous October or November. That first rig was too expensive. So we started horse-trading...

Paul Part of that horse-trading was we took on a whole pile of old Martin Mac 600s that White Light said we could have really cheap.

Rick Because again, an element of design is knowing where you want to spend your money. And certain lights, I knew I wanted their functionality and their brightness and at that time the VL3500 was my go-to spot.

Vic It was very much a workhorse.

Paul The other thing that dominated discussions about the rig was that we knew that occasionally during the show, the boys' voices would have to be pretty much unsupported. So, the noise floor for our rig was really low.

Rick Paul Arditti was the sound designer, and we developed that together. He still complained about how noisy it was. We made compromises for quiet, as we should have done, because sometimes it's just a kid with a radio mic talking on stage. And it's much more of a book musical than a razzle dazzle sound musical. One of the reasons why *Billy* works is because it's a great story, and it's a story that you engage in. If we did anything well, we enabled that to happen.

Emma So when you started with a blank sheet of paper, how did you start?

Rick Increasingly, I find that I'm in the situation as a lighting designer – I think we're all in this situation now – that you're having to design a rig for a show where you don't actually know what is going on. You don't have the luxury of watching a rehearsal. With many new musicals, particularly *Billy*, the show isn't actually fully written, and it will certainly change. You often don't have the luxury of actually having a conversation with the director and designer. Whereas with *Billy*, at least we did spend some time together.

So basically, you're doing the cover-your-ass rig, rigging the kind of opportunities you believe you need. What I learned on *Billy Elliot* and have repeated on other shows since is that I look at areas where I can fit lights and where I want light to come from, then I give myself the four basic flavours of light that I want: an arc spot that can shape, an arc washlight for soft-edged pools of colour, a tungsten spot that can shape to light people or things, and a tungsten washlight. If you look at the *Billy* rig, that's what you see in the main places. Any space that was left over, I rigged a few conventionals just to get out of jail.

I wish I still had somewhere the original paper sketches that I gave to Paul to draw, because I still do not draw by computer.

Paul That process of taking Rick's paper scribbles and turning them into the lighting plans was quite interesting because it was the first time I'd ever been given a 3D AutoCAD version of a set.

Rick What is good about it is I think it immediately gets your production electrician thinking about it the way that you're thinking about it. And it's good for a designer to have to explain what they've done and why they've done it. It's why I've decided I don't need to ever buy a CAD program, because for the amount of lighting plans left in me, I'd rather the theatre pays to have someone do it or I'll pay somebody to do it, because in that discussing things, it gets better.

Paul It very much felt like there was a rig for a style of lighting rather than a rig for a specific show.

Rick It's delivering opportunity. The luxury then is when you work with a brilliant programmer, you know you can respond quickly to things, and its which brushstrokes you choose rather than which brushstrokes you have rigged because you've got that flexibility everywhere. Ultimately it ended up being a value-engineered version of that. The tungsten washlights in those days became par cans with scrollers because the Martin TW1 hadn't been invented yet. Some of the arc washlights became what was on the shelf and cheap, which were those Mac 600s.

The VL3500s – the 'Q' supposedly quiet version – were our workhorses. I think we used them to great effect on the show. I'm more of a single-source than a multi-source-wash person. It gives me great pleasure in the opening moments of the show to see Billy on his own in the hall; everyone leaves and he's kind of dancing just with his own shadow on the floor. And there's just this one single shadow. Now does anyone else notice that? I don't know that anyone else really does, but it makes me very happy. It just looks clean and simple and unshowbizy in a way that's very appropriate for that show and hopefully sets up a language that we continue to use.

Rob Almost eighteen years on now, there is still no other light that will go wide enough to do that, and the LED ones that get close have multiple sources, so you don't get that single shadow. Even the most recent versions of the show still use the VL3500, which is more than twenty-one years old now, because nothing else will do what it does, and that look is important to the show.

Rick One of the things that was special about the show is that it's often in a box room. It's a very interesting box room and a much cleverer box room than I initially gave it credit for. It's raked, and not uniform. That's part of Ian's rather brilliant idea. The things he obsesses about are proportions. That gave a very good dynamic for a show that sometimes has a twelve-year-old boy standing on stage on his own. It makes him look important.

But it's a three-sided room. And when I saw it initially, my heart sank because, being a queen of sidelight and having earned a little bit of my living from sidelight, all of a sudden there were walls, and there was no way to get light on in the way that I wanted.

The box also splits up and fragments and goes off into the wings, and you do get a neutral dance space, and what I now know – but I did not know at the time – is there are four big, important dance numbers that we have to do in that space with very little scenery to help us. I knew I needed sidelight for those. So, we developed a system of flown lighting ladders. They're a pain in the ass – expensive and problematical – because they have to fly out to let the room on and off. And in the London production, the designer, particularly, was not so happy about the fact they weren't as well masked as they should have been. We hadn't addressed that as well as we might have, and he didn't like seeing those lights. On subsequent productions, we made that better.

One of the brilliant things that we learned we could do with the set, particularly towards the end of the show, is fragment it a bit more. You didn't need to bring it all back together again; you could just use a shorthand, a piece of it surrounded by blackness, leave the rest to the audience's imagination. It's very rare that you get a musical with so much darkness in it.

Rob And you did ultimately manage to get a bit of crosslight into that room...

Rick Oh, yes, my favourite two lights, the workhorses of the entire show. Revolutions just above head height out to the sides, front-of-house. They can go wide enough to light the strips of the wall. So, you get this very clean light on people from out front. They're perfect for giving you that simple, clean shadow on the wall. And they work all the time. The letterbox shifts a little bit when the walls are in slightly different places. They just give you the flexibility for people to move around anywhere and have their faces lit because the show doesn't overly rely on followspots.

Emma Did the rig then evolve in the theatre?

Paul It stayed static from the moment we went into the theatre until the moment we started turning the lights on. The minute you turn the lights on, you realize that they either do or they don't work.

Rick The rig did change a lot in the theatre. Originally, I started with three followspots. We had a followspot in the back and two in the high boxes on either side. I wanted high-side ones because I knew that people would be talking to each other, and it wouldn't be full-out presentational numbers. And then, because of the shape of the set, because of the shape of the theatre, I think after a couple of days of tech, I realized I was not using one spot very much, and it made much more sense to go to two in the front.

Paul Then I remember quite vividly, and all credit to Rick, he came in on Monday morning and said, right, we need to have a sit down and talk. I've been thinking over the weekend. He just went through all the changes he wanted to make to the rig over the next three days. There were some quite substantial changes: cutting some stuff, moving some stuff from front-of-house to onstage. It was probably a day's work for the crew, working flat out, to make the changes. But because he just presented it to us as a list of stuff, we could get on with it while he worked with Vic re-programming to deal with those changes.

Rick You just find out what's working and where. You don't want to have an expensive light just sitting up there not doing much, as I believe happens on certain shows. You want to make sure everything is earning its keep, or else it should go. But you also have to engender the right atmosphere that allows you to make those changes without anybody losing any face. I was lucky I had that. I would come and say I've had a sleepless night; you felt this groan between the team, as like what's going to change now? But we talked it through, and I was able to explain why I wanted to do it. And you could see already their minds were working out, oh, yeah, this is this then that simplifies this, this rationalizes this, this is a better use. I can see the point. And if you can just say, oh, I don't know, I'm just going to try this…

Emma It's about them coming on the journey.

Paul We started with ninety-two moving lights in the show, and we ended up with something like seventy-five.

Rick Because they just weren't earning their keep.

I do want to say, we didn't know that we had a hit. I think it is very fair to say we had a problem, and that was how to do the show. We had a problem to solve, and it was a problem all the time. And everybody was trying to solve the problem. We almost didn't know that it was any good most of the time.

I think I knew we had something very special when we got to 'Solidarity'. It's a very complicated seven-minute-long number that does what the best musical theatre does – you start at one place; you see things changing and you're somewhere completely different. And you've been told a big story in seven minutes about a boy who wants to dance, a community that's having a battle, a dad who doesn't want to know, a kid who's embarrassed, a kid who's got potential.

Then there's one moment when Billy strikes an attitude, I think it's called in the ballet. And I swear, it was the first time that kid looked up at the audience. It was electric. The only lighting response I could think of was to slowly but surely move the followspots in, the backlights came on, it got a little bit brighter and a little bit brighter. And then we were allowed to use our 45-degree frontlight to light his face when he finally looked up. And it was a moment of pure joy on stage. I think the lighting helped amplify that joy.

Vic The whole process of lighting 'Solidarity' was pretty special. We lit it on the go, and then we never changed it.

Rick We lit everything on the go! The great thing about having three actors alternating the leading role is that you have to keep on re-teching. It gave us a lot of time with people on stage, which is when I'm happiest because I like to light people, not just dress the air. We just lit the shapes they were doing, Vic just focusing away. In this very complicated number we'd never ask him to stand and wait for us, because that's another thing I like not to do. It drives some of my team crazy on occasion that I don't make people wait for lighting. I learned this on *Billy* because we always had enough time to catch up because it moved so glacially slowly.

Paul I don't know if this was the same for you, but this was the first show I'd done where we took the seats out to create a production desk area for you, with proper tables and big reclining chairs …

Vic Wheely chairs! That was awesome, wasn't it!

Paul And actually, that became a little bit of a social magnet in the auditorium.

Rick That was part of the idea. If you're going to be in for six weeks of tech, don't sit on a butt board because you will ruin your back. But also, make yourself the place where people want to be. If only so you can find out what's going on!

Vic *Billy* was after the indoors smoking ban. Steve Rebbeck was a smoker, Stephen and Julian, his associate, were smokers…

Rick So lots of things would get discussed amongst the smokers out in the proverbial alley…

Emma Was there any cue structure in place before you went into tech?

Rick What I tend to do with almost all my shows is I'll sit in a rehearsal and I'll develop a provisional cue list. When something happens where I feel there might be a lighting cue, I write it down, just a really long list, and I keep on adding or subtracting. So that when we're often lighting over the tech, that's my skeleton to hang cues on. I'll have a rough idea; I'll get that bit and that bit. I think there are about seven bits in between, so I'll leave numbers for those. It could be blocking things that inspire me, it could be musical things, it could just be a sense there's something you have to do with lights. Some of those cues ultimately get made, some don't.

Emma Did your shorthand with Vic help, because of having worked together before?

Rick Enormously.

Vic Definitely. Because of that, quite often, Rick would start pointing, and it would already be there.

Rick Occasionally, Vic would also say, you don't really mean that do you, and she'd come up with a better solution. But occasionally, I would push through and say, I do mean that. And I'd have to prove myself.

Vic The surprisingly helpful thing was that because there were so many stage lifts, the automation lady, Sian, who sat in front of us, had an overhead monitor. So even when they did stuff with the false iron in, when I couldn't see anything on stage, I used to focus from her overhead monitor.

Emma In terms of defining a colour language for the show…

Rick Every shade of grey I could manage…

Vic Well, you'd set a scroller list before the show. There were two colours on that scroller list that you used an awful lot.

Rick 728 is the one. It's a colour I actually made for Lee. I use it all the time…

I remember figuring out very early on that *Billy* had three types of musical numbers. Anthems, which is when the community sings about coming together. There were also ballads. Billy sings about his dead mother. Grandmother sings about her dead husband. And then there were the numbers. The numbers were what scared me the most. The 'Dancing Dresses' number, the 'Born to Boogie' number in particular, and to a lesser extent, 'Shine', the first number with all the ballet girls. Because originally, we didn't necessarily have any of the tools we needed for those. The original 'Dancing Dress' number was just done with a slash curtain, in a multi-million-dollar show! That was my suggestion to Ian when we couldn't think of what else to do. In later versions, we added a proscenium with rosettes that lit up and could chase. But it was meant to look like a cheap light entertainment show. Because the show works best when it looks like it springs from the kid's imagination. For those numbers, if it looks like we, the musical theatre makers, are doing them, then it's not so good.

But the colour palette was generally very limited so that most of the people are lit between open white, Lee 202 and L728. I tried some warmer colours and actually Ian was very against the warmer colours. He would literally stand on stage, and if he saw a bit of light straw in the rig, he'd call me out on it. He didn't want anything that looked marmaladey or warm.

I said, there are times when we have to make it look warm, it's got all these ballet girls in it. So, I did put a little bit of pink in the ballet girls. But I think he wanted it at all to be lit like it was Pina Bausch. It was a very restrained colour palette.

Then there was 'Born to Boogie', which just constantly eluded me. It's based on a number in the film where Billy starts to go to his first private lesson. I'd say it's a very derivative number by Elton John, and it's in three parts. First, they start to dance, then they do lessons, and then they can dance. The first part is the part that's always been very uncomfortable to me because they sort of dance too quickly, and we're trying to make it too much of a number too quickly. I don't think I've ever felt that I had the right lighting language for that. That's having relit it more times than any other part of the show.

I was very determined that it shouldn't just become a number. It needed to be driven by something. When I looked at this design, of this space that was a multi-purpose village hall that had to be everything for everyone, it felt to me like a kind of place where they maybe would have done some shows. So we worked in some vintage lights, Patt 23s and 123s with colour wheels. So even now, when that number is going super-colourful, especially now that much of the rig has become LED and can fade between colours, it's still trying to be motivated by those old-fashioned colour wheels.

Paul We just happened to find them, with those really old-fashioned Strand wall brackets, hidden in the depths of White Light's warehouse…

Rob But they're really hard to find now when you have to make a new version of the show!

Rick The other thing that was interesting is we had a bar of lights that we flew in for 'Electricity'. That started with just a chair and an empty stage. I said to Stephen, the only idea I have is it could be we're at the Royal Opera House, he's having his interview on stage, but maybe there's a lighting bar being flown in for maintenance, someone could come along and fiddle with it. Then maybe it could fly out, which was a reference to something he and Ian and I had done twenty years before on *Machinal* at the National.

My memory is that on the day that we came to teching it Stephen said, I just don't know if that idea of the lights is going to work. But let's try. And we did it, and the flyman, who was called Iain Gonoude, we didn't say, oh, take it out over 20 seconds, he just did it in time with the music, probably over twice as slow. And I think I had the grace to say to him, I think you just won me an award because it just flew out at the right time. It landed at the emotional moment where it needed to. The lights – originally Pirouettes, roughly period and with a lovely quality of light – did exactly what I'd hoped they would do, just kept us focused on the kid. It was just a beautiful, simple moment that was made of electricity. A happy accident. A little bit of inspiration. If he had flown it out badly that first time, it might have gotten cut.

Another number that I'm very proud of, and again it was done completely on the fly, is 'Grandma's Song'. At one point, they just stopped the tech so Stephen and Peter Darling, the choreographer, could try this new staging idea they'd had. Vic and I both had the idea that maybe we should light this as we're watching it because we might never have another chance. A group of men came on from stage left, infiltrated some of the secret doors, pushed the scenery out of the way, and then they became the line of people who were her memory of the dance hall. To this day, they are lit with one light that slightly tracks over and follows them and gets a bit bigger, then some specials on Grandma and Billy. When she idealizes what her husband had been, he had a Pirouette

'Grandma's Song' in *Billy Elliot*, directed by Stephen Daldry, choreographed by Peter Darling, set design by Ian MacNeil, costume design by Nicky Gillibrand, lighting by Rick Fisher, sound by Paul Arditti, from the Tokyo production of the show.

turn up on him which gave him that wonderful warm glow of memory. And eventually, they all left.

Paul Just the most magical choreography, how they all get there. And then they all just fade away.

Rick But it's super simply lit, partly because we just never saw it in rehearsals. We saw it on stage, and we kind of lit it that way.

Vic But again, it's that thing of the single source backlight, isn't it.

James All that smoke as well.

Paul They're all smoking – they bring their own smoke!

Rob I'm curious about 'Angry Dance', when it goes red. What point did you decide to make it go red? Because that's a very big shift in style from the rest of the show.

Paul It definitely happened during the tech. Because suddenly I was asked to get a load of red rotating beacons!

Rick I think I just was following the shapes, that it was like he's on top of the house, and he starts doing his what they call the nerve tap. So, it's like spot and spot. Then for the first time in the show you saw a really deep colour which was the red. Colour can be a fantastic thing.

Rob And then the shadows of Billy on the back wall?

Rick The people in the back two or three rows of the stalls at the Victoria Palace were sold as restricted view seats. They couldn't see Billy on top of the house. They could see him from the knees down. I thought, well, if I could see a shadow of the kid dancing on the back, when he's on the top. He's not up there very long. He's up there for 12 bars, 24 bars. If I could see a shadow of him dancing, at least I would know what I was missing, but I wouldn't feel left out. The Victoria Palace has two balconies, so we put some low lights on the balcony rails.

We had four shadows, and they were on two different levels. Now we just do it all as a band, and it just becomes another bit of the punctuation: it's the first time in the show where the lighting really does stabs.

Vic Remember also that the show never stopped changing, and as well as lighting each moment as we saw it, we were always trying to keep up with what was happening to it. The first timeline of the show was very different from the end timeline. For a long time, the preset cue was cue 597, and then we had to link around a lot of things because the order of the show kept changing, and the Strand 500-series desk we made the show on didn't just let you move cues around as easily as you can now.

'Angry Dance', from *Billy Elliot* – multiple shadows on the back wall.

Paul One of the things that was unique about this show that I've never met on any other show was that we had quite an extended preview period, but they decided not to do Monday or Tuesday performances. It meant we had Monday, Tuesday and most of Wednesday to make big changes to the show. You could plan, you could do it, you could practice it, you could do it right, rehearsing all three casts into it. It meant you could affect really big change and get it right.

Rick We were still changing it the day the critics arrived. About a week before we opened, after we'd been previewing for three weeks, someone got the idea that the audience didn't have enough knowledge of the miners' strike and the political situation at the time the show was set. So it was decided that we might want to put a bit of newsreel footage in at the very beginning of the show. That meant adding a video projector and making the video, which wasn't ready until the opening night. To his credit, Stephen addressed the company and said, we think this might help. It means coming in, doing some re-rehearsing and once again re-teching the beginning. We can do this if you're up for it, and if you think it's just too much, we'll leave it. Of course, everybody was willing to do it.

Emma So it opened in the West End. Did you immediately know it was going to end up being the show that had this ongoing life?

Rick Not until we had an audience. We started previewing it, and really from the first preview, which was four and a bit hours long, we all had glimmers that there was something good. That was even before the finale was in; the finale didn't come until two weeks into the previews. We used to just end with Billy walking out of the theatre.

We all thought the finale would get cut, and indeed the show is emotionally more satisfying with Billy just walking to his future. But the audience wants a feel-good moment as well.

Emma In terms of being able to catalogue the show in order for it to go on tour and move it, how did you do that?

Vic FocusTrack through and through for me; it was one of the early shows where we had tools to let us photograph what everything was doing.

James Their notes helped me enormously. I took over with little handover, and while the paperwork had all of the photographs of what things were doing, there were also lots of notes about feeling and mood and the shape of things. And about what not to do!

Rob I think it's about communicating intent. On this show, Rick very deliberately leaves a dark band at the front of the stage; the frontlight doesn't come right down to the front. It'd be easy to think that was a mistake in the paperwork unless it was very specifically noted.

Emma It's interesting you talked about intention. How do you communicate that intention as a lighting designer? I mean, I guess with a show like *Billy*, you can be quite separate from it at times because it has this continuing life. Do you think that initial team of people has been a really important part of making sure that that intention carries through?

Rick Oh, huge. We've always been blessed by a great team of people on *Billy*, and that's around the world. And something about this show, and I think it's because of the young performers, just invests everybody in it. You spend a lot more time doing it. And there's always maybe that sense that it could perhaps go wrong because it's based on these 12- to 15-year-old kids.

Vic You were never the hardest working person in the room. And they never complained. After being in the room with them for five minutes, you felt like you'd never achieved anything in your life!

Rick It's humbling, in the best sense of the word. You raise your standards accordingly.

Emma Did you ever get bored of re-inventing it or resolving some of the problems that maybe you felt you'd already solved?

Rick I must admit, I now know that I don't really need to re-tech it myself. I was very happy when Vic was there. After Vic decided she didn't want to be away from home so much and went to work for ENO, I'm very happy if Rob is there. I'm very happy if Hugh Hamilton, who's now the Australian associate, is there. I'm delighted to come and not sit in the tech, and I'll watch the dress rehearsals and just do a couple of notes, perhaps.

Emma What changed for you to feel comfortable with that?

Rick It's taken a long time because the show is special. And I think lighting is, I always say lighting and sound are the two things that have to be made fresh for each version, you know, that doesn't just come out of a box. I have been at most of the *Billy*s somewhere along the line, more than almost anybody else in the creative team.

Rob I do remember a definite point. Most successful shows go on an arc. You make the show. Then you do the next version where you take everything you've learned and make the version you now know that it needs to be. Then there's a third version where you get to do the polishing and scrubbing. Then it goes on tour, and you suddenly have to start compromising. None of the remaining *Billy*s have the big holes in the floor, for example. Then in America, particularly, it goes on a faster tour where suddenly you have to load it in in eight hours and perform that same night. *Billy* ended up with a company called NETworks, whose speciality is these fast-moving tours. Within the parameters they have to meet, they do them incredibly well. But it means compromises. And I think Rick felt he'd got the show to a point he was really happy with and didn't want to work backwards from there.

Rick One of the problems with *Billy* is it's very expensive to run. In America, where it's not a glamorous sort of show and there's a lot of swearing in it, it doesn't sell as many tickets as we initially had hoped, despite our ten Tony Awards and all that sort of stuff. So, we moved down the theatrical food chain very quickly in America.

Emma How does your mindset have to change, from something that had everything, and you were happy with to something where you had to scale back?

Rick You just have to look at what's strong and where the bang for the buck is. And what are you going to obsess about.

Rob You analyse. You figure out the bits that are really important – so, 'Angry Dance', the important bit is it snaps to red, it doesn't matter so much where that red is coming from. You keep in your mind that yes, you could do this better, but good enough sort of becomes the driving phrase.

The last British tour used that American touring set, but we fought to get back all the really critical bits that had got cut, scenic and lighting, and the show looks infinitely better as a result.

Rick It looks like the full West End show. I would even posit to say it looks better than the West End show, because after having brightened it up on Broadway the way you do, I would go back to see it in London, and I would think, oh, it looks like the school play version of *Billy Elliot*. It felt very dark, and it did feel quite tungsteny a little bit more tungsteny than I remembered. And then, by about a third of the way through it, I just kind of relaxed and said, oh yeah, this is how it was. This is what started it, and now we've maybe got a little bit too good.

Emma How does technology change the way the rig works?

Rob The core of the rig has been the same since Australia, which is more than 15 years now: VL3500 Spots and VL3000 Washes and VL1000 Arcs and Revolutions. Those Mac 600s from London have been all sorts of things over time but have lately settled as Auras, which work really well and are much more reliable. The thing that's changed in the last two versions is all the scrollers have gone away and become Lustrs.

Rick Which is better…

Emma I think what would be really interesting to hear is, over the arc of what is now this production's quite long life, what people have taken away from it and what changes that's made in your career. What you've learnt from it.

Rick The original tech was a very long period, but we had a very good team and we kept ourselves going. And when we were up against it, we solved the problems together. We tried things out. And we knew it was either getting better, or we knew something didn't work and that it had to be made better.

It's been a very wonderful part of my life. And it's brought me in touch with a fantastic team of people around the world. I'm very aware of the support that I've had as a designer from Vic and from Paul and from Chris Barstow, who looked after it in London originally, and all the people at the theatre, and Phil Marfleet, who looked after it for a while, Richard Pacholski, who looked after it in Australia until he sadly passed away. From James, you know, all these people who are just part of that family, who have looked after the show and made it their own and put in improvements, all around the world now.

Paul For me, it was the combination of having a great team, and then it just being this extraordinary show telling this remarkable story with those extraordinary boys. Your hairs standing up on the back of your neck every time you watched it. It's also responsible for the fact that I'm no longer a production electrician. I carried on being a production electrician for a year and a half after this, and I never really enjoyed anything quite as much. The magic had gone, and I just thought – time to go.

Vic Me too! I stopped being a programmer after *Billy*, though I don't think I've ever really realized it before. How could you go any further after this show? It was the best it could possibly be – what a show to go out on.

James That's so interesting because it was the last show I ever did as head of lighting. I never wanted to do another show.

Emma In terms of things which you've taken forward from *Billy*?

Rick I think one of the things I've taken forward, which is something I think maybe I felt even beforehand, is I know that if you're working with a good team and you've got a flexible rig, you do not need lighting sessions where you light an empty stage. I'd rather have my time after I've had people, to fix things.

Rob I think the other really interesting thing has been learning about the different places the show has been. About how the audience react to the show. But also about how the crew interact with it. Japan was amazing: they don't have anybody calling the lighting cues. The person running the lights has their own script with their own cues marked in it, and they just run it themself. And it was amazing.

Rick It completely freaks you out initially.

Rob There are a number of cues in 'Angry Dance' that have always been a cue and a follow-on because there's never been time for the DSM to say it, that we ended up giving to the Japanese operator to run himself. And the show is super-sharp because of that. So, it's really interesting. Also to watch the lighting crew on stage warming up with the cast each day...

Rick I think we're also at that interesting nexus, more than I think costume and set designers, although that's slightly untrue, we're at an interesting pinch point between technology and performance or technology and art or technology and whatever you want to call it.

Rob Though of course you need to protect yourself from when that technology fails. There are whole sequences in the show where there is only one light on, and that's a moving light. And if that isn't working halfway through the show, that scene is going to be in the pitch dark. What Vic set up very early on, which is amazing, is a whole hidden ballet of lights that are set to do the same thing and show up on the console as 'backups'. Then there's a list: if you get to act one, scene three and there's no light on stage, bring up this fader.

The closing moments of *Billy Elliot* – Billy downstage centre, lit only by the lights worn by the miners.

Rick Or you just get the follow spot on and just light them. And that does happen every once in a while.

Emma Last thoughts? Last highlights of the show?

Rick Doing a show about miners, the classic thing is, of course, they've got to have those lights on their heads. And I can remember one of the best moments in the show when we first made it in London was when they all went down on the lift at the back that had been so much work and money to get installed. And I was scared of letting them do it just completely in blackout. So I had a little bit of toplight to give some shape to it. I can remember it was Julian, Stephen's associate, who said, can't we get rid of that other light? Oh, it was only there for rehearsals, I bluffed, and we turned it out.

What you have is one of the great moments of the show – and there are no theatrical lights on whatsoever!

Emma Thank you all so very, very much.

GLOSSARY

ALPD – Association for Lighting Production and Design
An organization for anyone working in entertainment lighting. Descended from the Society of British Theatre Lighting Designers, which in 1961 grew out of the regular, informal lunches held by the pioneers of lighting design at Rules Restaurant in Covent Garden. The current name, adopted in 2022 to replace Association of Lighting Designers, aims to better reflect that creating show lighting involves a wide team of people around the lighting designer.

Arc Light
Type of light source which does not use a filament, but instead relies on a controlled spark jumping between two metal conductors. The name comes from carbon arc, which used carbon rods to control the spark. Gives a very intense light which cannot be dimmed except using mechanical flags. Used predominantly in followspots and moving lights. Now being replaced by **LED** sources.

Areas
Sub-sections of the stage lit individually but in a way where the light can be combined as a **cover**, described using stage terminology such as downstage left (the front of the stage to the left when facing the audience) or upstage right (the rear of the stage to the right when facing the audience), 'upstage' and 'downstage' based on stages that were raked – tilted so lower at the audience side than the rear.

Assistant Lighting Designer
A member of a lighting designer's team, particularly on larger shows. The Assistant is there to provide help as required.

Associate Lighting Designer
A member of a lighting designer's team, particularly on larger shows. An Associate is understood to be able to offer opinions or suggestions to the lighting designer, and to be able to deputize for the lighting designer if required. An Associate will often re-create a lighting design in later productions of a show if the lighting designer is not available.

Backlight
Light from behind. Such light helps separate performers from the background, giving a halo around the figure. May be directly from behind, or angled diagonally, which is known as three-quarter backlight.

Beamlight
A lighting fixture giving a near-parallel beam of light, different from most light sources where the beam gets wider the further you get from the light source. Can be used to simulate the effect of sunlight. Sometimes used as an alternative to the traditional **followspot**. Now often used for dramatic effects in concert lighting.

Birdie
A miniature version of a **Par Can**, perfect for use as a **footlight** or when it is necessary to hide a light in scenery. The name comes from golf, where a birdie is one under par.

Boom
A vertical lighting position standing on the floor supporting lighting fixtures for **crosslight**. Originally just a vertical scaffolding pipe, now sometimes a more structural tower, particularly for touring dance shows.

CAD
Computer Aided Design, here generally taken to mean using a computer to draw a **lighting plan**, rather than the older technique of hand-drawing using pencil, pen and stencils containing symbols for different kinds of lighting **fixtures**.

Glossary

Cans / Comms
A communications system allowing production staff in a theatre to communicate with each other, normally in the form of a headset with microphone (the 'cans') that can be worn while keeping the hands free.

Channel
An individual lighting **fixture** or set of lighting fixtures plugged so that they operate together in a lighting **rig**, which most lighting **consoles** can only identify as a number rather than a name. A lighting designer will create channel numbering systems to allow them to work quickly with combinations of lights.

Chinagraph
A pencil using hardened wax, making it able to be used to label glossy surfaces such as lighting **gels**, allowing them to be identified in use or when stored for later re-use.

Cinemoid
An early type of lighting colour filter (**gel**) made by **Strand Electric** as a more robust, fireproof replacement for the earlier filters made from gelatine.

Clay Paky
A pioneering manufacturer of moving lights. Creator of the Knight of Illumination Awards for lighting design, for which each winner received a custom, hand-crafted sword!

Colour Temperature
A way of measuring or describing the 'whiteness' of light. A lower colour temperature is a warmer light. A traditional **tungsten** domestic light bulb has a colour temperature of about 2400 K, daylight on an overcast day of about 6500 K.

Console (Desk)
A device used to control the lighting **fixtures** in a show. Originally manually operated mechanical devices, consoles are now computerized. They store combinations of **channels** at different levels and the settings for **moving lights** into individual looks called **cues**, and then play them back in specified times. May now just be software running on a laptop rather than specific hardware. Also called lighting desks. Often operated by specialist **programmers**.

Conventional
A lighting **fixture** that must be manually configured, requiring an **electrician** to access it to **focus** it. Sometimes called generics. Still in common use because of their low cost and ready availability.

Cover (General Cover)
A system of lighting fixtures positioned and **focused** each to light a different **area** of the stage, but which when used together provide an even wash of light across the whole stage. Different covers might come from different directions – a 'front' cover or a 'high side' cover, or might be in different colours – the 'warm' cover vs the 'cool' cover.

Creative Team
The group of people, sometimes abbreviated to the 'creatives', who conceive the physical production of a show, including a show's **director** and **designers**.

Crosslight (Sidelight)
Light from the side of a stage **focused** across the stage. Sidelight from different heights gives different effects, with both 'head high' lighting and 'shin' lighting (the lighting fixture positioned as low as possible) able to light a performer without lighting the floor or scenery, giving a light that is invisible until a performer steps in to it and then makes them the brightest, most dominant thing on stage. Originating in dance lighting, these crosslight, sometimes called sidelight, techniques are now often used in lighting drama.

Cue
Used interchangeably to mean one individual lighting look – a combination of different lights at different levels to create one 'picture' on stage – and the transition between one lighting look and another. Some **consoles** let cues be broken into parts with separate timing, or allow separate times to be assigned to each channel, to help shape these transitions.

Cue Synopsis
A lighting designer's breakdown of the points in a show where they believe a lighting change is required, whether as called for by the script, as required for the movement of scenery or performers, to punctuate the show, to shift the mood on stage or for any other reason.

Glossary

Cyc
Short for cyclorama; a representation of the sky on-stage, created using a plain or painted cloth or plastic material or sometimes created from plaster as a permanent part of a stage. May be lit from the front and/or rear, top and/or bottom (from a **groundrow**) depending on the cyc's material and the desired effect.

Designer
The person (usually an individual, sometimes a team) tasked with creating each element of a show. The most common design elements in a theatre production are the set/scenic design, the costume design (these two roles sometimes combined), the lighting design, the video/projection design and the sound design.

Dimmer
The electronic device allowing the brightness of a traditional tungsten lighting fixture to be controlled remotely. Depending on its size, a theatre may have tens or hundreds of dimmers. Touring shows may bring their own portable systems. New **moving light** and **LED** fixtures do not need external dimmers as they have their own internal dimming electronics.

Director
The person responsible for the overall creation of a stage production, from picking the show to casting the performers to leading the **creative team** to running rehearsals, to delivering a show onto the stage and to an audience.

DSM – Deputy Stage Manager
In British working practice, the person with direct responsibility for running a production during each performance, following through a script marked up with every action and cue point and calling the cues to each department at the correct moment. In America, the Production Stage Manager also takes on this task. Outside theatre, this role is called the show caller. In some countries, each department follows their own script and takes their own cues.

Electrician
People who actually bring a designer's show lighting to life, rigging and cabling the lights to give a complete working system. Sometimes called lighting technicians or lighting crew.

Eos
A family of computer lighting **consoles** manufactured by **ETC** from 2006 onwards, which has become the de-facto standard lighting control for theatre productions in many parts of the world.

ETC
Electronic Theatre Controls: a US-based manufacturer of lighting equipment founded by the late Fred Foster in 1975. The company's products are now the standards in most parts of the world.

Fixture
A lighting instrument designed to project a controllable beam of light. Depending on the type of fixture – **spotlight, Fresnel, washlight, flood** – the beam's size and shape can be adjusted. A lighting design will use many fixtures each with different purposes within the overall design.

Flood
A lighting **fixture** giving a wide but not very controllable spread of light, usually – but not always – used for evenly lighting large areas such as **cycloramas** or other painted cloths.

Fluorescent
A light source which uses electricity to energize a gas which then illuminates a phosphor coating on the inside surface of the lamp to create light. Most familiar as the fluorescent tube, which gives a wide coverage of light from a compact source.

Flying
Raising or lowering items in a theatre. May be by pulling directly on ropes (hemp flying), adding weight to balance the weight of the items to be raised (counterweight flying) or motorized in various ways. In theatre productions, lights will normally be hung on fly bars lowered to stage level before being flown out to their correct working height.

Followspot
A light used to highlight a performer, the light beam moving around the stage with that performer, most obviously as a hard-edged white circle of light. Followspots are traditionally manually controlled by

Glossary

an operator positioned at the light, though systems that have an operator controlling the light remotely or even have **moving lights** automatically following transmitters worn by performers are now available.

Focus
How any given lighting **fixture** is set: where its beam of light is set to land, what size the light is, what its edge looks like (sharp or soft-edged), the shape of the light if framing shutters have been used to alter it from a round shape, whether a **gobo** has been installed to project a pattern. Setting the light is described as focusing. For **conventional** lights, each light will have to be set by an electrician by hand. For **moving lights** the lights can be adjusted remotely at any time by the **programmer** from the lighting **console**.

Footlight
Lights rigged along the front edge of a stage providing light up into a performer, potentially also creating large, dramatic shadows of them on scenery behind them.

Fresnel
A lighting **fixture** creating a soft-edge wash of light by using a stepped Fresnel lens. The beam of light from a Fresnel can be controlled using barndoors – movable flaps attached to the front of the fixture that allow some degree of beam shaping.

Fringe
Small-scale theatre productions, often in unusual spaces not originally created for performance, and usually with limited equipment and budgets. Where many theatre careers begin . . .

Frontlight
Light directed onto a performer from the direction of the audience, either straight in, or in the practice first described by Stanley McCandless in his pioneering 1932 book **A Method of Lighting the Stage**, from 45 degrees to either side of the performer, or indeed at any other angles a designer prefers or a theatre's architecture allows.

Gel
Coloured plastic filters inserted into the front of lighting **fixtures** to colour the light coming from the fixture. Designers can choose from hundreds of colours using swatch books from manufacturers such as Lee, Rosco and GAM, the gels identified by numbers such as Lee 201 (a very pale blue tint) or Rosco 26 (primary red). The name is a legacy of early filters which used gelatine as a base material rather than today's heat-resistant plastics.

Generics
See **Conventional**.

GLP
German Light Products: Manufacturer of lighting fixtures, notably the X4 Bar LED **light curtain**.

Gobo
A disc usually made of metal containing a cut out pattern or image, which when inserted into a **profile spot** will cause that pattern to be projected onto the stage. Has many uses, the effect of light through foliage being just one.

Groundrow
Lights positioned at the bottom of a **cyc** to light it upwards. The word is also used to describe a low scenic cutout placed in front of these lights to conceal them.

Haze
A fine smoke created using a special fluid heated in a specialist machine and, ideally, distributed evenly across the stage, which allows light which is normally invisible until it hits something to be seen in the air. Usually under the control of the lighting team.

Hire Company (Rental Company)
Supplier which can rent lighting equipment to theatre productions – whether a few extra fixtures for a theatre that has its own stock or the complete rig to a commercial production where the producer doesn't want (or doesn't have the cashflow) to purchase all the equipment required – which may be millions of pounds worth for a musical. In effect, rental companies are eco-friendly operations recycling lighting equipment between shows!

Glossary

House Lights
The lighting system that illuminates an auditorium as an audience enter. Usually, though not always, provided by the theatre and so not part of a designer's lighting rig, though they will decide on the fade point and time so critical for establishing the start of a show.

Incandescent
See **tungsten**.

Ladders
A vertical lighting position to hold lighting **fixtures** used for **crosslight**, suspended from above and so leaving the stage space beneath clear, usually to allow scenery on and off stage, as compared to a **boom** which rests on the stage. Named for their resemblance to traditional ladders, which are also used in theatre.

LED
Light Emitting Diode technology is increasingly replacing **tungsten** as the standard light source in entertainment (and other) lighting fixtures. LED fixtures can contain a white LED, mimicking the single-colour behaviour of a tungsten fixture, or multiple colours of LEDs allowing different colours to be mixed under the control of the lighting **console**. The simplest fixtures will use just red, green and blue sources. More complex fixtures will use seven or eight colours of LEDs to allow the creation of richer colours and more subtle colour variations.

Light Curtain
A lighting fixture creating an intense sheet of parallel light. When used with **haze** in the air, it can create an apparently solid wall of light through which performers can appear or disappear. Pioneered by the Czech designer Josef Svoboda and later a signature of lighting designer David Hersey on shows such as **Les Misérables**.

Lighting Desk
See **Console**

Lighting Plan
The technical drawing or drawings showing the location and configuration of all of the lighting **fixtures** in a lighting **rig** to **scale**. Producing the lighting plan may be delegated to an **associate** or **assistant** on large shows. For **rep** theatres with a permanently installed rig, the venue team will maintain the plan. In America, known as the light plot.

Lustr
A family of LED lighting **fixtures** made by **ETC**, which established seven and now eight colours of LEDs, rather than the more usual three or four, to create a higher quality of light. With a form familiar from the **tungsten Source Four** spotlight and a colour system integrated with the **Eos** console allowing colours to be selected using familiar gel numbers, the Lustr won over many lighting designers who had been resisting using LED fixtures in their work.

LX
Commonly used abbreviation for 'lighting' or 'electrics' in reference to lighting: 'lx plan', 'lx session', 'lx desk'.

Magic Sheets
A graphical representation of the fixtures in a lighting **rig** by purpose or function, rather than by location as in a lighting **plan**. Originally a paper-based tool favoured by American lighting designers, the term is now also used to describe the ability to create custom graphical layouts in a lighting **console**.

MIDI
A protocol originally designed for connecting together synthesizers, now used to connect all kinds of performance equipment – for example, allowing a sound effect such as thunder to trigger a corresponding lighting cue.

Modelbox
The **scale** model of a set used by a scenic designer to present their design for a show. In early discussions, this will be a 'white card' model showing the overall structure but without details or finishes. The final modelbox will be a precise, highly-detailed presentation that will ultimately be used as a reference by those building the full-size version. Still preferred by many to 3D CAD or virtual reality alternatives.

Glossary

Moving Light
A lighting **fixture** where functions of the light are motorized to allow them to be controlled remotely from the lighting **console**, with no need to physically access the light once it is rigged, and with the light able to be used for many different purposes during the show. Sometimes called automated lights, or Vari-Lites from the first brand to successfully commercialize this type of product.

Paperwork
A collective term describing all of the information required to specify a lighting rig for a show and then, once the lighting has been created, to allow a show to be maintained over its run or re-created in future versions. It will include at least a **lighting plan**.

Par Can
A simple lighting fixture that consists of a sealed, fixed-beam 'par' lamp mounted inside an aluminium 'can'. Popularized originally by rock-and-roll lighting for its high light output, low weight and ruggedness for touring.

Patt Numbers
In its heyday, **Strand Electric** identified its lighting **fixture** types using a 'pattern' or 'Patt' number, the most famous being the Patt 23 baby spotlight. Though long out of production, examples are still found in many theatres; they are therefore the tools currently active lighting designers have grown up with.

Plotting / Plotting Session
The process of creating each lighting look or **cue** on stage: turning on different combinations of lights and balancing them at different levels to create the overall stage pictures. In the days of manual lighting **consoles**, plotting would often take place overnight because of the time to manually write down – 'plot' – the level of each light. Now designers often prefer to plot during **technical rehearsals**, with the performers on stage.

Practicals
Non-theatrical lighting fixtures or light sources used on stage as part of a scenic design: the bedside light in the bedroom scene, the bare light bulb in the prison scene. These fixtures will still be connected to a **dimmer** and controlled by the **lighting console**, even when it looks like they're being switched on and off by the performers.

Press Night (First Night / Opening Night)
The night a show officially opens: the press are invited to review the show, and the lighting designer's work is finished!

Previews
Early public performances of a show where the understanding is that the audience pay a lower ticket price, in return accepting they may not be seeing the finished version of the show. Previews give the creative team a chance to judge how an audience react to a show and make changes accordingly.

Pre-Visualization
Creating lighting states in advance using a detailed computer model of the scenery and lighting **rig** connected to the lighting **console**. Increasingly this kind of functionality is starting to be built into the lighting **consoles** themselves.

Production Desk (US: Tech Table)
Temporary work spaces created in theatre auditoria, either by laying planks of wood over the seats or, on bigger shows, by removing groups of seats to create more robust structures with room for more comfortable seating than perching on the up-turned theatre seat. A designer's home during the technical rehearsal period – and since it's where they light a show from, arguably the best place to then watch the show from.

Production Electrician
The head of the team of **electricians** who install a show's lighting; on commercial shows, they are usually employed on a production-by-production basis. On some musicals, all of the electricians are now termed production electricians, with the head of the team called the senior production electrician. In theatres with permanent staff, the chief electrician fills this role.

Glossary

Production Manager
The person ultimately responsible for delivering all of the technical elements of the show to the stage, ideally within budget, and so almost certainly, the most demanding job behind the scenes in theatre.

Production Meeting
Regular meetings of all those involved in mounting a show to ensure co-ordination between all of the different department and design elements.

Profile Spot (US: Ellipsoidal spot)
The entertainment lighting **fixture** which gives the most controllable beam of light: beam size, sharp or soft edge, straight edges using adjustable framing shutters, or pattern projection by installing a **gobo**. In America sometimes called an ellipsoidal, after the shape of the reflector, or a Leko, after one of the first US products of this type. The **Source Four** is the most common fixture of this type today.

Programmer
Though there has always been a 'board op' running the lighting console, the rise of **moving lights** led to an increasingly specialist role providing the interface and translation between the vision in a designer's mind and the practicalities of the lighting fixtures and control system. Known as the Vari-Lite programmer or moving light programmer, as consoles integrated the control of **conventional** and **moving lights** the job title became lighting programmer, now often just programmer.

Prompt Copy
The script used by a **DSM** or show caller, the name is taken from the original role of this script to allow an actor to be 'prompted' if they forgot a line. Sometimes called the prompt script, prompt book, book or calling script.

Rehearsal Room
A location away from the stage (and, in a commercial production, usually away from the theatre in which the show will be performed) where the director and cast work together to create the show. Rehearsal rooms usually have few or no technical facilities and so do not allow the addition of most of the technical elements to a show during the rehearsal process.

Rep
Theatre scheduling where different shows are performed in the theatre on different days, from a catalogue of shows which may not be seen for some time, then brought back onto the stage at a later date. Quite different from the commercial model of performing the same show in the same theatre each night.

Re-Lighter
Person tasked with re-creating the lighting for a show, most usually on a tour where they will be responsible for adapting the lighting rig to each new venue then focusing the lights and making any small changes required.

Rig
The set of lighting **fixtures** used to light a particular show. A lighting rig may be designed just for a particular production, or it may be a more permanently installed, versatile set of equipment in a theatre working in a **rep** style.

Robert Juliat
French manufacturer of lighting fixtures, including followspots and versatile high-output zoom **profile spots**, which are popular in large opera houses and rep theatres.

Scale
A proportionally smaller – 'scaled down' – representation of something, in theatre including set plans, set models and lighting plans. 1:25 and 1:50 scales provide a good balance of details and size for most theatre productions with metric drawings; in the US the equivalents are 1:24 (1/2" = 1') and 1:48 (1/4" = 1').

Scroller
A device created to add the ability to change the colour from a **conventional** lighting fixture. Two motorized rollers tensioned a scroll made of individual cuts of coloured gel taped together. Now largely superseded by **LED** lighting fixtures.

Glossary

Show Caller
See **DSM**.

Showfile
The data file from a computerized **lighting console**. Particularly when using colour-changing and moving fixtures, this increasingly becomes the only complete record of how a show is lit, and so the key element when re-creating the same production elsewhere.

Site Specific
Shows created in non-theatrical spaces which use that space as part of their design so that show and venue become deeply interlinked (which of course makes it harder to then re-locate that show to a different venue if it is a hit!).

Smoke
A theatrical effect created by using specialist smoke machines to heat a custom fluid to create a visible smoke on stage. Related to **haze**, and like that, generally under the control of the lighting team.

Source Four
The most common theatrical spotlight in use today. Sold by **ETC**. Revolutionary on its 1992 launch for using just 575 W of power yet being brighter than rivals using 750 W or even 1000 W. The traditional tungsten version is still in production, joined by the LED **Lustr** variants.

Special
A lighting **fixture** set for one very precise moment or effect in a show. Contrast with **wash**.

Spot (moving light)
Moving lights which can give a precisely controllable beam of light able to be set to have a very sharp edge if required, and able to project patterns of light by setting the fixture to have a **gobo** in its beam or sometimes cutting sides of the beam using motorized shutters. The automated equivalent of a **profile spot**.

Stage Management
In theatre, the team of people who are in overall control of the backstage elements of a production. In British practice led by a Stage Manager or sometimes Company Stage Manager, with the **DSM** and then one or more Assistant Stage Managers. In American practice the Production Stage Manager (PSM) heads the team while also taking on the work of the DSM.

Strand Electric / Strand Lighting
A pioneer in and leading manufacturer of stage lighting across the world for much of the twentieth century. Strand equipment can still be found in theatres everywhere. The company also left behind a unique record of lighting and theatre history via its **Tabs** magazine.

Technical Rehearsal (Tech)
The point at which all of the elements of a show, from the actors' performances to the scenery, costumes, lighting, sound, video and other elements, are assembled into a finished show. It will begin after the fit-up or load-in, when the scenery is built and the lights are installed, and lead up to dress rehearsals, when the performance is run without an audience, previews performed to an audience, and then an opening night.

Timecode
A way of synchronizing devices to the nearest 30th of a second. In lighting, it allows complex cue sequences to be precisely triggered alongside, most commonly, a pre-recorded soundtrack, especially sequences with so many cues it would be impossible for a **DSM** to call. Though less useful for live shows where an actor might vary their timing every day…

Tungsten
A light source where the light is created by applying electricity to a metal (tungsten) filament encased in a sealed glass envelope – in effect, controlled fire and so a miniature version of the sun, the light source we are most familiar with. Rapidly being outlawed on ecological grounds because of their relative inefficiency and falling out of production as a result, replaced by notionally more efficient (and always more expensive) LED sources. Sometimes called incandescent.

Wash
    Lighting **fixtures** set to blend together to give an even coverage of light across the stage, able to be used individually to illuminate a particular **area** or in combinations to light larger areas. Contrast with **special**.

Wash (moving light)
    Moving lights which give soft-edged beams of lights designed to be blended together into larger areas of light. The automated equivalent of a **Fresnel**.

Workshop
    Experimental rehearsals leading to private or invited-audience-only performances, usually with little or no technical provision, used to experiment with potential new shows before committing them to full-scale new productions.

ACKNOWLEDGEMENTS

We'd both like to express our undying gratitude and thanks to:

- Everyone interviewed for this book. All those you've read here, of course. But also a number of other people in lighting roles beyond lighting design, who didn't make it here as the focus of this book shifted – but who will be a key part of the follow-up volume…
- All of the photographers whose work features here, the yang to the lighting designer's ying, and the providers of the only long-term record of our ephemeral work.
- All of the other lighting designers out there. Your work is a constant inspiration, your stories would all be just as interesting and we wish we had room to tell them all.
- Joshua Carr, there at the beginning of the journey and a staunch supporter all along the way.
- The ALPD, for letting us call out to their membership for information and inspiration.
- Helen Mumby at The Soho Agency for support, encouragement and all those things agents do!
- Anna Brewer and Aanchal Vij at Bloomsbury, for support, encouragement and all those things editors do, particularly understanding that lighting works best when shown in colour! Sandra Creaser, copyeditor extraordinaire, uncomplaining at having to listen to two opinions, happy to argue about every comma. And all of the design and production team who make mere words into an actual book.
- And The Society for Theatre Research, who, in the closing stages when we thought we wouldn't be able to show the work of the designers as we'd imagined, awarded us a grant that let us do so.

Then from Emma:

- For the wonderful support of my family, from my parents, who believed in allowing me to follow my dreams, to Dom and Imogen, who support me through thick and thin, and to Elliot, our greyhound. Thank you!

And from Rob:

- This is for my gang: Mary, Emily, Ben and Leo, who have no idea what I've been toiling away at but should know everything I do, I do for them. And Lexi, the lockdown hound, whose late-night puppy eyes drag me away from more fiddling with punctuation!

ABOUT THE AUTHORS

Emma Chapman

Emma discovered theatre at boarding school, falling into all of the backstage roles when the other students wanted to be performers – but in doing so, very much discovering her tribe. This led her to the Bristol Old Vic Theatre School, officially taking their Stage Management and Technical Theatre course, but actually finding a love of lighting that ultimately fuelled her career.

From Bristol she joined the Salisbury Playhouse as an assistant electrician under Peter Hunter, before venturing out as a freelance lighting designer, some of her career highlights include Katori Hall's Olivier Award-winning *The Mountaintop*, *Kiss Me Kate* at the Théâtre du Châtelet in Paris, *Ghost Quartet*, the opening production at the Boulevard Theatre in London, a new musical of *The Third Man* at the Menier Chocolate Factory, and *The Lion* at the Southwark Playhouse and then touring the USA.

Emma's passion for lighting has always been matched by a passion for innovation. It was this that led her to be part of the trio, alongside Lucy Osborne and Howard Eaton, who designed and realized the rapidly relocatable touring theatre Roundabout for Paines Plough, which won the Theatre Building of the Year in the 2015 Stage Awards. This led the trio to found studio three sixty and develop a follow-up venue, The Mix, currently providing a performance space for Theatr Clwyd as their theatre undergoes a major refurbishment.

Emma is also a founding member of the Association for Lighting Production and Design's Wellbeing Group, and a passionate advocate for reducing the stigma around mental health.

Between all of those things and interviewing lighting designers for this book, she spends time with her husband, Dominic, and daughter, Imogen.

www.emmachapman.co.uk

About the Authors

Rob Halliday

Rob began lighting at school and then at the National Youth Theatre almost thirty-five years ago, and hasn't stopped yet.

In that time he has lit shows of his own, and programmed the lighting, sometimes also serving as associate lighting designer, for many other designers. His favourite show of his own is *Tree of Codes*, which he created at the Manchester Festival in 2015 with Wayne McGregor, Olafur Eliasson and Jamie xx and which has since been seen around the world. Of shows with others, highlights include *Les Misérables* with David Hersey and *Billy Elliot* with Rick Fisher.

Somewhere along the way, Rob started writing about lighting and technical production, his work appearing in publications including *The Stage*, *Lighting Dimensions*, *Live Design*, *Theatre Crafts*, Lighting & Sound America and, most frequently, *Light+Sound International*. Many of those articles have been collected together in the *Entertainment In Production* books; others can be found online.

He has also spoken about lighting at numerous drama schools and events around the world, including several appearances at the Showlight lighting symposium, has acted as lighting consultant to a number of pioneering new theatres including Leicester's Curve, Doncaster's CAST and Chester's Storyhouse, and has helped represent entertainment lighting in discussions about lighting regulation with the EU and UK Governments.

Between all those things, he's happy to hang out with his wife, Mary (when she's not off working on shows of her own!), and kids, Emily, Ben and Leo.

www.robhalliday.com

INDEX

Aberg, Maria 92
ACL – Aircraft landing lights (Aeros) 193
Acting 13
Actor 8, 13, 14, 24, 34, 35, 36, 40, 41, 47, 51, 75, 77, 80, 106, 113, 116, 120, 131, 133, 135, 137, 148, 149, 150, 151, 163, 168, 189, 194, 195, 196, 197, 207, 216, 223, 224
Agent 94, 112
Aladdin ix, 118
Albertina Museum, Vienna 176
ALD – see also ALPD 112
Aldwych Theatre, London 162
A-level 100, 113, 128, 188
Almeida Theatre, London 9, 72
ALPD 25, 59, 111, 112, 187, 217
Amargo, Rafael 146
Amateur dramatics 85, 86, 188
America 6, 15, 16, 72, 77, 122, 138, 171, 191, 213, 219, 221, 223
American Ballet Theatre, USA 125
American Utopia 175
Amies, Gerry 114
Anatol 73
Anderson, Laurie 175
Anderson, Paul 25
Ando, Tadao 102
An Inspector Calls viii, 59, 67, 68, 71, 72
Appia, Adolphe 8
Apprenticeship 114, 189
Arabian Nights 184
Arblaster, Anthony 145
Arc (discharge) 6, 166, 193, 204, 213, 214, 217
Architect 102
Architectural lighting 101
Architecture 89
Arcola Theatre, London 73
Arditti, Paul 34, 39, 40, 203, 210
Area cover 151, 154, 217, 218
Ariadne in Naxos 117
Aristocrats 73
Art 15, 17, 20, 49, 60, 61, 65, 85, 86, 89, 100, 102, 103, 116, 117, 124, 128, 158, 173, 174, 175, 176, 190, 199
Art exhibitions 61, 117, 200
Artist 15, 56, 61, 64, 86, 92, 102, 103, 106, 128, 159, 174, 180
Arts Threshold 19
Ashford, Rob 96
Ashmore, Catherine ix, 169

Assistant lighting designer 47, 69, 95, 114, 116, 158, 167, 202, 217, 221
Assistant Stage Manager 48, 224
Associate lighting designer 13, 16, 69, 114, 116, 136, 171, 202, 207, 213, 217, 221
Audience 8, 13, 16, 17, 24, 26, 27, 28, 40, 41, 50, 53, 55, 67, 75, 80, 81, 97, 108, 122, 135, 153, 154, 155, 167, 168, 184, 189, 192, 193, 197, 205, 206, 212, 216, 217, 219, 220, 222, 224, 225
Austin, Neil viii, 5, 9, 11, 95
Australia 191, 214
AutoCAD 204
Automated light (moving light) 222
Automation 12, 13, 208

Backcloth 67, 115
Backlight 8, 14, 21, 27, 62, 106, 116, 120, 124, 134, 136, 151, 152, 154, 163, 207, 210, 217
Backup Tech 59
Ballet 49, 101, 111, 113, 118, 121, 167, 206, 208
Barcelona, Spain 121, 122
Barn Theatre (at Rose Bruford), London 100
Barrow Street Theatre, New York 135
Barry Lyndon 61
Barstow, Chris 214
Batsheva Ensemble, Israel 173
Battersea Arts Centre 6
Bausch, Pina 175, 208
Beamlight 12, 217
Bechtler, Hildegard 190
Becoming Sheas 101
Bennett, Ned 105
Benn, Roanna 47
Benson, Keith 114
Beyond The Beautiful Forevers 54
Bhatia, Milli 109
Billington, Ken 1
Billy Budd 45
Billy Elliot ix, 45, 59, 66, 69, 71, 202, 203, 204, 207, 208, 210, 211, 212, 213, 214, 215
Billy Elliot Team 201
Binkley, Howell 53
Bintley, Sir David 118
Bird, Dick 118
Birdies 38, 130, 131, 134, 135, 136, 137, 138, 160, 217
Birmingham Royal Ballet 118
Björk 157
Blane, Sue 118
Board op 223

Index

Bologna, Italy 97
Boom 71, 116, 151, 200, 217, 221
Boomtown Festival 101
Boritt, Beowulf 1
Boswell, Laurence 148
Bourne, Matthew 45, 53, 57, 59, 63
Boyle, Danny 168, 169
Branagh, Kenneth 17, 85, 95, 96
Brenner, Marc viii, 34, 79
Bretton Hall 31
Bridge, Andrew 114
British Council 142
Britten, Benjamin 145
Broadcast performances 49, 123
Broadway, New York 12, 16, 19, 65, 72, 85, 87, 202, 214
Brotherston, Lez 63
Brüggen, Frans 146
Bryan, Robert 114
Buckhurst, Bill 130
Budget 8, 17, 25, 39, 57, 65, 78, 94, 115, 130, 134, 145, 152, 162, 192, 193, 203
Buether, Miriam 38, 40
Bury, John 114
Bush Theatre, London viii, ix, 60, 73, 79, 177
Byrne, David 175

Cabaret Circus 101
Cairo, Egypt 183
Caldwell, Finn 50
Calico Museum of Textiles, India 141
Campbell, Jim 175
Candles 118, 120, 130, 133, 134, 137
Cans (communication headsets) 15, 24, 33, 116, 165, 175, 218
Capture (pre-visualisation software) 192, 193
Caravaggio 61, 117
Car Cemetery 76
Carpentry 114
Carr & Angier 202
Carr, Joshua 2
Carson, Heather 175
Carter, Lucy 181
Castellucci, Romeo 175
Cats 48
Ceilings 13, 21, 32, 33, 38, 39, 40, 41, 62, 76, 115, 159, 168, 170, 182, 192
Centrelight 151, 154
Centreline 152
Changing Destiny 173
Channel 218
Charcoalblue 202
Châtelet Theatre, Paris 64, 70
Chelsea College of Arts, London 85, 86
Chief Electrician 175, 222
Children of the Sun 18
China 97
Chinagraph 149, 218

Chivers, Natasha viii, 19, 22, 28
Choreographer 1, 9, 13, 22, 24, 55, 63, 75, 78, 82, 87, 115, 118, 123, 144, 146, 162, 167, 177, 181, 209, 210
Choreography 88, 133, 175, 181, 196, 210
Christie, Bunny 9, 18, 55
Christophers, Harry 190
Cinderella 124
Cinemoid (Strand) 52 149, 218
Circus 101
Clarke, Ed 169
Clark, Jon viii, 31, 34, 40
Clay Paky 218
Clayton, Linda 158
Clayton, Tim 190
Cockpit Theatre, London 113
Co-design 171
Collaboration 7, 8, 9, 12, 13, 14, 18, 21, 28, 29, 45, 55, 62, 64, 86, 92, 93, 94, 108, 131, 133, 152, 158, 168, 176, 177, 178, 191
ColorForce (ChromaQ) 39
Colour 6, 7, 9, 10, 12, 16, 17, 23, 24, 26, 27, 33, 35, 52, 53, 66, 67, 75, 80, 81, 82, 83, 88, 89, 90, 91, 92, 94, 95, 97, 99, 102, 103, 105, 115, 116, 117, 118, 120, 128, 130, 131, 132, 134, 138, 141, 145, 147, 148, 149, 159, 160, 163, 164, 165, 166, 170, 176, 178, 179, 180, 181, 182, 183, 184, 185, 192, 193, 194, 195, 196, 204, 208, 209, 210, 218, 220, 221, 223, 224, 227
Colour libraries 7
Colour path 120, 185
Colour shift 6
Colour temperature 26, 33, 35, 137, 218
Colour wheel 209
Commercial theatre 65, 199
Company viii, 6, 8, 9, 14, 17, 220
Company Stage Manager 224
Composer 105, 179, 198
Computer Aided Design (CAD) 204, 217, 221
Concert touring 157, 166, 167, 171, 175, 191, 222
Conductor 144
Constable, Paule viii, 31, 45, 47, 50, 53, 74, 80, 107, 134, 138, 158
Contemporary dance 34, 159, 166, 175, 181
Conventional 218, 220, 223
Cooke, Dominic 55
Corps de ballet 123
Cosi Fan Tutti 49, 149
Costume 7, 8, 13, 16, 27, 74, 106, 178, 185, 194
Costume design 13, 210
Costume designer 1, 7, 8, 11, 13, 16, 22, 40, 49, 50, 87, 118, 169, 216, 218, 219
Costumes 88, 89, 91, 131, 224
Cover 218
Craig, Edward Gordon 8
Crazy For You 1
Creager, Jessica 13, 136
Creative team 218

232

Crew 13, 16, 69, 70, 71, 72, 100, 101, 197, 199, 206, 216, 219
Crewdson, Gregory 24, 61
Crimp, Martin 9
Crosslight (sidelight) 53, 89, 91, 150, 151, 152, 197, 205, 217, 218, 221
Crowley, Bob 34
Crucible Theatre, Sheffield 7, 88
Cubist painting 154
Cue 218, 222
Cues 14, 36, 68, 78, 88, 92, 160, 195
Cue sheet 20, 31, 51, 68, 79, 121, 142, 160, 178, 195, 207
Cue synopsis 121, 195, 207, 218
Cue time 120, 123
Cumming, Alan 28
Cummiskey, Stephen ix, 190
Cyclorama (cyc) 112, 120, 149, 219, 220

Daldry, Stephen ix, 31, 34, 38, 40, 41, 59, 66, 68, 202, 207, 209, 210, 212, 216
Dance 23, 24, 31, 67, 73, 77, 83, 101, 121, 157, 170, 173, 181, 185, 205, 206, 208, 209, 217, 218
Dance of Death 73
Daniels, Ron 113
Danish National Opera, Denmark 73, 121
Darling, Peter 209, 210
Davies, Howard 18
Davis, Andi 145
Davis, Fly 50
Day-Lewis, Daniel 113
Deamer, Bill 55
Death of England: Delroy 173
Dennis, George 79, 179
Denton, Daniel 177
Deputy Stage Manager (DSM) 13, 14, 15, 20, 36, 51, 79, 88, 93, 105, 167, 195, 216, 219, 223, 224
Designers 60, 219
Desire (ETC) 152
DIALux 101
Dickinson, Ian 9, 50
Dick Whittington 99
Digital Light Curtain (DLC) 11
Dimmer 219
Director 1, 5, 6, 7, 8, 9, 11, 13, 14, 15, 17, 19, 20, 21, 22, 23, 24, 25, 26, 28, 31, 32, 34, 35, 36, 37, 38, 40, 41, 47, 49, 50, 54, 55, 59, 60, 61, 63, 64, 66, 68, 71, 73, 74, 75, 78, 79, 81, 82, 85, 86, 87, 90, 92, 93, 95, 96, 99, 100, 101, 104, 105, 106, 107, 109, 113, 115, 116, 117, 120, 121, 122, 124, 128, 129, 130, 135, 138, 144, 146, 147, 148, 153, 159, 160, 162, 163, 165, 166, 168, 169, 177, 178, 179, 180, 181, 189, 190, 191, 192, 193, 194, 195, 196, 197, 198, 200, 203, 210, 218, 219, 223
Director of movement 169
Donmar Warehouse, London 5, 72, 73
Dorfman Theatre (at the National Theatre) 50
Drama 46, 73, 100, 111, 113, 115, 121, 128, 146, 173, 174, 218

Drama Desk Awards 19
Drama school 100, 114, 134, 138, 142, 146, 188
Dress Rehearsal 81, 92, 93, 153, 213, 224
Duke, Ben 173, 177
Duncan, Isadora 128
Dunn, Nina 190
DV8 47
Dyslexia 188, 189

Ear for Eye 54
Eaton, Howard 114
Edinburgh Festival 202
Effects (chases) 88, 106, 162, 164, 175
Eglin, Morgan ix, 99
Electricians 5, 9, 16, 60, 65, 71, 72, 78, 97, 111, 114, 115, 116, 158, 168, 173, 174, 200, 218, 219, 220, 222
Electronic Theatre Controls (ETC) 7, 100, 219, 221, 224
Elerian, Omar 173, 177
Eliasson, Olafur 102
Elliott, Marianne 9
Encore (Martin) 39
English National Opera (ENO) 45, 114, 202, 213
English Shakespeare Company (ESC) 15
English Touring Theatre (ETT) 105, 160
Eos lighting console (ETC) 78, 88, 122, 164, 219, 221
Equity card 114
Equus ix, 99, 105, 108
Europe 38, 45, 70, 97, 111, 122, 142, 173, 183

Farncombe, James 157
Featherstone, Vicky 21, 28
Ferguson, Matthew ix, 111
Festivals 47, 99, 101
Figueiredo, Miguel 182
Film 56, 61, 76, 80, 90, 102, 104, 105, 117, 132, 149, 174, 175, 190, 208
Film editor 80
Finborough Theatre, London 95
First night 222
Fisher, Rick viii, 59, 63, 68, 112, 136, 202, 204, 206, 210, 212, 213
Fit-up (load-in) 224
500-Series console (Strand) 95, 211
Fixture 217, 218, 219, 220, 221, 222, 223, 224, 225
Flavin, Dan 90
Fleischle, Anna 22
Floodlight 14, 41, 132, 133, 135, 219
Florence, Italy 122
Fluorescent 27, 39, 42, 53, 131, 135, 137, 170, 219
Flying 219
  Flying – counterweight 219
  Flying – hemp 219
  Flying – motorised 219
Flyman 5, 15, 209
Focus 16, 21, 36, 41, 42, 60, 69, 77, 97, 102, 107, 115, 121, 122, 124, 136, 145, 163, 166, 167, 175, 195, 197, 199, 207, 208, 218, 220, 223

Index

Focus magazine 111, 112
FocusTrack 212
Follies viii, 54, 55
Followspot 12, 40, 88, 89, 91, 93, 121, 123, 150, 174, 205, 206, 217, 219, 223
Followspot operator 16
Footlights 27, 167, 217, 220
Foster, Fred 219
France 42, 122, 223
Frankenstein ix, 157, 168, 169, 197, 198
Franklin, Paul 202, 204, 214
Franks, Elliot ix, 146
Frantic Assembly 19
Freelancers Make Theatre Work 45
Fresnels 15, 16, 38, 39, 41, 122, 132, 133, 151, 219, 220, 225
Fringe theatre 25, 46, 47, 48, 60, 62, 78, 85, 86, 95, 99, 101, 220
Frith, Suzanne 144
Frontlight 220
Frost, Sebastian 82
Fry, Gareth 11
Fugard, Athol 188
Fuller, Craig 190

Gaborit, Delphine 109
Gaiman, Neil 49
Galloway, Ian William 28
Gam 7, 365 147, 149
Garrick Theatre, London ix, 96, 146
Gasparetto, Angelo 198
Gate Theatre, London 76
GCSE 100, 128
GCSE drama 100
Gel 6, 7, 26, 52, 82, 83, 91, 103, 115, 118, 137, 149, 160, 166, 218, 220, 221, 223
Generic (conventional) 220
Gibbons, Tom 23
Gielgud Theatre, London viii, 9
Gillian Lynne Theatre 1
Gillibrand, Nicky 210
Gilmour, Soutra 79, 82, 83, 87, 179
GLP 8, 10, 11, 12, 14, 220
Glyndebourne Opera 45, 111, 114, 202
Göbbel, Wolfgang 48
Gobo 10, 62, 131, 132, 134, 151, 197, 199, 220, 223, 224
Goldberg, Andrew 28
Goldsmiths, London 46, 48
Gonoudem, Iain 209
Gothenburg Opera, Sweden 73
Goulding, Andrzej 22, 87
Grandage, Michael 5
Grange Festival, 190
Great American Market (GAM) 220
Greece 141
green, debbie tucker 54
Grenfell, Colin ix, 187

Groothuis, Paul 55, 68
Groundrow 219, 220
Groups 25, 48, 60, 149, 163, 181, 195, 222
Guardians of the Galaxy 99
Guards at the Taj viii, 73, 79
Guildhall School of Music & Drama 5, 73, 74, 187, 189
Guys and Dolls 86

Haggerty, Dan 10
Halliday, Rob 202, 213
Hall, Peter 114
Hamilton 53
Hamilton, Hugh 213
Hamlet 148
Hammershoi 61
Hampstead Theatre, London 72
Happy Days 19
Harada, Kai 1
Harlan, Manuel viii, ix, 11, 28, 50, 82, 162
Harold Pinter Theatre, London 179
Harringtons Pie Shop, London ix, 130
Harry Potter and the Cursed Child viii, 5, 10, 11, 12, 13, 17, 18, 95
Haydn, Joseph 116
Haze 8, 11, 132, 137, 143, 181, 197, 220, 221, 224
Head high crosslight 218
Henderson, Mark 5, 18
Hensel, Merle 28
Hersey, David 8, 47, 221
His Dark Materials 45
HMI 149
Hoggett, Steven 11, 19, 28, 50
Holland 141, 142
Hopper, Edward 61
Hopkins, Robert Innes 190
House lights 220
House rig 37
Houston Ballet, USA 118
Howell, Richard viii, 73, 79, 82
Hudson, Howard vii, ix, 85, 87, 96
Hue/Saturation 164
Hugh Chinnick 114
Hughes, Mick 114, 189
Hung Han Yun, Jessica 99, 105, 109

Ice shows 157
Icke, Robert 19
Imagination 5
Immersive theatre 101
Incandescent (tungsten) 221, 224
India 184
Inheritance, The viii, 32, 34
Instagram 89
In the round 113, 154, 155, 196
Iphigenia 148
Ivey, William 1

Japan 71, 102, 103, 111, 216
Jekyll & Hyde viii, 82, 83
Jensen, Ashley 47
Jerry Springer: The Opera 202
Johannesburg, South Africa 122
John, Elton 208
Jonathan, Mark ix, 111, 118, 123
Jones, Christine 11
Judd, Donald 90
&Juliet ix, 85, 86, 87, 88, 90
    Lighting desk (console) 95, 216, 220, 221
    Scenic designer 50
    Scenic designer (set designer) 7, 8, 13, 14, 16, 19, 20, 21, 32, 35, 38, 49, 62, 89, 95, 104, 135, 168, 178, 181, 191, 192, 193, 197
    Tech (technical rehearsals) 181

K10 B-Eye (Clay Paky) 145
Kalman, Jean 48
Kenny, Simon 130, 131, 133, 134, 137
Kenton, Tristram ix, 177
Kidman, Nicole 11
Kiln Theatre, London 72
King's Head Theatre, London 101
Kiss Me Kate 86
Knapp, Steve 102
Knight of Illumination Awards 73, 79, 127, 218
Kodicek, Catherine 40
Koons, Jeff 90
Korea 102
Kubrick, Stanley 61, 175
Kyncl, Ivan viii, 68

La Crimosa 173
LAMDA, London 19
Larlab, Suttirat Anne 169
Laxton, Emma 190
LED 6, 7, 12, 16, 26, 39, 52, 66, 81, 82, 91, 103, 117, 120, 130, 131, 134, 138, 143, 149, 150, 160, 163, 164, 166, 168, 170, 180, 182, 192, 193, 194, 204, 209, 217, 219, 220, 221, 223, 224
LED tape 21
Lee colour 7, 52, 83, 149, 163, 208, 220
    Lee 103 149
    Lee 120 116
    Lee 161 147
    Lee 169 194
    Lee 200 7, 111, 116, 120, 131, 132, 137, 138, 163
    Lee 201 11, 53, 83, 91, 116, 120, 131, 164, 220
    Lee 202 11, 53, 83, 91, 120, 131, 151, 208
    Lee 203 53, 83, 91, 120, 151
    Lee 204 164
    Lee 205 53, 149
    Lee 241 131
    Lee 366 131
    Lee 506 136
    Lee 650 53
    Lee 709 27

    Lee 711 27, 193
    Lee 728 208
Lee, Jackie 189
Lehman Trilogy, The viii, 31
Leitmotivic structure 148
Leko 223
Les Misérables iv, viii, 45, 221
Lewis, Geraint viii, 9
Light bulb 157, 168, 170
Light curtain 220, 221
Lighting Christmas Lunch 111, 112
Lighting design 9, 13, 26, 31, 32, 33, 46, 53, 60, 74, 77, 86, 100, 101, 112, 114, 124, 127, 158, 164, 165, 173, 174, 175, 181, 188, 200, 210, 217, 219, 224
Lighting designer 5, 6, 7, 8, 9, 10, 11, 13, 14, 15, 16, 22, 25, 28, 31, 32, 34, 40, 45, 46, 47, 48, 49, 50, 55, 56, 60, 61, 62, 63, 64, 65, 66, 68, 75, 79, 81, 82, 85, 87, 95, 96, 101, 105, 109, 110, 111, 112, 114, 115, 116, 117, 118, 121, 123, 124, 127, 133, 141, 143, 144, 146, 152, 153, 157, 162, 165, 167, 169, 170, 171, 173, 174, 175, 176, 177, 179, 180, 182, 183, 189, 190, 191, 193, 198, 199, 200, 202, 203, 204, 212, 214, 217, 218, 219, 220, 221, 222, 223
Lighting desk (console) 7, 13, 14, 20, 35, 36, 37, 60, 76, 81, 82, 88, 92, 93, 95, 106, 113, 114, 116, 120, 121, 122, 123, 135, 160, 163, 164, 182, 188, 196, 218, 221, 222, 223, 224
Lighting ladders 205, 221
Lighting manufacturers 6, 10, 100, 111, 137, 164, 220
Lighting plan 9, 24, 25, 26, 32, 37, 39, 53, 60, 65, 66, 70, 77, 78, 82, 90, 94, 106, 107, 115, 121, 132, 135, 136, 138, 142, 150, 151, 153, 154, 160, 161, 164, 178, 179, 180, 192, 195, 199, 204, 217, 221, 222, 223
Lighting programmer 7, 9, 10, 12, 13, 26, 51, 52, 56, 65, 70, 78, 79, 92, 93, 95, 106, 107, 110, 111, 114, 116, 120, 122, 124, 129, 145, 161, 163, 164, 166, 181, 182, 194, 196, 202, 204, 215, 218 220, 223
Lighting rig 218, 221, 222
Lighting session 21, 63, 68, 120, 196, 203, 216
Lighting states (see Cues) 115, 142, 222
Light installation 102
Light plot (lighting plan) 221
Light Relief 59
Lightstrike 12
Lindsay, Katrina 11, 19
Little Shop of Horrors 92
Lloyd, Jamie 31, 79, 179, 185
Lloyd, Phyllida 162
Lloyd Webber, Andrew 48
Load-in (fit-up) 224
Longborough Festival Opera 143, 144
Los Angeles, USA viii, 111, 117
Lowe, Georgia 105
Lumiere and Son 46
Lustr (ETC) 7, 26, 82, 83, 138, 149, 164, 193, 197, 214 221, 224

Index

LX (lighting / electrics) 221
Lyttelton Theatre (at the National Theatre) 18, 68, 69, 95

Mac 600 (Martin) 203, 204, 214
Mac 700 (Martin) 145
Mac Aura (Martin) 214
Macbeth viii, 27, 28, 148
Machinal 209
Mackintosh, Cameron 56, 134
MacNeil, Ian 59, 68, 202, 205, 208, 210
Mae, Amy ix, 127, 130
Magic sheet 37, 221
Making Theatre Podcast 157
MA Lighting 100
Marfleet, Phil 214
Marko – see Jonathan, Mark 111, 112
Martin, Justin 40
Masking 8, 125
Mason, Monica 123
Maxwell, Shelley 105
Maybanks, Helen viii, 22
McCandless, Stanley 151, 220
McCarthy, Siobhán 130, 133
McEwan, David 22
Mcfarlane, John 49
McGregor, Wayne 181
McInnerny, Tim 113
McOnie, Drew 82
Melville, Mark 198
Mendes, Sam 31
Message In A Bottle viii, 22
Messel, Oliver 123
Method of Lighting the Stage, A (McCandless) 220
Metropolitan Opera, New York 125
MIDI 221
Midsummer Night's Dream, A (Britten) 145
Millennium Dome 5
Milroy, Sacha 168
Miss Saigon 161, 167
Misty ix, 177
Mitchell, Katie 31, 42
Moment Factory 102
Mood boards 104, 105
Mortimer, Vicki 18, 54, 55
Movement director 11, 50, 105, 109, 198
Moving lights 12, 21, 25, 42, 52, 53, 66, 71, 77, 88, 90, 92, 97, 115, 121, 122, 124, 138, 145, 150, 152, 160, 161, 162, 163, 166, 182, 193, 206, 216, 217, 218, 219, 220, 222, 223, 224, 225
Mozart, Wolfgang Amadeus 116
Mumford, Peter 149
Murfin, Dan 12
Murray, Helen ix, 109
Museum of Home, London 99
Music 20, 23, 35, 46, 78, 87, 115, 116, 124, 128, 143, 146, 157, 162, 166, 173, 174, 185, 209
Musical 6, 13, 14, 16, 17, 25, 53, 54, 59, 67, 71, 73, 80, 85, 86, 87, 88, 89, 91, 95, 111, 121, 127, 137, 145, 148, 153, 157, 161, 163, 202, 203, 205, 206, 207, 208, 220, 222
Music hall 149
Music supervisor 162
My Name is Rachel Corrie 187
My Neighbour Totoro 99

Naito, Rei 102
Naoshima, Japan 103
National Ballet of Japan 118
National Gallery 17
National Theatre, London viii, ix, 6, 10, 12, 17, 18, 26, 39, 45, 47, 50, 53, 54, 55, 59, 65, 67, 68, 69, 70, 72, 74, 95, 99, 107, 111, 114, 168, 169, 173, 209
National Youth Theatre of Great Britain 111, 113
Negus, Anthony 144
Neon 170
NETworks Presentations 213
Newton, Anthony 39
New York 5, 16, 17, 28, 39, 69, 70, 127, 135, 136, 187
New York, USA 125
9 to 5 89
1984 19
Nishizawa, Ryue 102
Noël Coward Theatre, London 11, 34
Norris, Rufus 19
Northen, Michael 25
Northern Europe 183
North Pole 170, 191
Notes 13, 16, 20, 35, 37, 57, 61, 71, 72, 81, 94, 97, 120, 121, 122, 123, 165, 167, 178, 182, 194, 195, 212, 213
Nowell, James 202, 214

Ocean At The End Of The Lane, The 49, 50
Oedipus 141
Off-Broadway 16, 72
O'Keeffe, Georgia 56
Old Masters 180, 183
Old Vic Theatre, London viii, 82, 83, 202
O-levels 188
Olivier Theatre (at the National Theatre) 5, 18, 19, 54, 55, 59, 74, 169
On The Town 86, 93
Opening night 222, 224
Open White (OW) 83, 88, 92, 182, 185, 208
Opera ix, 31, 35, 36, 45, 49, 54, 55, 56, 70, 71, 73, 77, 80, 87, 97, 101, 111, 113, 114, 117, 120, 121, 123, 143, 148, 157, 158, 161, 166, 167, 170, 171, 173, 223
Opera North 161
Oram, Christopher 5, 7, 13, 95, 96
Orchestrator 162
Orfeo ed Euridice, 190
Ormerod, Ben ix, 47, 139, 141, 144, 146, 148, 150, 151, 155, 158
Osram 12
Other Richard, The 105

Oval House, London 59, 60, 66
Owen, Gareth 87

Pacholksi, Richard (R2) 214
Painter 180, 183
Paintings 117, 180
Palace Theatre, London viii, 11
Pantomime 99, 107, 112, 203
Pantone 7, 16, 164
Paperwork 69, 135, 136, 212, 222
Par cans 15, 25, 132, 133, 149, 150, 152, 154, 192, 204, 217, 222
Patt 23 (Strand) 222
Patt 123 (Strand) 209
Patt 743 (Strand) 25, 149, 194
Patterson, Tamykha 110
Patt numbers 222
Pelléas and Mélisande 117
Peña, Elena 109, 177
People Show 46, 47
Performers 60
Performer tracking 170
Persson, Johan iv, viii, ix, 5, 55, 87, 96, 123, 198
Petipa, Marius 123
Pet Shop Boys 157
Phantom of the Opera, The 82
Philistines 18
Photograph 51 11
Photographer 61, 104
Photography 17, 20, 61, 90, 102, 175
Pilbrow, Richard 13
Pink, Andy 175
Pinterest 104, 132, 134
Pinter, Harold ix, 114
Pipe-end 151, 152
Piper, Tom 146
Pirouette (Strand) 209
Playhouse, Liverpool 187
Playhouse, Oxford 158
Plays 31, 32, 86, 111, 142, 148, 157
Playwright 54, 188
Plotting session 21, 80, 88, 105, 120, 143, 163, 181, 195, 222
Poet, Bruno ix, 142, 157, 162, 169
Pollock's toy theatre 113
Popp, Ethan 162
Pop shows 159, 161
Portfolios 192
Potter, Mick 146
Practicals 38, 130, 152, 159, 168, 222
Praxis Makes Perfect 19
Press night 17, 192, 200, 222
Previews 13, 16, 17, 24, 35, 36, 37, 57, 66, 67, 68, 81, 93, 107, 121, 123, 137, 153, 167, 168, 194, 212, 222, 224
Pre-visualization 36, 88, 161, 192, 222
Prince, Kate 19, 22
Privacy 73

Privett, Alan 144
Producer 8, 13, 28, 88, 94, 95, 137, 162, 175, 220
Production desk (US Tech table) 115, 143, 207, 222
Production electrician 15, 25, 51, 52, 53, 65, 100, 114, 129, 136, 164, 202, 204, 215, 222
Production manager 25, 39, 48, 94, 122, 168, 189, 200, 203, 223
Production meeting 223
Production stage manager (PSM) 13, 219, 224
Profile spot (US ellipsoidal) 15, 122, 136, 142, 220, 223, 224
Projection 64
Projection designer 87, 162
Prompt copy (prompt book, calling script) 20, 51, 56, 65, 105, 120, 160, 195, 223
Props 60, 70, 114
Proscenium arch 197, 199
Public Theater, New York 73
Puplett, Leon viii, 40
Puppet designer 50
Puppetry director 50
Pyant, Paul 114, 153, 175
Pyne, Vic 54, 55, 202, 206, 207, 208, 209, 213, 214, 215, 216

Ravenhill, Mark 10, 12
Read through 20, 104, 195
Rebbeck, Steve 203, 207
Red 5
Regent's Park Open Air Theatre, London 92, 93
Regional theatre 72, 78
Rehearsal 181
Rehearsal room 8, 14, 24, 32, 35, 36, 40, 78, 79, 88, 92, 104, 115, 117, 120, 123, 160, 161, 178, 181, 191, 192, 194, 223
Rehearsals 8, 9, 14, 24, 32, 34, 35, 36, 40, 41, 42, 50, 51, 62, 63, 68, 78, 79, 90, 92, 93, 107, 115, 120, 121, 123, 131, 132, 143, 150, 160, 161, 163, 167, 171, 175, 178, 181, 188, 191, 193, 195, 203, 207, 210, 216, 219, 222, 223, 225
Rehearsal video 20
Reiche & Vogel (R&V) 12
Reid, Christopher 34
Re-lighter 223
Rembrandt 61
Renshaw, Christopher 146
Rental company (hire company) 17, 25, 65, 111, 116, 162
Rep 37, 70, 71, 123, 161, 197, 221, 223
Resistible Rise of Arturo Ui, The 47
Revit 101
Revolution (ETC) 205, 214
RGB 12
Richardson, Josh 130
Richter, Max 19
Rickman, Alan 190
Rig 222
Ring Cycle, The 141, 143, 144, 145, 147

237

Index

Rite of Spring, The 175
Robert Juliat 97, 149, 223
Robertson, Mike 95
Rogers, Tom 89
Romeo and Juliet (ballet) 53, 57
Romeo and Juliet (Branagh) ix, 85, 95, 96
Room 59
Rosco colour 7, 149, 163, 220
    Rosco 26 220
    Rosco 78 7
    Rosco 371 91
    Rosco 372 91
    Rosco 373 91, 194
    Rosco 608 149
Rose Bruford College, London 10, 99, 100
Rose Theatre (at Rose Bruford), London 100
Rosenthal, Jean 174
Ross, Finn 11
Rothko, Mark 175
Rothwell, Mike viii, 63
Royal Academy of Dramatic Art (RADA) 127, 145
Royal Ballet, (RADA) London 123, 124
Royal Court Theatre, London ix, 21, 27, 41, 54, 72, 108, 109, 114, 133, 187, 188, 190, 199
Royal Exchange Theatre, Manchester ix, 188, 189, 197, 198, 199
Royal Opera House, London ix, 36, 114, 120, 123, 161, 167, 209
Royal Scottish Academy, Glasgow 47
Royal Shakespeare Company (RSC) 72, 75, 99
Royalties 170
Rudd, Katy 50
Rules Restaurant, London 217
Run-through 14, 24, 90, 193
Russian Avant Garde 180

Sadler's Wells, London viii, 22
Santa Fe Opera, USA 71
Saint Joan 54
Satyagraha 45
Savoy Theatre, London 89
Scale 221, 223
Scandinavia 171
Scenic design 13, 32, 47, 62, 83, 87, 89, 90, 115, 117, 118, 159, 161, 175, 178, 181, 222
Scenic designer 1, 5, 7, 9, 10, 11, 13, 15, 21, 22, 25, 27, 28, 31, 32, 34, 37, 40, 47, 48, 49, 50, 54, 55, 56, 59, 61, 63, 68, 71, 74, 75, 76, 78, 79, 82, 85, 87, 89, 92, 95, 96, 101, 104, 105, 109, 112, 114, 115, 117, 118, 120, 123, 130, 131, 144, 146, 148, 158, 159, 160, 162, 168, 169, 174, 176, 177, 179, 180, 181, 182, 183, 185, 190, 192, 198, 200, 203, 210, 216, 218, 219, 220, 221
Scenic painting 17, 64, 86, 89, 114, 117, 175, 180
Schiele, Egon 176
School of Visual Theatre, Israel 173, 174
Schubert, Franz 146
Scottish Opera 121, 124

Script 8, 13, 14, 20, 24, 31, 32, 35, 36, 51, 60, 61, 62, 78, 87, 88, 104, 108, 115, 131, 147, 160, 189, 191, 192, 194, 195, 196, 197, 216, 218, 219, 223
Scroller 7, 12, 26, 27, 116, 152, 204, 208, 214, 223
Sculpture 86, 175
Scutt, Tom 92
Seagull, The ix, 179, 180, 185
Secret Cinema 99
Sedgwick, Toby 169
Set 7, 8, 9, 13, 14, 21, 22, 24, 27, 32, 36, 42, 60, 61, 62, 64, 67, 68, 76, 79, 83, 88, 89, 91, 94, 105, 106, 107, 117, 118, 119, 120, 123, 124, 127, 129, 132, 147, 150, 159, 161, 166, 175, 180, 181, 182, 184, 185, 192, 193, 194, 196, 197, 200, 202, 203, 204, 205, 206, 209, 214, 217, 218, 220, 221, 222, 223, 224
Set electrics 94
    Jeremy Secomb 130, 133
Set model (modelbox) 8, 13, 16, 21, 38, 51, 76, 89, 104, 115, 118, 131, 136, 138, 147, 148, 159, 160, 185, 192, 202, 221, 223
Sets 13, 15, 76, 117, 118, 159
7:84 theatre company 47
Seven Methods of Killing Kylie Jenner ix, 108, 109
Shadows 14, 39, 118, 132, 150, 183, 184, 211, 220
Shaftesbury Avenue, London 123, 134, 135, 136
Shaftesbury Theatre, London 87
Shakiry, Rajha 109, 177
Sharp, Bronwen ix, 130, 133
Shaw Theatre, London 113, 114
Shemesh, Jackie vii, ix, 173, 177, 179
Sheppard, Luke 87
Shin crosslight 218
Show Caller 224
Showfile 36, 224
Shutt, Christopher 96
Sigur Rós 157, 162, 166
Silver Tassie, The 18
Sinclair, Rob 175
Site-specific 224
Skilbeck, Nick 162
Slater, Daniel 190
Sleeping Beauty ix, 123
Smallman, Sam 35
Smith, Rae 47, 55
Smoke 174, 197, 210, 220, 224
Society of British Theatre Lighting Designers 217
Sodium 53, 159, 170
Sondheim, Stephen 134
Son-et-lumière 128
Sound 5, 6, 8, 13, 14, 15, 23, 60, 114, 170, 178, 197, 213, 221, 224
Sound design 28
Sound designer 1, 6, 8, 9, 11, 22, 28, 34, 39, 40, 50, 55, 79, 82, 87, 96, 105, 109, 130, 146, 162, 169, 176, 177, 179, 181, 190, 198, 203, 210, 218, 219
Source Four (ETC) 7, 97, 134, 194, 221, 223, 224
Source Four Par (ETC) 16

Index

South Bank, London 47
Southern Europe 183
Southwark Playhouse, London 85
Spall, Timothy 113
Sparks (lighting supplier) 25
Special 224, 225
Spotlight 219
Stage and orchestra rehearsal 143
Stage management 19, 60, 74, 79, 101, 127, 167, 178, 181, 188, 224
Stage manager 15, 60, 114, 115, 120, 123, 224
Stamp 35
Starlight Express 48
Stationhouse Opera 47
Steel, Liam 9
Steinberg, Nevin 162
St John's Passion 49
Stones, Ben 22, 198
Strand Electric / Strand Lighting 95, 112, 209, 211, 218, 222, 224
Stroman, Susan 1
Sugg, Jeff 162
Sunday In The Park With George 19, 64
Sun flood 25, 33, 39, 40, 41, 42
Sunset at the Villa Thalia 26
Superbeam beamlight 12
Sustainability 45
Svoboda, Josef 8, 43, 174, 221
Swan Lake viii, 49, 59, 63
Swatch book 6, 7, 52, 66, 91, 103, 116, 138, 147, 149, 164, 220
Sweeney Todd ix, 127, 128, 130, 131, 132, 133, 137
Systems 16, 32, 33, 90, 91, 151, 170, 218, 219

Tabs magazine 112, 224
teamLab 102
Tech (technical rehearsals) 6, 14, 15, 18, 20, 21, 35, 36, 37, 40, 41, 51, 62, 66, 68, 69, 75, 77, 79, 80, 81, 82, 83, 88, 90, 91, 92, 93, 94, 95, 104, 105, 106, 107, 108, 128, 133, 135, 142, 143, 145, 148, 150, 153, 160, 163, 164, 165, 166, 167, 178, 181, 184, 192, 193, 196, 200, 206, 207, 209, 210, 212, 213, 214, 224
Tel Aviv Opera House, Israel 173, 174, 175
Television (TV) 46, 73, 101, 102, 123
Tennant, David 47
Teshima, Japan 102, 103
Theatre Critics of Wales Award 19
Theatre de Complicité 45, 48, 55
Theatre Royal Stratford East, London ix, 99, 105, 108
The Cherry Orchard 18
The Curious Incident of the Dog in the Night-Time 53
The Jungle viii, 31, 33, 38, 40
The Other Richard ix
Thomas, Giles 105
Thompson, Mark 162
Three-quarter backlight 152, 217
Thrust stage 154

Tiffany, John 11, 19, 28
Tildesley, Mark 168
Timecode 10, 13, 224
Time Out magazine 113
Tina: The Tina Turner Musical ix, 157, 162, 163, 167, 170
Tipton, Jennifer 48
Titanic 85
Tokyo, Japan 141, 210
Tony Award 5, 31, 59, 213
Tooting Arts Club, London 130
Tooting, London 128, 130, 135, 136
Toplight 91, 151, 216
Toronto, Canada 85, 97
Torriset, Kjell 144
Tosca 101
Town, Johanna vii, ix, 187, 190, 198
Trafalgar Studios, London 73
Tramway, Glasgow 28
Treatment, The 9
Tungsten 6, 7, 11, 12, 15, 27, 33, 39, 45, 52, 120, 145, 147, 148, 150, 166, 168, 170, 193, 204, 214, 218, 219, 221, 224
Turkey 183
Turner, JMW 89
Turner, Lyndsey 9
Turrell, James 61, 102
Tusing, Scott 13
TW1 (Martin) 149, 204
Twombly, Cy 90

UAE National Day 157
UK Theatre Award 19
Underworld 169
Union 97, 171
United Kingdom (UK) 15, 16, 59, 60, 69, 70, 72, 73, 111, 122, 128, 135, 141, 171, 183, 187, 214, 219, 224
United States of America (USA) 13, 15, 16, 59, 60, 65, 69, 70, 72, 86, 128, 135, 136, 152, 202, 214, 219, 221, 223, 224
University 46, 47, 100, 106, 129, 158
University of Winchester 127
Urban Electric (lighting supplier) 101

V&A Museum, London 8, 99
Van Laast, Anthony 162
Vanstone, Hugh 74
Vari-Lite (moving light) 222, 223
Vari-Lite programmer 223
Vaults Festival, London 101
Victoria Palace, London 202, 211
Video 6, 13, 35, 123, 143, 153, 166, 175, 178, 212, 224
Video designer 6, 11, 22, 28, 40, 64, 87, 177, 190, 218, 219
VL1000 Arc (Vari-Lite) 214
VL3000 Wash (Vari-Lite) 214
VL3500 (Vari-Lite) 203, 204, 214

239

Index

Voller, Andrew 10
Vor 13

Wagner, Richard 143, 145, 148
War Horse 45, 54, 72
Wash 225
Washlight 219
Wash (moving light) 225
Webber, Julian 207, 216
Welsh National Opera 121
West End (London) 11, 15, 39, 65, 72, 85, 95, 99, 116, 127, 134, 212, 214
White card model 8, 22, 62, 76, 182, 221
White Guard, The 18
White Light (lighting supplier) 101, 203, 209
Whitson, Stevie 47, 61
Who's Afraid of Virginia Woolf 24, 27
Williams, Jack 133
Window 62, 75, 115, 120, 135, 182, 194, 199

Woodward, Ash J 11
Workshop 225
Writer 105, 189
Wyer, Samuel 50
WYSIWYG (Cast Lighting) 161, 162, 170

X4 Bar (GLP) 8, 10, 11, 12, 14, 220
Xia, Matthew 198

Yavroyan, Chahine 61
Yoga 127
Young, Campbell 162
Young, Paloma 87
Young Vic, London viii, 39, 40, 41, 54, 142, 173
Yvonne Arnaud Theatre, Guildford 202

Zorro: The Musical ix, 141, 145, 146
Zulu 122